The Wrong Side
Of the Ball

MIKE ZIMMERMAN

ISBN-13: 978-1517060930
ISBN-10: 1517060931

To Al and Ruby Zimmerman,
for teaching me to do what I love.

To Elizabeth and Jack,
for your endless patience, support, and love.

And to Coach Carl,
for your experience, wisdom, knowledge, and passion.

I couldn't have pulled this off without all of you.

CONTENTS

ACKNOWLEDGMENTS

The Bible says, "Every good and perfect gift is from above" (James 1:17), and that is how I am compelled to view this book. The idea came to me in a flash, driving home from the first (and I'm sure only) half-marathon I'd ever run. I'd suffered an injury about a week before the race, and knew that to have any chance of running (or staggering) 13.1 miles that day I'd have to put it all in the Lord's hands. So I did. And I finished the race.

Driving home to Milwaukee that evening, I was listening to worship music (as I had during the race), praising Jesus, and thinking about what my next challenge might be. I'd always wanted to write a book, probably about golf, and out of nowhere came this idea to explore the left-hand/right-hand phenomenon in golf by learning to play left-handed myself. Usually, when I come up with an idea like that, the more I think about it the more half-baked it seems. In this case, the more I thought, prayed, and discussed it, the more fully baked it became. That's how I knew it was from God. So I dedicated a year to the process and had the time of my life.

Finishing the book was more of an ordeal than I anticipated, but I kept my eyes on God and never gave up, trusting that I would finish the book in God's time, not my own. And that's exactly what happened.

That is why, above all in the most literal way possible, I acknowledge the Lord Jesus Christ and present this book for His glory.

INTRODUCTION
A Sinister Proposition

David Letterman: Fifty percent of the most recent winners
have been left-handed, is that true, at Augusta?
Bubba Watson: Yeah. Fifty percent are right-handed, too.

– "Late Night with David Letterman," April 10, 2012

Want to win a few bets at the 19th hole? Ask the others in your
foursome to name four lefties who have won major championships
in golf. Your knowledgeable friends will quickly reel off the names
Bob Charles, Mike Weir, Phil Mickelson, and Bubba Watson.

Imagine their shock and surprise when you tell them – as you
hastily collect your winnings – that only one of those guys, Bubba
Watson, is a true lefty. The other three are actually right-handed, but
play golf from the sinister side.

Now imagine their rage when they realize you've tricked them.
Fisticuffs ensue. Since you're outnumbered three-to-one, they easily
beat you to a pulp and take back your winnings. They also take your
watch and the rest of the cash in your wallet, just for good measure.

Man, who are these guys!? Why you would want to play golf with
three jerks like them is beyond me, but who am I to judge another
man's friends?

Later, in the E.R., you tell your wife what happened and she asks
the obvious question: "Well …? If not Charles, Weir, and Mickelson
[your wife is very knowledgeable about golf; that's why you married
her], what's the answer? Have any other true left-handers ever won a
major professional golf championship?"

A smile creeps across your bloodied face, but you wince only
slightly at the pain. "Johnny Miller," you gasp. "Greg Norman. Curtis

Strange. Nick Price. David Graham. Byron Nelson."

A hush falls as doctors, nurses, assorted orderlies, and the little old lady in the waiting room stop what they're doing and draw silently closer, hanging on your every word. Everyone is astonished by the revealed wisdom that has already passed your swollen lips, but you're not done yet. With strength fading, you summon another breath and whisper, like Charles Foster Kane spitting out "Rosebud": "Hogan."

A nurse faints. In the hallway, a bedpan crashes to the floor. Across the pond, a chill wind blows through "Hogan's Alley" at Carnoustie.

"They're all naturally left-handed," you explain. "They only play golf right-handed."

A tear runs down your wife's cheek as she turns to the attending physician and says, "Doctor, my husband is obviously delirious and in great pain. Can you do something?"

Shaking his head with a sad and concerned look, the doctor lowers a mask to your face. Moments later the room goes dark and all is quiet.

In retrospect, maybe you should have just stuck to the conventional wisdom. Or at least made the stakes a little lower.

• • •

Ever since I was a kid first taking up the game of golf, I was taught that the left hand is, or should be, the dominant hand in a right-handed swing. "You're using too much right hand!" was my dad's most frequent input. "Let your left hand pull the club through; don't push it through with your right."

How can that be? I always wondered. I throw with my right hand. I write with my right hand. I hit my annoying younger brother with my right hand. Why wouldn't I use mostly my right hand to swing a golf club?

And, assuming it's true that I shouldn't, wouldn't it make sense for me, as a right-handed person, to play golf left-handed?

That thought has haunted me ever since. And so when Phil the Thrill, the right-handed lefty, first burst onto the scene by winning the U.S. Amateur and a boatload of college titles (not to mention a PGA tournament) as a young amateur, I assumed he was a product of just such a theory. Surely, I thought, someone must have groomed him to play as a southpaw with an eye toward turning him into a world-class player.

The truth, as it turns out, is more mundane – but just as interesting. When Phil was first taking up the game as a wee lad in San Diego, California, he learned to swing a club by standing in front of his father and literally mirroring the elder Mickelson's movements. He did everything else right-handed, so they tried to turn him around. But Phil was a stubborn cuss, and he would have none of it. So a "lefty" he remained, albeit only on the golf course. The question is: Did it make him a better golfer?

Meanwhile, Mike Weir, like most young boys in Canada, first fell in love with hockey. A natural right-hander, Weir found he could swing a hockey stick more easily with his left hand low. So that's how he played. In fact, he may have been encouraged to do so, since in hockey it's helpful to have left-handed shooters playing on the left side of the ice, putting southpaws in demand.

When "Weirsy" later took up golf, it only made sense for him to swing from the "wrong" side of the ball – using a partial set of left-handed clubs handed down by a family friend. Good thing, too. If none had been available, he may have been forced to turn things around – and who knows where his golf may have led him then. To obscurity? Or to possibly even greater heights? The world will never know.

Decades before, Bob Charles, the patron saint of left-handed golf, did everything right-handed except "play games requiring two hands." Turns out that both his parents were excellent golfers, and lefties. That is, his mom was a natural lefty, his father a righty – but they both played golf left-handed. So when young Bob, a natural right-hander, took up the game himself, the clubs he found lying around the house were all left-handed. And that's how he learned to play.

Charles's situation mirrors the challenge routinely faced by young lefties all over the world: You're a southpaw, and interested in playing golf, but the only clubs you can find to use are right-handed. So you "make do." Could it be that's actually an advantage?

While some 15 percent of the population at large is left-handed, only about 10 percent of golfers overall play that way. The percentage is even smaller at the professional level. The worldwide shortage of left-handed equipment (especially in the olden days) probably explains why so many natural lefties such as Norman (world #1 for 331 consecutive weeks), Strange (a back-to-back U.S. Open champion), and Miller (U.S. and British Open titles) play golf right-handed. And play it so well. Even the great Ben Hogan – winner of nine major championships, perhaps golf's most enigmatic and compelling character ever, and author of one of the great comeback stories in the history of sport – wrote that he was, in fact, "born left-handed" (though he would later refute his own claim).

Yet certain questions remain unanswered: What role, if any did "the big switch" play in the success of these top golfers? Would they, could they, have succeeded as righties? Given the success of these great champions, is a golfer potentially better off learning to play from the opposite side?

And what about the strange case of David Graham (PGA Championship and U.S. Open titles), who grew up learning to play golf left-handed, but switched to right-handed as a teenager? Or Mac O'Grady, a right-handed pro and one of the PGA Tour's greatest eccentrics, who played so well left-handed he once petitioned the USGA to grant him amateur status as a left-hander? And then there was the legendary gambler Titanic Thompson, who bested many top golfers of his day – pros and amateurs alike – by playing left- or right-handed.

What is it about the game of golf that invites such high levels of "crossover" success? And more to the point: Could it just be possible for a 47-year-old underachieving right-hander to fix his lifelong swing flaws and become the golfer he always wanted to be by turning things around and "relearning" the game as a lefty?

Let's look at a few of the obstacles such a "hypothetical" golfer – that is to say, that I – would face:

Habit. Think about how natural your golf swing feels to you. It didn't get that way overnight, but through many thousands of repetitions. Perhaps over the course of a lifetime. Now think about how unnatural an opposite-handed swing would feel. How long would it take to make the foreign motion feel natural? Maybe it never would. It's tempting to believe that my bad habits would go away while my good ones would carry over. But that's not likely to happen. With my luck, my touch and feel, meticulously developed over a

THE WRONG SIDE OF THE BALL

lifetime of ball-striking, would go out the window while the nearly overwhelming massive bending arc (NOMBA™) of my tee shots would stick to me like goose poop to FootJoys.

Age. According to wisdom handed down through many generations, old dogs and new tricks go together like peanut butter and mayonnaise. Like Tiger and Phil. Like Jordan Spieth and shaving. Is 47 too old to learn a whole new way of doing things? Is my muscle memory too set in its crotchety old ways? (Hey, you kids! Get off my lawn!)

Physiology. And that's not even considering the physical obstacles that come with getting older. My back is not what it used to be. My flexibility (what little I ever had) has gone the way of the hickory shaft. In fact, replacing my rickety spine *with* a hickory shaft might be an improvement. Plus, it's a known scientific fact that the little aches and pains everyone develops now and then take longer to go away once you start wanting to go to bed at 9:30.

Family. I'm pushing 50. I have a son, Jack, who's 9. A wife, Elizabeth, who's ... forever young. They are very important to me. Is it possible to put in the work that will be required to succeed without them forgetting who I am? My son already tells his friends that all I do is watch golf and read about golf. And sometimes I play golf – hopefully with him. At least he shows signs of learning to love the game as much as I do. Perhaps I can incorporate him into the learning process, take him to the range and par-3 and such. He'd like that! And so would I. But what about the missus? I don't think she would enjoy tagging along the same way my son would, and I doubt I have enough "marital capital" stored up to carry me through. (Note to self: Start doing more laundry and vacuuming. And dusting ... yeah, dusting.)

What's the point? Already my idea has been greeted with some skepticism from friends and loved ones – to say nothing of the outright derision dished out by my mortal enemies. They don't understand why I would want to do this – or doubt that learning to play from the left side would be an effective method of improving my golf game. But that's not really what it's about. The point is to try it and see what happens. And to see what I can learn – about the golf swing, left-handedness, myself, and perhaps life – along the way. No matter how good or bad a left-handed golfer I one day become, I believe an adventure awaits down this path.

Commitment. Is it going to be fun to start over? Will I hate being bad? At what point in the learning process does golf become enjoyable? Such a quest would probably mean giving up right-handed golf completely. Perhaps for a time, perhaps forever. Progress will likely be slow – will I miss playing decent golf too much to carry this plan to fruition? One reason I consider myself a golfing underachiever is that I've never been willing to put in the work (on the range, that is) required to improve the way I'd like. Will I be willing and able to stick to my guns and practice hard? I'm starting to feel tired already.

That last question – about commitment – if appraised by one of those guest experts on "Pawn Stars," would probably produce a value somewhere in the range of $64,000. Well, that would be the auction price. Chances are, after not-too-gently explaining to me how he's running a business here, Rick would probably offer me something just north of half that amount.

But there's only one way to find out if I'm holding a rare and genuine gem of an idea or a cheap and ordinary piece of costume jewelry. I going to have to just do it and find out for myself. So let the quest begin.

So help me Hogan.

CHAPTER 1
A Golfing Memoir

"You tried your best and you failed miserably.
The lesson is, 'Never try.'"

—Homer Simpson

It's quite a trick to get kicked out of band at age 9. But there I was, on the verge of tears, face to face with Mr. Picker: "If you're not going to practice," he said sternly, "you may as well not come back next week."

Practice. Ugh. The very word sent shivers of disgust through my body. I mean, why practice when you could *play*? This was my attitude throughout most of my young life (and to a lesser extent, today). It's not that I didn't want to be good at things — whether it was baseball, piano, football, tennis, trombone, or golf. I enjoyed doing them all. I just didn't want to practice. Not in the traditional sense, anyway.

Take my trombone. Please.

When I was in grade school, my mom, a former music teacher, thought it was outrageous that the school system didn't have us learning band instruments prior to the fifth grade. So she convinced the powers that be to let me start trombone lessons a year early. True, the trombone was my choice (I was drawn to the cool "slidey" thing), but I don't remember having any urgent desire to learn a musical instrument.

Oh, I *played* it. I just paid little attention to the notes on the page. I loved making noise with it, and figuring out how it worked, and by and large doing my own thing. But I had a complete aversion to performing the prescribed drills. And since my parents weren't great at enforcing good practice habits (and I'm sure it had nothing to do with my resistance!), there were times when the entire week would go by without my trombone ever once being liberated from its case.

But as much as I hated to practice, I dreaded even more that moment when Mr. Picker would realize I hadn't kept up my end of the deal. He would put down his little white stick, sigh, pause for dramatic effect, look at me with disapproval and say something like, "Did you practice *at all* this week?"

"Yeah!"

Yeah, right! would be more like it.

Eventually he suggested maybe I shouldn't come back. I think he meant it rhetorically, but I took it as, "Don't ever darken my doorstep again. You're hereby officially *banished* from band!"

Getting scolded by my band director was one thing; disappointing my parents – my mom, in particular – was quite another. I knew how important music was to her, so I couldn't quite bring myself to tell her I'd been kicked to the curb. I think I would rather have told her I'd been caught peeing in the sink. So when band day arrived a week later I tried to sneak out of the house without my trombone. But my mom saw me leaving: "Don't forget your trombone, Mike!"

Busted.

Now, I suppose I could have tried to sustain the charade and just brought the blasted hunk of brass to school anyway. But I hated carrying that thing those four long blocks – both ways! It was heavy. Oh, how I envied those fifth-grade girls carrying around their tiny little flutes.

So I chose confession over physical labor and burdensome guilt. "Mom, I need to tell you something," I started to say, with tears welling up in my sad little eyes.

Somewhat to my surprise, my mom was very understanding as I told her my pathetic tale. Yet, what she did *not* say was, "Don't worry, if you don't want to take trombone lessons, you don't have to." What she *did* say was, "Don't worry, I'll talk to the band director and straighten things out."

Not quite what I had in mind.

Against steep odds, I did learn to enjoy playing the trombone and by high school became modestly proficient – without hardly ever practicing. And if I hadn't kept at it, I never would have met and fallen in love with the sweet and lovely Barb Alexander, a fellow freshman and lady trombonist. Our relationship lasted nearly four years, all through high school. Who knows, it might have lasted even longer if I had ever summoned the courage to ask her out.

This same pattern was generally true of my sporting career. I loved to play, hated to work at it. Even more significantly, I hated the pressure of playing team sports. This is perhaps best exemplified by my big Little League choke in the all-city tournament.

When I was 11, I was on a pretty good team: Youthfit Shoes. We only lost a few games during the year and went into post-season play confident that we could do well. After winning our first-round game rather handily, we faced a veritable goliath in the second: Sholem Shoes. (And yes, the competing shoe sponsorship made for a natural rivalry, a precursor to the great Nike-Reebok wars to come.) Sholem was undefeated and heavily favored to win it all. Yet, we managed to give them a good game and led by a run going into the sixth and final inning. But then some sloppy fielding (perhaps by me?) in the top half gave Sholem a one-run lead.

Wouldn't you know it, I soon found myself in one those situations great players crave and adequate ones soil themselves over: trailing by a run, runner on second, two outs, full count. And Yours Truly at the plate. The wind-up (*How old is that pitcher, anyway, like 15?!*), the pitch (*Oh, good, it's low, I won't have to do anything but stand here*), and the call: strike three! (*Wait ... what!?*)

Game over.

I actually held it together pretty well for a while. Everyone consoled me and agreed that the pitch was low. But just as I was starting to feel a little better, John Karich (I'll remember that name forever!) glared at me with his narrow, yellow eyes and hissed, "Why didn't you swing?"

That's when I lost it. I cried and cried and cried. And cried some more. The experience left a scar, no doubt. I was never quite the same player after that, and the following season would be my last of organized baseball.

Not coincidentally, that's when I started gravitating toward individual sports.

Tennis was big with me for a while. And here I should clarify what I mean by "practice." Because I worked at tennis pretty hard; I just never got much in the way of formal instruction. But I beat balls against the garage door relentlessly. How and why my parents put up with it I'll never understand – especially since our garage door had four windows in it. One by one I broke them all. And one by one my dad replaced them with plexi-glass panes. But even they would crack on occasion when met with the force of one of my ferocious forehands.

I don't know; maybe my parents just liked the idea that I was putting some actual *effort* into something. Anything!

After a time, my folks signed me up for some group tennis lessons with the local park district. To my surprise and delight, I was the best one in the class.

But I found out the hard way that being the best in a park district class is not the same as actually being, you know, *good*. I was so excited by my perceived tennis prowess that I convinced my parents to enter me in a local youth tournament.

I showed up that first morning innocent and undaunted, as a lamb to the slaughter – as Greg Norman to Nick Faldo on Sunday at Augusta. I was excited, but not really nervous. What was there to be nervous about? I was best in class! My opponent was a nice, polite young man about my own age. I remember it had rained the night before, so when we shook hands across the net before the match, he asked me very nicely to try not to let the balls roll into any of the puddles around the court.

"I have gut strings," he said.

Blank stare. I had no idea what that meant, but I understood that it was important to him for some reason to keep the balls dry.

Three-and-a-half minutes later, I turned around after retrieving a ball from a puddle, only to see Chip standing at the net again. In the blink of an eye he had beaten me 6-0 6-0. I scarcely remember winning a point. I was so discouraged by my thrashing that I literally would not play the game again for years.

Decades later, I was telling this story to Tom Scaggs, an old friend who is a serious tennis player. "Do you remember the guy's name?" he asked.

"Yeah," I replied. "Chip Sweeney."

Tom's eyes widened. "Chip Sweeney?" he said. "*Chip Sweeney?!*" he repeated, this time with a bit more volume.

"You quit tennis because you lost a match to Chip Sweeney!? He was one of the best players in the whole state!"

Well, what do you know about that? Live and learn, I guess.

That fall, perhaps motivated by my latest athletic humiliation, I won the job of starting quarterback on my school's 5th and 6th grade YMCA flag football team. My brother – 18 months younger, 10 pounds heavier, and less athletically inclined than I – was my center. To this day I shudder at the memory of having to place my hands against his upturned buttocks to receive the snap.

My quarterbacking career was quite forgettable. I had a good, accurate arm, which is how I won the job, but I had the steely nerves of a traumatized baby kinkajou. I was much more concerned about not screwing up than about trying to do something good. Our coach had me calling my own plays, and I quickly learned that the safest thing was to hand the ball off nearly every time to our talented running back. Three yards and a cloud of confusion.

When fall turned to winter, the YMCA action moved indoors to the basketball court, where I promptly got elbowed in the mouth while fighting for a rebound during a game. Blood and tears flowed amidst the sweat.

The damage to my mouth was pretty significant, with the most extensive trauma being to my two lower front teeth. One was snapped off basically in half, requiring many visits to the dentist – and ultimately a root canal – to repair. And that was the easy part. X-rays revealed that my other tooth was broken into several pieces below the gum line. Ultimately, it took a crack team of oral surgeons to slice open my gum and pick out the pieces.

It was *not* a pleasant time in my life.

I share this painful tale to help explain the effective end of my career in team sports. My mother was horrified by the grisly turn of events – and ticked off that the YMCA was not held financial responsible for all the resulting dental bills. I can't prove this, and my mom always denied it, but I believe she quietly applied pressure to my dad (maybe without even realizing it) to stop encouraging me to play such dangerous sports. It also didn't help that so many of my friends from grade school ended up going to the other junior high school after 6th grade. When I arrived at the doorstep of Jefferson Junior High, I suddenly found myself in a much bigger school, with a lot fewer friends, and less self-confidence than ever before. Going out for any team sports did not appeal to me at all.

Which ultimately just made it easier for me to turn my full attention to golf.

• • •

My golfing memories go back to about age 7, when I started playing in the yard with some of my dad's old clubs; he had a bag full of them, hardly ever used. Though I vaguely remember my dad having a regular golf game at some point, he was one of those guys who basically gave it up once the kids came along.

It was an eclectic mix of clubs; a few of them even had names on them – such as mashie or spoon – rather than numbers. A couple had fake plastic wood layered over steel shafts. There was even a 2-wood.

Eventually my dad cut down a couple clubs to fit me – one iron and one wood – and fashioned crude grips out of electrical tape. For the most part, I worked on my game alone in the front yard – with real golf balls. Gradually, my proficiency increased, until one day I caught one flush with my miniature 3-wood and sent it sailing across the street and over our neighbor's hedge. *THUD!* The ball hit the side of the house with authority. Fortunately, no one was around to witness my transgression. Unfortunately, no one was around to witness *the best shot of my life*!

One day, I believe it was the summer I turned 8, I was playing front-yard golf with two friends, Andy Stallman (more about him later) and Tim Holmes. The problem was, we couldn't find any golf balls. So we used a baseball. One baseball, shared by the three of us.

After taking a shot, each player would "mark" his ball with his foot before handing the ball and club off to the next player. Ours was not a large yard, and our 8-year-old brains were highly undeveloped, so you might imagine what happened next. Andy got too close to Tim while marking his ball and Tim *whacked* him square in the nose on his follow-through. Much blood, many tears, and loud screaming followed.

My mom was inside baking a cherry pie – which I remember because she didn't bake very often and I *loved* cherry pie. She rushed out when she heard the uproar and took Andy inside. There she patched him up, and once he settled down and the bleeding stopped, she sent him home, about two blocks away, on his bike.

That evening, Mom was horrified to learn that Tim had, in fact, broken Andy's nose. She felt so badly about not taking Andy's injury more seriously that she brought that fresh-baked cherry pie over to his house. She never forgave herself for not driving Andy home that day. And I never forgave *her* for giving him that pie.

As I got older, the local Par-3 course – 27 holes of modestly manicured wonder – became my primary golf stomping grounds. Andy, by then firmly entrenched as my best friend, was my primary playing partner.

All things considered, "Par-3" (as near as I could ever tell, that was the actual name of the place) was a pretty nice facility. In addition to the three 9-hole courses, two of which were lighted for night play, there was a small pro shop and driving range. It was run by a PGA Professional by the name of Bob Nelson – who I would later learn was also a math teacher, golf coach, assistant football coach, and former wrestling coach at the local high school. Running Par-3 was his summer gig.

"Bulldog" Bob, as the high school kids called him, didn't look much like a golfer. Short and stocky with stubby fingers and no neck, he looked more like a football player or wrestler than golf pro. I never saw him actually play, but I did see him hit balls, and he was the real deal.

Andy and I would play at the Par-3 whenever we could scrape up a few bucks and a ride to the course. Some years we purchased season passes, making transportation the only issue. Fortunately, our parents were frequently willing to make the 10-minute drive and drop us off. It was probably a small price to pay, in retrospect, for keeping us occupied for a few hours. I once played 54 holes in one day, all by myself. I was also the proud maker of two aces there: one with a bladed 7-iron that bounced the 76 yards to the hole; the other a couple years later with a well-struck, 110-yard 5-iron.

In addition to being my best friend, Andy in those days was someone I looked up to – in spite of the abuse he sometimes dished out. He was a little bit taller than me, a little bit bigger, and generally a little bit better at everything. It frustrated me that he generally got the better of me on the golf course, but it motivated me to improve.

Most frustrating of all was the way he mocked me when I started trying to hit a 3-iron to one of the two 140-yard holes, the longest on the property. Historically, we both needed drivers to reach those greens. But I *knew* I could hit a 3-iron that far, because I had done it several times when Andy wasn't there. The problem was, I would invariably miss-hit the shot in the face of Andy's merciless taunting.

"Told ya!" he would cry out as my ball dribbled halfway to the hole or far off to the right.

Andy passed away unexpectedly at the age of 29, and whenever we talk about him, we remember his friendship, his sharp wit, his love of working for the Ford Motor Company in Detroit, and his mean streak. We miss you, buddy.

As much time as I spent on the Red, White, and Blue, rarely did I grace the driving range with my presence. Beating balls held virtually no appeal to me. Again, why practice when you could play? Limited funds, I'm sure, were also a factor. Still, the course was an excellent training ground, even as I continued to ingrain bad swing habits.

As Andy and I got older, our golf outings sometimes took us to the ancient University of Illinois 9-hole course – which I believe the university kept in operation primarily to serve as a parking lot for football games. We called it "Dogpatch" or "Rinky-Dink." It was not a very impressive course. But this is where my dad occasionally took me to play after work. After dinner. After dessert. He knew that if we waited until it was almost dusk, the tiny little clubhouse would be closed and we could walk on and play a few holes for free. Those days were the best of my young life, as I enjoyed playing golf with my dad more than anything.

More often, however, my playing partner there would be Andy or Mark Sweeney (no relation to Chip).

Mark Sweeney. Now there's a name that brings back memories! It was Mark who introduced me to caddying at the local country club. It was Mark who introduced me to the Beatles. It was Mark who introduced me to certain kinds of "literature." And it was Mark who introduced me to almost burning down my house.

In fairness, this particular incident was as much my doing as Mark's. But I'm sure it wouldn't have happened without Sweeney's nefarious influence. He had a certain effect on me.

One fine summer evening during our junior high school years, Sweeney (we hardly ever called him "Mark") and I were hanging out in my backyard just after dark. I don't remember where the rest of my family was, but I had somehow finagled permission to stay home alone. So Sweeney came over. We had grilled out for dinner that night, so there was a pile of smoldering coals in the bottom of our little grill. Sweeney and I were sitting around what was left of the fire talking – likely about our growing appreciation for boobs and who amongst the 9th grade girls might be considered an "ultra-fox" – absent-mindedly poking at the coals with the thin metal skewers we used to toast marshmallows. Somehow, we figured out that the little circle on the handle end was just the right size and shape for picking up a hot coal.

Fling!

Next thing you know, a hot coal was exploding against a tree in a burst of glowing orange cinders. *Wow, that was cool!*

Fling! Fling! Fling!

After a few flings, however, that tree wasn't providing quite the same level of excitement anymore. Somebody – coulda been me, coulda been Sweeney – eyed the steeply pitched roof of my house. *Are you thinking what I'm thinking?*

Now, wait just a second! Lest I create the impression that Sweeney and I were a couple of crazed, brainless, 13-year-old pyromaniacs, I want you to know that before any red hot coals were flung onto the backside of the Zimmerman abode, I, being the responsible one, smartly watered it down with our garden hose. Safety first!

Fling! POOF! Fling! POOF! Fling! POOF!

In a matter of moments, we were enjoying a fireworks display rivaled only by the carefully controlled and properly licensed shows we witnessed each Fourth of July at Memorial Stadium – from a proximity to which we had previously only dreamed of. *This ... is ... AWESOME!*

Sure, it's awesome until someone loses an eye – or flings a flaming fireball so far it flies over the roof and into the front yard.

In a mild panic, I ran around the house, only to be greeted by a woman walking her dog. "What was *that*?" she asked with appropriate alarm.

Confession, they say, is good for the soul – but bald-faced denial comes more quickly to the tongue: "I don't know!" I replied. "Something just came flying over the house!"

Thinking I had dodged a bullet, and undoubtedly proud of my

brilliant cover story, I ran and rejoined Sweeney in the back yard. A few minutes later, after we had gone inside, we heard sirens. They came closer. And closer. We quickly realized they were coming down my street – toward my house. Again with minds focused solely on "doing the right thing," we hid, cowering in the kitchen as the fire trucks rolled slowly by, presumably scanning the skies for glowing chunks of Kingsford's.

But they never found one. And they never found us. Our secret has remained safe – until now. (Sweeney, if you're reading this, I blame you completely!)

Despite his propensity for helping me find trouble where none had previously existed, I also have Mark Sweeney to thank for a short game that later helped earn me a spot on the high school golf team. When we weren't up to no good, Sweeney and I spent many summer evenings "chipping around" in his yard. We made up a game: Each tree was assigned a number, and we designed "holes" that were described something like this: "Go to the left of #2, around #6, and back to #3" – meaning you had to hit the trunk of tree #3 with your ball to "hole out." We played for something like a nickel a hole, and whoever lost the hole got to choose/design the next.

The game called for us to hit a wide variety of shots with just one club – I used a pitching wedge. You might have to open it up to get a high bounce off the concrete walkway (which was treated as a water hazard when you were not required to hit it as part of a hole). You might need to close the face to hit it low, under the branches. And, what I think was most important of all, we played the ball as it lay, which required shots from all manner of challenging lies on the not-so-beautifully manicured lawn.

I would need that strong short game as I moved from Dog-Patch/Rinky-Dink to the 18-hole Orange and Blue Courses at the "new" U of I golf courses by the airport in nearby Savoy. What distinguished both back then – the Blue Course especially – were the wide-open spaces.

Both the airport and its adjacent golf courses were built on what used to be cornfields. The natural landscape is flat, treeless, windswept, and flat. The Blue Course was and still is the easier course, with no real trouble to speak of. With no proper rough, it was "bomb and gouge" without the gouge. I'm not sure they irrigated at all in those days, making the entire course run faster than Tiger through a pack of autograph hounds. I especially looked forward to the ninth hole on the Blue, a 470-yard dogleg right par-5, where the prevailing southwesterly breeze made it possible for even barely pubescent 14-year-old boys to think about hitting the green in two.

The Orange Course was more challenging – more of a real golf course. Whereas I don't think they moved any earth to build the Blue, they compensated for the lack of topography on the Orange by elevating a few of the greens and sloping most others sharply from back to front. Large sand traps also gobbled up shots that wandered too far left or right. Over the years, they gradually added more trees to give the course some definition. It was not a pretty track, but it was not an easy one. And it suited my scrambling style.

Though the University of Illinois golf team has since moved its operations to a newer, better course across town in Urbana, the beloved Orange Course (as I now refer to it) is what Steve Stricker called "home" during his Big Ten Championship seasons. Which I think gives the place some lingering prestige.

Neither the Orange nor the Blue, however, adequately prepared me for my stint on the high school golf team.

• • •

Mike Hagan hated me – and I really don't know why. No, wait … I think I do. I think he hated me because it drove him crazy how I played golf.

My swing back then was not at all pretty to look at. I had a very strong grip and played the ball way forward in my stance. With my hands thrust forward, I slashed at the ball with a vicious out-to-in motion, producing a wildly unpredictable slice. It was very unrefined, and I'm sure it offended Mike's more-sophisticated golfing sensibilities.

Hagan was a country club guy – his dad was one of the men I would occasionally caddy for. I'm sure he had gotten all the appropriate lessons and learned to swing a club in all the right ways. His swing was pretty. And yet … whenever we played together, he couldn't seem to beat me. He would hit a nice drive down the middle of the fairway and a nice approach to the green. Then he would two-putt for par. On the same hole I might drive it wildly right, hit a desperate recovery shot left of the green, but then chip close and sink the putt. There was no question he was the better golfer, but when we played together I got into his head – big time. The whole situation reminds me of what Bobby Jones once said about Walter Hagen, a legendary scrambler and showman:

> I would far rather play a man who is straight down the fairway with his drive, on the green with his second, and down in two putts for his par. I can play a man like that at his own game which is par golf …. But when a man misses his drive, and then misses his second shot, and then wins a hole with a birdie – it gets my goat! (From *Sir Walter: Walter Hagen and the Invention of Professional Golf*, by Tom Clavin)

I had first tried out for the golf team as a sophomore – a broken leg had taken me out the fall of my freshman year. But to illustrate my level of interest, I didn't find out about the tryouts until the day they started. So I made hasty arrangements to get out to the driving range at the Par-3 after school to have my game thoroughly evaluated by Bulldog Bob.

Over the course of the next two days, I showed Bulldog enough to make what was essentially the practice squad. This meant I was invited to come practice (free of charge) at the range every day after school but would not be taking part in practices at the team's home course or compete in matches.

In retrospect, this was a golden opportunity I did not truly appreciate. I showed up dutifully for a while but soon got bored with the proceedings. I wanted to *play*; this was *practice*. Eventually I just stopped showing up. Truth is, I couldn't bring myself to face the coach, much in the way I couldn't face my mom when I was banned from band.

And nobody ever said anything.

When next fall rolled around, I didn't bother to try out again; I figured I had blown my chance. And the truth is it just didn't matter that much to me. I loved playing golf as much as ever, but playing on a team was not high on my list of priorities. Perhaps my previous sporting humiliations were a factor. I was learning to fear letting my teammates down.

By then my caddying career had pretty much come to an end, but I always had some sort of a job with which to earn my greens fees. At 9, I became the youngest paperboy in town. Once I got old enough to caddy, about age 13, that became my primary summer job. There wasn't much I didn't like about it – except the prospect of having to talk to people. I loved being out on the course and just being around the game. I learned a lot simply through osmosis.

I was a pretty good caddy, but never got a good reputation for it because I was so quiet. I envied the older boy who worked in the pro shop, and desperately wanted that job to one day be mine. But when the position opened up a few years later, I had no shot, as I had never done anything to garner the club pro's attention. Nor did I ever feel compelled to make my ambitions known. More than anything, my goal in life at that age was to blend in.

In the winter months I worked a couple days a week cleaning my dad's office; he owned a small advertising agency downtown. I really hated this job, and my dad was always on me to do it better. But I was handicapped by being naturally lazy. It wasn't my fault, you see. It's something I was born with – much to my dad's eternal frustration.

The one nice thing about the job was that there was a little golf shop a couple blocks away. After I had put in my two hours pushing the dirt around the office, I would wander over and kill time window shopping for clubs, bags, balls, and assorted gadgets, gizmos, and swing-aids. I don't know what the guy who owned the place thought. He was friendly and always nice to me. But now, as an adult, I wonder how much I might have annoyed him, spending so much time there without ever actually buying anything. Who knows – maybe the thought of a 14-year-old kid so deeply bitten by the golf bug made him smile.

Ultimately I did buy something there: a set of used Johnny Miller woods – 1, 3, and 5 – for something like $40. They went nicely with the used Walter Hagen irons I had bought for $75 at the pro shop where I caddied. My first full-size complete set.

Another significant event in my world in those days was the annual birthday golf outing with my dad. Even though he rarely played anymore, he knew how much I loved it – and was proud that I was getting good. So once a year he took off work, took me out to the Lake of the Woods Golf Club, and played 18 holes with me. The best part? We rented a *cart*, which was still something of a novelty back then. And he let *me* drive it! Wahoo!

It was the day of the year I most looked forward to, even more than Christmas.

In high school I started buying a summer student pass for the U of I courses in Savoy. It cost $90: an absolute steal, even in today's dollars. It gave me unlimited greens fees for the months of June, July, and August. With pass in hand, the only thing limiting my golf was time and opportunity (i.e., transportation). But I had plenty of time on my hands and found various ways to get out to the course pretty frequently.

At home, I began tracking all my scores, hole by hole, on graph-paper charts. Many a Saturday night was spent in my room designing graph-paper golf courses, analyzing my scores, and dreaming about taking Julie the Cruise Director to Mr. Roarke's special island. To this day I remember charting three straight 82s on the Orange and thinking to myself that was pretty darn good. And it was.

The first time I broke 80 came in my first opportunity – which is something of an aberration considering my history of choking under pressure. But when I came to the 18th on the Orange, a 160-yard par-3, needing a par for 79, I stuck it to three feet and calmly (the pressure was off!) made the birdie for 78.

Despite my increasing skills, the fall of my junior year went by without a thought of playing on the golf team. Some of it may have had to do with my dad getting sick. He hadn't been feeling well for months, and I don't think encouraging me to try out again was top of mind. In December, he was diagnosed with lung cancer. It was bad. A heavy smoker for 30 years, he had put off going to the doctor for too long. There was very little they could do, and in April of the following year, 1980, he passed away.

My dad had always been the primary source of what little motivation I could muster. And without him there I just kind of drifted through life for a while. When my senior year began that fall, I had no intention of trying out for the golf team. Again, I never even gave it much, if any, thought.

But then, on what must have been one of the first days of school, I happened to run into Coach Nelson in the hallway. I didn't expect him to remember me, but if he did, I was sure his feelings toward me would be ill, considering how I had bailed on the team two years previously. I tried to avoid eye contact as we approached each other, but to no avail. He caught my attention and said something like, "Got your sticks? Tryouts are tomorrow."

Perhaps my "betrayal" was bigger in my mind than in reality. And how could I refuse a personal invitation from Bulldog Bob? I tried out again, and this time made the team – the *real* team.

It took a while to crack the starting lineup, however. Playing at Lincolnshire Fields Country Club was a shock to my system. Unlike the wide-open Orange and Blue courses, Lincolnshire wound through an upper-middle-class subdivision on the outskirts of town. There was water or out-of-bounds lining nearly every hole, so the penalty for wayward shots was severe. In the first nine-hole practice round I shot 54 – or maybe it was 57. Keeping my driver in the bag, I gradually learned to play a more controlled game. My scores improved each round, and by the end of the second week I had carded a nifty 38, which got me into the starting lineup.

I usually played in the #4 spot, but sometimes, Coach Nelson put me at #3, in place of Brad Miller, who was cocky and kind of obnoxious. Truthfully, I found him extremely obnoxious. I think Coach did it because, in contrast to Brad's "challenging" personality, he appreciated my mild-mannered, cooperative nature. In retrospect, I think he just liked me.

At one tournament, I started out hot and shot 38 on the front nine. With stars in my eyes, I let the pressure get to me and shot 10 strokes worse on the back for a total of 86, probably pretty close to average for me in those days. We did well that day, finishing third overall as a team. I remember we were ten strokes out of second, and some of the guys pointed out that that's exactly how much I "choked" by. But Bulldog came to my defense, saying that 86 was a solid score and pointing out that if I hadn't shot 38 on the front, we might not have even finished third.

If you're reading this, Coach, thanks for that.

My rivalry with Hagan continued; it probably hadn't helped that I ignorantly showed up for the team's first match wearing shorts – which Hagan quickly, and none too tactfully, informed me was a no-no. Hey, it was warm out and I was used to playing at Savoy. He should have just been happy I was wearing a *shirt*!

Our rivalry even reared its ugly head on the course once in the middle of a dual match. He and I were paired together (not our usual lineup; I think Bulldog had mixed things up to try to gain an edge) with two members of the opposing team. As usual, Mike let my presence get to him. He was not playing well and seemed ready to explode. Mid-way through the match, Mike found himself in a fairway bunker; I was standing next to his bag at the edge of the trap near the fairway. Mike muffed the shot and promptly whipped his club at his bag in anger. His aim, however, was a little high. The club hit *me* instead, right across the knee, snapping cleanly in two. The club, not my knee. He begged me not to tell the coach, and I never did.

At the golf team banquet that fall, Coach Nelson told the assembled parents and loved ones that I had one of the best short games he had ever seen. I beamed. My long game ... let's just say I'm glad he didn't mention it.

After graduation that spring, I really had no idea what to do next. With my dad gone and my mom still grieving, I was not pushed in any particular direction – though I really could have used it. I hadn't done anything in the way of college prep, so I did the only thing I could think to do: buy myself a beautiful set of Wilson Staff woods as a graduation gift.

My grades, thanks to my poor-to-nonexistent study habits, were respectable, but not stellar – a solid B average. Armed with a strong sense of "I guess I don't know what else to do," I enrolled at the local junior college in the two-year broadcast technology program.

I probably could have had a shot at making the golf team there, but didn't consider it. I'm not sure why. If you had asked me during my high school years what I wanted to do for a living someday, I would have said "professional golfer." I was enough of a realist to know I wasn't good enough, but it was the only thing I could think of, and the only thing I ever dreamed of.

Back at the Orange Course, I used to envy the young guys working there, driving the lawnmowers and what not. I thought it would be awesome to have such a job, but again, I never bothered to look into it, such was my lack of initiative. I think I also assumed you had to "know somebody" to get what was so clearly a fun and glamorous job. At least, that was my excuse for not trying. I would have *killed* to get a job in the pro shop – but was not willing to risk a blow to my fragile self-esteem by actually *asking*.

In retrospect, I never realized there were *other* career paths in golf to follow besides "touring professional." If someone had steered me in that direction, I would have jumped at the opportunity. Or maybe not. I was pretty lazy and clueless.

After three years of on-again, off-again study at Parkland Junior College, I made my way to the University of Illinois to start over as a freshman, studying animal science with an eye on becoming a veterinarian. I was 21 by then and figured I had matured sufficiently to study hard enough to get into vet school (which is very difficult).

I was wrong.

I had clearly underestimated the temptations and distractions of full-time campus life and it didn't take long for me to wander off the academic straight and narrow. I blame Mike "Scruffy" Neuses for this. The weekend before my first big biology test, Mike, who had moved to Champaign from Iowa before our senior year in high school, convinced me to take a road trip to Iowa with a bunch of others for a football game.

"Well, okay," I finally said. "But I'm going to bring some books and study in the car."

"If you do I'm going to throw them out the window!" he replied.

I believed him. He seemed so wise and mature. So I left the books at home and went to Iowa. Had a blast. And got a "B" on my biology exam. Not a disaster, but B's weren't going to get me into vet school. And a pattern had been set.

The vet school dream died relatively quickly, and without that as a goal my grades began to really suffer. I soon found myself on the verge of flunking out. Eventually I steadied myself, changed majors (to agricultural communications), and found my groove. I also discovered the Illini Union.

During the winter of my sophomore year I took advantage of being a hometown boy to get a job at the Illini Union bowling alley over the holidays. I had bowled some as a kid, so it was a good fit. And I enjoyed learning to fix pinsetters. But the job also involved working in the pool hall, which was overseen by the same office. This, it turns out, was where my true weakness (and latent talents) lay. Before long I had become a highly skilled pool player, a very good bowler, and a passable student. A renaissance man!

One of the other regulars in the pool hall was Chuck Fiser, a member of the U of I golf team – which also included Mike Small, now the Illini men's golf coach. But Steve Stricker was the big star, what with his multiple Big Ten championships and All-American status and such. I got a glimpse of him once when he stuck his head in the pool hall, presumably looking for Chuck. I don't think he noticed me, though. Sigh. Another unrequited love.

After what felt like about 17 years I finally graduated. My career path took me briefly to New Jersey and then to the Milwaukee, Wisconsin, area, where I've lived ever since.

My golf game survived my college years pretty much intact, but in the working world it started to suffer a bit. Still very much single, it wasn't an issue of time or opportunity, but my motivation seemed to slip. My game had peaked, and as it became harder to improve (always my primary motivation), I began to enjoy it less. Improving from where I was would have meant (gasp!) practice and hard work. And I wasn't really willing to do that. As I started to play less, my scores crept up and the fun factor crept down. Eventually, I had to make a very conscious decision to enjoy the game for its own sake and not depend on improvement as a measure of gratification. So I settled in to become a somewhat satisfied high-80s kind of player instead of a frustrated low-80s kind.

And that's where it has stayed pretty much ever since, even as my game has evolved considerably. My ball striking has improved since then – I play a much more "controlled" game off the tee. I don't slice it as much, but partly because I don't swing as hard or hit it as far. I hit more fairways (or at least stay out of the trees more often) and more greens in regulation than I used to. Meanwhile, my short game has deteriorated through lack of use. Though it's still solid compared to most people's, I'm not the master of getting up-and-down I once was. Now that I'm married (God took pity on me and found me a wonderful wife, Elizabeth) and the ridiculously proud father of an amazing 9-year-old boy, I don't get to play nearly as much as I'd like. And so it goes. It's a very good life.

And yet ... there's still this thought in the back of my brain: "What if?" What if I had practiced more and gotten more formal instruction? What if I'd pursued golf as a career path when I was younger – would I perhaps be a golf writer now? And what if I ever had the opportunity – and took advantage of it – to rebuild my swing from the ground up? My answer to the "what would you do if you won the lottery" question had always been: I'd quit my job and learn to play golf full-time, tearing down my swing completely and then rebuilding it from the resulting rubble.

Then one day it hit me: Why not "start over" by learning to play left-handed? For one thing, I told myself, it would give you a head-start on tearing down your swing. You could write a book about it and justify the time and potential expense to your loving wife and family as a "career move." Find an experienced pro to guide you. Wherever possible, include your son (who was already learning to love the game – he's probably digging a sand trap in our front yard as I write). Finally, don't just write about yourself, write about the science and theory of playing golf from the opposite side. Write about famous left-handed golfers. And don't base your "success" on how proficient a lefty you become; base it on how much you learn and how much fun you have along the way.

The more I thought and prayed about it, the better idea it seemed, despite the challenges and misgivings previously discussed. Once I got Elizabeth on board the deal was sealed in my heart, mind, and spirit.

This is going to be awesome!

There was just one problem. That pro … he'd probably expect me to, you know, practice.

There's that word again. What was I getting myself into?

CHAPTER 2
Small Ball

"There is no similarity between golf and putting;
they are two different games, one played in the air,
and the other on the ground."

—Ben Hogan

For my money, Ben Hogan is the greatest golfer of all time – if you measure the man at the peak of his prowess: 1948; 1950-'53 (I give Hogan a medical exemption in 1949; more about that later). During that stretch, Hogan won eight of the 12 major championships he played, never once finishing outside the top 10. Which is pretty remarkable when you consider the man hated putting. So much so he considered it another game entirely. "Putting is not golf," was his attitude.

Yet, if Hogan had devoted any effort at all to "that other game" – even a tenth of what he devoted to full swings – it's almost unfathomable to think about all the tournaments he might have won. Could anyone ever have beaten him?

Hogan's answer to his inadequate putting was simple. According to legend (and as reported in James Dodson's amazing *Ben Hogan: An American Life*), it came from his wife:

> On one occasion about this time, after coming close but faltering yet again and bitterly wondering aloud to his bride, "Why the hell can't I make more birdies, Val?" ...
>
> "Why, Ben," she supposedly replied calmly, "why don't you just hit it closer to the hole?"

Of course, it was a different game back then. Byron Nelson writes in his autobiography that pros in general didn't work much on their putting. He attributed this to the wildly inconsistent greens and putting conditions encountered on tour in his day, much slower and bumpier than the billiard-table-smooth greens pros play on today. Putting back then involved a lot of guesswork, Nelson said, and "it just didn't pay to spend a lot of time on putting."

Today, however, the axiom "Drive for show and putt for dough" is alive and well. So I didn't think I'll be able to afford neglecting "that other game" as I re-learn the game. In fact, I intended to start there.

I'm pretty sure legendary teacher Harvey Penick would approve. In his famous *Little Red Book*, when talking about teaching beginners the game, he advocates starting at the hole (with putting) and working your way out (with chipping, then pitching, etc.):

> Golf should be learned starting at the cup and progressing back toward the tee.
>
> I'm talking about with children. The same thing applies to adult beginners, but adults think that is too simple. An adult beginner – especially a man – thinks he's not getting his money's worth if you ask him to spend an hour sinking short putts. He wants to pull out his driver and smack it, which is the very last thing he will learn if he comes to me.
>
> If a beginner tries to learn the game at the tee and move on toward the green, postponing the short game until last, this is one beginner who will be lucky ever to beat anybody.

This is how I've tried to teach Jack. When I take him to the driving range, he's content to hit only a few dozen balls before moving to the putting green, where he happily chips and putts for as long as I let him.

I like this approach. Plus, though the thought of taking a full left-handed swing seemed preposterous at the outset, putting left-handed seemed doable. So I resolved to putt, putt, putt, then putt some more, until my left-handed stroke felt as natural as my right. By then, I theorized, the left-handed motion would feel natural enough to help me start chipping, then pitching, etc.

If I was patient, it may be months before I even started *thinking* about taking a full left-handed swing. Oops, I just thought about it. Couldn't help it.

Step one, of course, was to acquire a left-handed putter. Easy enough for many people, I suppose. Difficult for me, given my finely honed stinginess. So, one beautiful late-September Sunday evening, when I saw a left-handed putter at the driving range pro shop, for the low, low price of just $20, I still couldn't pull the trigger.

Jack was outside on the putting green having a ball. I was inside pacing a hole in the carpet near the bag of bargain-bin flat sticks. I took it out. I put it back. I took it out again and put it back again. I took it out and fashioned a crude left-handed putting grip and stroked it back and forth a few times. I put it back again.

It was new, with the shrink wrap still on the head. But it was a cheapie – a "Hippo" brand Ping knock-off. It's only $20, I told myself. Buy it! But 20 bucks is 20 bucks, I countered. What if I buy it and decide I don't like it – or change my mind about left-handed golf? Twenty dollars is dinner for three at Culver's!

Hating myself for being such a wimp, I shoved the putter back in the bag and went back outside, where I sat and sulked for a while before convincing Jack it was time to go home (not an easy task).

At home I told Elizabeth about my dilemma and she gave me a look that says, "What, are you an idiot? Just buy it already!"

You see, my lovely wife and I have very different approaches to this type of purchase decision. While I tend to think, "I'd better not buy this, in case we don't need it," she thinks, "I should buy this, in case we need it." To say more would be to risk our carefully crafted marital bliss.

The next day at work I wasted a good part of the morning thinking about that stupid putter. I should go back there at lunch and buy it, I thought. But it's a 15-minute drive each way – how much gas is that? It would be silly to make a special trip just to buy a $20 putter. Then I had a better idea: the worldwide interwebs. Within minutes I identified an Odyssey brand knockoff (I've always liked the look of those) I could have delivered to my front door for $19.98 – two cents cheaper than the Hippo! And no sales tax or gas usage!

Three hours later, with beads of sweat forming on my brow and my hand beginning to cramp from holding it over the "submit your order" button, I sent the order on its way. The quest had officially begun.

The putter was slated to arrive in about a week, the first week of October. In the meantime, I was already crafting a strategy for learning to properly play with my new toy. One of the keys to this project was to *do things right*. That is, re-learn my golfing skills in a proper and orderly fashion, not just by slapping balls around and figuring out what seems to work. But I hadn't yet lined up an instructor, and I didn't want to wait. My hope was to spend the winter months honing my lefty skills indoors, so that by the time spring rolled around I'd be ready to hit the course.

As it happened, a recent issue of *Golf Digest* had a special 30-page putting section, so I decided to start there. And the place to start with putting is with the grip.

I've always been a pretty solid putter. And for as long as I can remember I've used what is basically a looser version of my interlocking golf grip. It's a bit unorthodox, but it's comfortable and seems to work well. Almost immediately I had the thought that maybe I should just keep this same grip and putt cross-handed as a lefty. But I dismissed that idea right away. It would feel like cheating, as the whole idea was to start over and learn from the ground up.

So I consulted several sources to get the lowdown on a "proper" putting grip. What I discovered is that *how* you hold the putter isn't really that important. Putting guru Dave Stockton puts it this way: "Grip the putter any way you like, as long as it doesn't hinder your left [my right] hand's role in the stroke. But make sure to grip the club in your fingers."

After all, you see all manner of different putting grips on the PGA Tour (though the more unusual ones typically belong to golfers who have struggled on the greens). After a little bit of experimentation using my regular putter, I settled on what you might call a double-overlapping grip, with the pinky and ring finger of my left hand nestled in the gaps between the index, middle, and ring fingers of my right. It felt pretty natural, and allowed me to keep my shoulders a little more level than usual.

I found it was useless, however, as much as I tried, to hit left-handed putts with my right-handed putter. So I settled in by the front door and waited for the UPS man to come. It was a long wait.

Finally, on October 4, 2010 (a day that will live in revelry), I found a golf-club sized box on the doorstep after work. My new putter was here!

After ripping the box to pieces, I was immediately taken aback by the "geometry" of the new club. I had read that putters with the shaft more in line with the center of the face, such as this one, were better for the straight-back and straight-through stroke I try to make. This is not, however, something I normally think much about; I mostly just hit it. In fact, I'm generally of the mind that putters are putters. And that far too much thought, effort, and money is put into putter choice, as evidenced by my success with my $10 flat stick. Not to mention Jim Furyk winning the $10 million FedEx Cup bonus in 2010 using a used putter he picked up in a pro shop for 39 bucks.

Putting is simple – or at least it should be. Yips (a mental affliction that causes golfers to stab jerkily at putts), something I've never had a problem with, are generally caused by over-thinking. So I would need to be careful about thinking too much now. What better way to avoid this than to start hitting some putts right away? So I grabbed Jack and headed to nearby Brown Deer Golf Course, a Milwaukee County track that was formerly home to the U.S. Bank Championship, formerly the Greater Milwaukee Open (may it rest in peace).

I have fond memories of this course, even though I've rarely actually played it (it's more expensive than most other public courses in the area). It's where PGA Tour journeyman Skip Kendall, who grew up down the road in Fox Point, honed his skills as a young man. It's also where I once witnessed – from a distance of about 10 feet – the muscular Jim Thorpe splinter his driver shaft on his downswing.

Back when I was young, carefree, and single – with vacation days to spare – I often volunteered as a marshal at the GMO. It was awesome – though not recommended to anyone who doesn't really, really enjoy watching golf. Our ranks were mostly comprised of genial retired guys, many of whom have been sitting in the same spot at the same hole for years (just during the tournament, I mean; not continuously).

But I was a young (by comparison) renegade, and always requested to be moved around each day. And on this particular Friday morning I was assigned to work the tee at the par-4 12th, a lonely outpost in a back corner of the course, all but deserted in the early hours. In the presence of perhaps a half-dozen spectators, I watched in awe as Thorpe and his huge forearms strode to the tee box and prepared to swing away.

We privileged few then watched in amazement as the graphite shaft (no doubt somewhat primitive by today's standards) on Thorpe's driver splintered on his downswing. The clubhead made glancing contact and the ball squirted about 45 degrees to the right, traveling perhaps 50 yards into a grove of trees. If there had been any kind of a crowd there, it surely would have struck someone.

While the players and caddies scratched their heads and tried to figure out what happened, I in my stylish marshal shirt and matching cap, along with perhaps three enthusiastic fans, scurried to see where the ball ended up. As we scanned this forgotten area of the course – surely only some weekend hacker had ever hit a ball there before – one of my helpers gave a quiet shout: "Here it is!" I looked up, in horror, to see him proudly *holding* the ball, apparently assuming Thorpe would be entitled to some sort of equipment-malfunction do-over.

"Don't pick it up!" I whisper-yelled, prompting the perp to drop the ball immediately. Clearly, he respected my authority – or sensed and feared my rising panic.

As a deputized marshal, I was the law in those parts. I had sworn an oath (well, not really ... but I vaguely recall signing some forms). Yet the last thing I ever wanted was to actually have to *do* something, especially if it could affect the course of play. Sure, holding up the little QUIET PLEASE sign gives one a feeling of power, but as Spider-Man says: "With great power comes great responsibility." And responsibility is something I've always shied away from (ask anyone!). Yet there I was with a situation on my hands.

So what did I do? I leapt into action – and by that I mean I kept my mouth shut. No one saw what happened, and if I had told someone, there would have been a delay. We might have had to summon a rules official, who would then have to find his way to our remote corner of the course and issue a ruling. My nightmare. Instead I assumed my well-practiced marshal stance: legs shoulder-width apart, arms raised, palms out in mock-authoritative fashion. Stand back, everyone! Marshal at work here! Everything's under control! Picture Barney Fife quieting a crowd on Main Street Mayberry – without the crowd.

After a moment, Thorpe, his forearms, and his caddy strode purposefully toward us. A bead of flop sweat rolled down my temple as I shushed the imaginary gallery, but Thorpe never even looked up. He made quick work of the matter, whacking the ball between some trees and into the fairway without much thought or fanfare. Almost as suddenly as it gathered, the storm passed.

Is there a penalty for unknowingly hitting a golf ball that a fan picked up, when the act was subsequently covered-up by a spineless marshal? If there is, Thorpe signed an incorrect scorecard that day and should be retroactively disqualified immediately!

But I digress.

In addition to this storied history of marshal malfeasance and cover-ups, Brown Deer also has a nice big practice putting green out front, which is more or less open to the public. I say "more or less" because I've never actually asked; but I considered it so until I was told otherwise. There's also a nice chipping green with a large sand trap. A great place to practice your short game.

As Jack and I walked to the green my belly button was puckering and un-puckering in excitement (to quote the ever-quotable Hawkeye Pierce). Jack wandered off to practice his chipping (at least, I think that's where he went; I kind of forgot about him, frankly) as I prepared to stroke my first left-handed putt. I expected those initial jabs to be awkward, and they certainly were. But what I did *not* anticipate was to have so much trouble lining up. In fact, this was the *opposite* of what I expected.

One of the key things I had discovered in my initial research was that your dominant eye has a lot to do with whether you'll have more success as a left- or right-hander. The theory is that with your dominant eye closer to the hole, closer to the line of your shot, you get a better visual read on things. My right eye is clearly dominant, so I was looking forward to this enhanced view of life on the putting green.

This was not at all what I experienced.

I looked down at the putter, then up at the hole. Down at the putter, up at the hole. Down, up. Down, up. But there mysteriously seemed to be no relation between the two views! It was as though whatever synapses in my brain were responsible for connecting the two pictures had ceased to function. I had no idea whether I was aiming at the hole or lined up 10 feet off.

This was a very discouraging development, but I tried not to panic. This was, after all, my very first foray into the sinister side of golf. Perhaps my brain was just so used to processing data from the mirror image of what I was now seeing that it would just take a while to recalibrate things. Patience, please.

I decided to concentrate on shorter putts, about five feet, and think primarily about the stroke, not my alignment. I also practiced hitting putts using only my right hand, as suggested in that *Golf Digest* article. Repetition was going to be key, I reminded myself. Just ask Hogan, who honed his deadly ball-striking by spending countless hours "digging it out of the dirt," as he put it – back when such a relentless practice routine was unheard of.

After a while Jack re-appeared (perhaps he had been starting fires somewhere or throwing rocks at geese down by the pond) and I challenged him to a putting contest. He readily agreed – but here's the thing about competing with Jack: He loves competition and *loves* making up games. I get a huge kick out of his creativity in this regard, but it tends to manifest itself in constantly changing rules. More accurately, he tends to add *new* rules as the game progresses.

Conveniently, the new rules always seem to be to his advantage. My attempts to explain the inherent unfairness of this, however, fell on deaf ears. So after just a few holes of competition (and my gentle but continuous objections to his ongoing regulatory manipulations), Jack decided to end the contest and return to practicing on his own. We shook hands, as good sportsmanship dictates, and went our separate ways. We kept at it until darkness made it all but impossible to continue and then went home to a delicious late dinner of macaroni and cheese. Extra juicy, just how he likes it.

Over the next few weeks, I spent most of my lunch hours on the Brown Deer practice green – the course is less than ten minutes from my house and three minutes from where I work. Fortunately, we had been experiencing a lengthy stretch of beautiful fall weather. It was bliss.

I experimented quite a bit with different techniques and practice approaches. I had read that Jack Nicklaus is left-eye dominant, which makes him "cross-dominant": right-handed, left-eyed. Again, this is said by some to be an advantage – and also now applies to me, as a right-eye dominant "lefty." So I was very interested in what he has to say about alignment.

In *Golf My Way*, Nicklaus writes that it's important to keep your eyes directly over the *line* of the putt, though not necessarily over the ball. In fact, the Golden Bear finds that he prefers to line up with eyes slightly behind the ball, which he feels gives him a better angle on alignment.

I also experimented with using an open stance – with my feet fairly close together – an approach I used with much success years ago. At some point I realized that I was having better luck getting long chip shots close to the hole than long putts – mostly an issue of distance control. I theorized that perhaps it was because my chipping stance was quite open. Maybe, I thought, opening my shoulders and facing more toward the hole would give me a better visual sense of distance. I tried using this stance on long putts and it worked like a charm. For a while I even used it on short putts.

I played around with this approach for a while left-handed, and it maybe, kinda, sorta seemed to help. But I decided to abandon it anyway, reasoning that I would rather develop a sound "conventional" stroke before resorting to any unorthodox practices.

It was also interesting to discover just how little I'm aware of my right-handed technique. Often, I would stand over a putt and realize I had no idea where to position my hands, or the ball, or how much to tilt my shoulders, or whatever. Many times I resorted to assuming a right-handed stance in order to "remember" how I do things as a righty. Even so, what seemed natural as a righty often felt weird the other way, so I would do something different altogether.

After considerable experimentation, I settled on a set-up position that put my feet slightly farther apart than usual, the ball about two-thirds forward in my stance, my hands pressed forward, my shoulders slightly tilted, and my right eye looking straight down at the face of my putter.

I'm still not sure if it's all technically "correct," but it felt comfortable so I went with it.

As much as I enjoyed my noontime practice sessions, I often caught my mind wandering and my concentration lapsing as the reps piled up. I knew that I would have to figure out ways to keep my practice interesting to stay productive. So I charted out a triangular three-hole course on the green. I would play it twice – once clockwise, once counter-clockwise – with three balls, which added up to 18 "holes" total. Each was a par-2, with distances of approximately 25, 30, and 35 feet.

My initial trips around this course were disastrous, accumulating 18-hole scores in the neighborhood of 9 over par. Over the course of a couple weeks, I managed to get my career best score down to -1. I celebrated by heading back to work.

As you might expect, I continued to have good days and bad days on the green. At times I got very frustrated. Other times I would let my ego get away from me a little bit and I'd start fantasizing about how good of a left-handed putter I'd already become! Occasionally, I'd think to myself, "I'll bet I'm already a better putter than _____," filling in the name of one of my less-proficient golfing buddies. (Don't worry, Keith, I won't say who!)

It's terrible, I know. But I'm only human. Besides, the true test won't come until there's a real score on the line in a real round on a real course. Which I wasn't planning to have happen until spring.

One thing I would do when my stroke seemed to leave me was to "PLK," which stands for "Putt Like a Kid." It's what author James Dodson's father advised him to do in *Final Rounds*, Dodson's account of his and his dad's golf trip to Scotland during the final months of his father's life. Dodson describes his dad as one of the best putters he's ever seen, and one of his key pieces of advice is to simply not over-think the process. Putt like you're a carefree child and you'll stroke the ball better and make a lot more putts.

It's an idea that's consistent with what Johnny Miller writes in *I Call the Shots*. It's remarkable, he says, how many kids are off-the-charts awesome with the flat stick. Miller himself – a man who later in his career resorted to putting with his eyes closed – was one such "kid" who seemed to make everything as a young man. But it's startling how many top pros seem to eventually lose their putting strokes. Miller was one. So was Palmer. And Tom Watson. Hogan – who never had a great stroke to start with – ultimately reached a point where he could barely make himself swing the putter. He would stand frozen over the ball for what seemed an eternity just waiting for – who knows what? For whatever feeling it was that gave him an ounce of confidence to make a simple five-footer.

It's why you see so many belly putters and long putters and weird "claw" and cross-handed putting grips at the highest levels of professional golf. Especially on the over-50 Champions Tour (commonly known as the Senior Tour).

I'm 47. Is it bound to happen to me sooner or later? Is my

putting fate sealed? I do know this: The more I think about it the greater chance I'll be afflicted. So it's definitely a balance between trying to make sure I'm teaching myself good technique and not analyzing things too much. "Paralysis by analysis," as they say.

So I made a point, every now and then, of trying not to think at all as I whacked the ball around the green. Sometimes it helped, sometimes it didn't.

Dodson's father also counseled him that he should concentrate on *pulling* the putter through with his *left* hand. I was glad to read this, because it supports my proposition that perhaps your leading hand should be your dominant one. I later realized, however, that this approach is far from universally advocated. Nicklaus, for instance, writes in *Golf My Way* that putting is primarily a right-handed stroke.

Dave Stockton, on the other hand, writes (referring, of course, to right-handed strokes): "Lead with your left …. The left hand is the direction hand, and it's just as important as the right."

Confused? Don't worry. Putting, the simplest part of golf, has confused some of the world's greatest golfers.

To help with my alignment issues, I relented and tried drawing a straight line on the ball with a marker, and used that to identify my line when placing the ball on the green. I have seen many pros, including Tiger, use this method, but it always seemed a little bit like cheating to me. Not literally, it's quite legal – but it seems like it ought to be against the rules. Something akin to using an outside aid, like a range finder. But Tiger does it, so I decided to give it a try – and immediately started making everything.

Holy smokes! I thought. This is amazing! Why doesn't everybody do this? It works because once you place the ball properly, all you have to do is make sure the line on your putter lines up with the line on the ball – and then make a good stroke. So simple, so effective. It doesn't help in distance control, of course – at least not directly. But by freeing your mind of one thought – "Am I lined up properly?" – it opens up brain space to think about distance.

Unfortunately, the magic of this particular technique turned out to be made of W.O.O.D., which is Johnny Miller's term for "Works Only One Day." When I came back the next day, it was still helpful, but not as dramatically as when I first tried it. I also realized that it wasn't helping me learn to line up my putts visually. And it's time-consuming. Slow play is a growing problem in golf, and if everybody used this technique things would only get worse.

So I decided to scrap it altogether.

One thing I find interesting about life on the practice green – aside from the increasing concentration of goose poop as the season approached its end – is how much it's like an elevator. Or a men's room. Words are seldom exchanged. But one day, I heard a man comment to his friends, "Is there anything more boring than practicing putting?"

In my "previous life" as a golfer I probably would have agreed with him. Warming up for a round was the only time I ever "practiced" putting. But so far, as a lefty, I'd spent nearly every lunch hour practicing, weather permitting. Had I really turned over a new leaf? Time would tell. It could still turn out like vet school: a brief period of dedication followed by gradually diminishing returns. But I had a good feeling so far. As monotonous as practicing putting sometimes seemed, it beat the heck out of studying biochemistry.

I did strike up a putting green conversation once – but only because the other guy started it! Noticing that I was putting left-handed, he commented, "Hey, you're doing that backwards!" Apparently, left-handers hear such comments – like, "You're standing on the wrong side of the ball!" – all too often. But it was a first for me. "Maybe that's why it's so hard," I replied cheerfully.

It was only then that I noticed that he, too, was putting the wrong way 'round. Curious, and feeling a little less reserved than usual, I asked him if he was a true lefty or if he does other things right-handed. It turned out that swinging golf clubs and baseball bats are the only things he does left-handed. His father was a baseball player and a lefty, he said, and taught him to swing a bat left-handed. So when he took up golf later in life, going lefty seemed like the natural choice.

What are the odds, I thought, that the first left-handed golfer I would engage in conversation would be a natural righty? Maybe this phenomenon is more common than I realized.

Meanwhile, I started to think more about moving from the putting green to the chipping green. My original plan was to spend the winter chipping balls in the basement. But things were progressing nicely. As October became November – the weather continued to be remarkable. I wanted to take advantage of the chance to practice outside while I still could, so I started looking for a left-handed pitching wedge.

Again, price was an object. And pitching wedges, it turns out, are primarily sold as part of a set of irons. Gap wedges, sand wedges, lob wedges, even "approach" wedges (which I'd never heard of before), could be bought singly, but I found nothing marked PW. Eventually I found a sand wedge at a discount website that could be mine for about $23, including shipping. So I pulled the trigger (it was getting easier) and ordered it.

The next day, browsing again on the same site, I found a cheap gap wedge (between a pitching wedge and a sand wedge), which was closer to what I really wanted. So in a bold move of fiscal irresponsibility, I ordered that one, too. A week later, I was the proud owner of two new left-handed wedges.

Again, I couldn't wait to try them out. So I grabbed Jack and headed to Brown Deer. It was cold. And windy. And I mean *really* windy. Trees were bending sideways. Geese were flying backwards. Houses were falling on witches. But we had a *blast*. Jack especially.

But the golf was hard. In anticipation of this moment, I had already been working on a new grip. Right-handed, I use an interlocking grip (with my left index finger tucked in between my righty pinky and ring finger) – because that's what my dad taught me. Plus, it's the grip Jack Nicklaus uses. And if it's good enough for the Golden Bear ….

Later I learned that an interlocking grip is not common, that an *overlapping* grip, a.k.a. the "Vardon grip," is considered more standard. So in retooling for my switch to lefty I decided to trust Harry Vardon. As the only six-time winner of the British Open, he must have known something.

Again, I did a bunch of reading to get the lowdown. But in the end I decided to listen to Ben Hogan (why wouldn't I?). In his famous and highly influential book, *Five Lessons: The Modern Fundamentals of Golf*, Hogan spends the entire first chapter, 19 pages, extolling the importance of a proper grip. "The grip is the heartbeat of the action of the golf swing," he writes. He then goes on to describe, in great detail, a proper overlapping golf grip.

The main thing I learned – and realized I'd been doing wrong for the last 40 years – is to hold the club more in my *fingers* than in my palm. I'd heard the old adage (I believe from Sam Snead) about holding the club as you would a baby bird – just tightly enough to keep it from flying out of your hands. But this is not something I've been successful putting into practice. Still, I could see how a lighter, more finger-based grip might help with touch and feel.

Hogan is a stern taskmaster. One of his instructions in the book (written in all caps), is:

> TO GAIN A REAL ACQUAINTANCE WITH THIS PREPARATORY GUIDE TO CORRECT GRIPPING, I WOULD SUGGEST PRACTICING IT FIVE OR 10 MINUTES A DAY FOR A WEEK UNTIL IT BEGINS TO BECOME SECOND NATURE.

OKAY! I GET IT! NOW PLEASE STOP SHOUTING AT ME!!

But seriously, I have to *practice* my *grip*!? How do you *practice* a grip? But I suppose that just means gripping, ungripping, and regripping the club repeatedly in order to "gain a real acquaintance with" what a proper grip feels like.

Fortunately, I already had Jack's old whacker* at my office as a keepsake. So I took it from the shelf and kept it by my desk, all the better to gain acquaintance with my new and improved left-handed grip.

(*A "whacker" is the equivalent of a modern-day child's 7-iron. It is approximately 24 inches long with a lightweight metal head, a yellow shaft, and a narrow black grip. It is often the first real golf club given to a child, at about the age of 4 or 5. The name is organically derived by the child himself, apparently as the result of the father repeatedly encouraging the child to "give it a good whack" with said club.)

So I was ready when it came time to hit the practice area with my new lefty wedges. Or so I thought. Again, as with the putting, there were a few surprises. An excerpt from my journal that day:

> It was fun! Definitely weird, though, hitting with the lefty SW. Had to think about everything. Tried lots of things. Experimented with position in my stance and had best luck putting it farther back than I normally would. Had to stay on top of my grip to make sure I kept it in my fingers instead of my palm. … And harder than the first day of putting, that's for sure. Was never really quite sure what to do with my wrists. They don't seem to want to bend and flex in a manner similar

to my right-handed swing. I had best luck when I kept them very stiff and didn't try to hit far, or when I "flipped" the ball up in the air with my wrists, which doesn't seem very correct. I had a hard time keeping my hands ahead of the ball as I would with a normal chip. Just felt weird all around. It was fun, but it was also discouraging in a way. It's going to be hard, that's for sure. Jack had a ball, as usual. We played until it was almost too dark to see, and even then Jack didn't want to quit. Afterward we saw the empty parking lot and so I let Jack sit on my lap and steer for a while. A nice father-son evening.

(Don't tell Jack's mom about the steering! I'm not sure if she approves of that sort of thing.)

It was nearly Halloween by then, but the nice weather (other than that cold and windy first day with the wedges) continued. I spent every lunch hour I could at the practice area. It was nice because, being so late in the year, I usually had it all to myself.

I worked on a variety of things, such as putting the ball in different positions in my stance. The very short chipping stroke was starting to feel fairly natural, but it was really just a big putting stroke. When I took a bigger swing, it still felt very strange. I had very little sense of where the clubhead was during any part of the swing.

At one point, when chipping from about 25 feet, I put all eight balls within two feet of the hole. Of course, hitting the same shot over and over like that can be pretty easy. But it helped with my confidence nonetheless. And just repeating that left-handed motion so many times helped it all feel more natural, a tiny bit at a time.

In some respects I was already ahead of schedule – though I was trying very hard not to *have* a schedule. About a month previously I wrote in my journal, "If I can hit spring time with a bit of feel for left-handed chipping and putting I think I'll have accomplished something." Well, here it was barely November and I felt like I had already accomplished that much. Not to sound over-confident, but things were shaping up very nicely indeed.

I also continued to think about a coach. I knew that for a nobody like me to sell this book idea, it would help to have someone with a reputation.

Not long after being graciously rejected by a couple of high-profile golf coaches, I found myself seated at dinner next to my wife's boss, Michael, an avid golfer. Elizabeth made me tell him about my book idea (she twisted my arm). He asked if I had gotten a professional opinion on it. "Not yet," I replied.

"You should call Carl Unis," he said. "Here's his number. Tell him I said to call, he's an old family friend. A great guy."

Awesome!

Carl Unis, I soon learned, is something of a local legend. For 23 years he was the head professional at nearby Brynwood Country Club, where my wife worked as a lifeguard in high school. She remembered him, but didn't remember much. I also learned that he not only played in, but made the cut at the 1967 U.S. Open at Baltusrol.

I called him cold (which is always hard for me), explained who I was, and asked him if I could send him some information about my book. "You could do that," he replied. "Or, we could get together for lunch when I get back in town."

"That would be great!" I said, trying hard not to sound like Peter Brady when it's time to change.

A couple of weeks later I found myself waiting nervously in the back room of the Silver Spring House for "Coach Carl" to arrive. At the appointed time, in walked the man I recognized from an online video.

After exchanging pleasantries, we sat down and started chatting. A moment later the waitress approached and asked for drink orders. "I'll have an Arnold Palmer," Coach Carl replied.

An Arnold Palmer? *How perfect is that?* A slight smile crossed my lips. I think this might be the beginning of a beautiful friendship.

CHAPTER 3
A Guiding Hand

"Hmm ... let's fix that grip."

—Anonymous PGA Professional

Poor Arnold Palmer. The mid-1960s weren't working out for him quite the way he'd hoped. Sure, he continued to be the world's most famous, wealthiest, and most beloved golfer. But he just couldn't seem to get the better of Jack Nicklaus. Not in the big ones, anyway.

In 1962, Arnold won the Masters in April, finished second in the U.S. Open in June, and won the British Open in July – while claiming six other PGA Tour victories throughout the year (not the mention the Canada Cup, paired with Sam Snead). By any standard, it was a phenomenal year. Palmer had clearly established himself as the "King."

But that narrow U.S. Open loss was tough to take. It was also a harbinger of things to come. Held practically in Arnie's own backyard, at Oakmont in Pennsylvania, in front of legions of adoring fans, Palmer lost the title in an 18-hole playoff to a 22-year-old Nicklaus. It was the Tour rookie's first professional victory, a big upset, and a huge disappointment to Arnie's Army.

Palmer bounced right back with his second consecutive British Open title the very next month, but winning the big ones became a lot more difficult after that, thanks in large part to the emergence at Oakmont of the man they called "Fat Jack."

By the time the 1967 U.S. Open at Baltusrol rolled around, Jack had clearly displaced Palmer as the world's best golfer. And Arnie's fans were growing uneasy. Palmer hadn't won a major championship since the 1964 Masters. The triumph at Augusta National was his seventh major overall, but his first since the 1962 British. In the meantime, Nicklaus had nabbed five more major victories, including the 1966 Masters and British Open.

But 1967 had not started well for the Golden Bear. He missed the cut at the Masters (something he would not do again until 1994, at the age of 54) and seemed to be mired in a putting slump. Plus, Baltusrol is located in Springfield, New Jersey, close enough to Arnie's home turf to ensure a full complement of passionate legions.

And that's exactly what he got.

In his wonderful book about golf's most celebrated rivalry, *Arnie & Jack*, author Ian O'Connor writes of the Baltusrol Open, "Not since Oakmont [in the 1962 Open] had Nicklaus confronted a pro-Palmer gallery that, in his words, was so 'blatantly partisan.'"

If ever there was a time and place for the "King" to wrest his crown back from the heir apparent, this was it.

But little did Arnie or his fans know that a new putter (nicknamed "White Fang") and a timely tip from Gordon Jones, an old pal from Ohio, would help bring Jack's short strokes back to life.

Palmer's best friends that week were, indeed, his ever-vocal fans. Buoyed by their boisterous support, Palmer came out of the gate strong, and found himself alone at the top of the leaderboard at the completion of the second round. With White Fang working its magic, Nicklaus lurked just a stroke behind.

The two were paired together for round three – and perhaps their intense rivalry and focus on each other hurt their play, as neither emerged as the third-round leader. That honor instead went to unknown amateur Marty Fleckman.

It had been 44 years since an amateur had won the U.S. Open. The last to do it was Johnny Goodman in 1933 – and the feat hasn't been repeated to this day. But Fleckman, a 23-year-old former University of Houston star, seemed determined to make a run at it. After opening with a 3-under 67 to take the first-round lead, most assumed he would quickly fall out of contention. It was not uncommon, after all, for a relative unknown to come out hot and lead the Open after the first day. Most were never heard from again.

Instead of stumbling, Fleckman backed up his stunning 67 with a solid 73 on Friday to remain even par for the tournament. On Saturday, following a shaky start, the young amateur ground out an impressive 69 to reclaim the lead – while Palmer and Nicklaus were busy trying only to beat one another. (Though accounts differ about which golfer said it, one suggested to the other on the eighth tee that they "stop playing each other and start playing the golf course.")

In the end, Fleckman staggered through a pressure-packed final round to a disappointing 80 and a tie for 18th.

Meanwhile, Palmer and Nicklaus, who began the day one stroke behind Fleckman in a three-way tie for second with Billy Casper, staged a battle for the ages. Arnie, with his 1-under 69, was one of only two golfers among the top 11 finishers to break par that day. The other, of course, was Jack, who put the hammer down for a stellar 65.

As his lead (and his legend) grew on the back nine, Nicklaus had the U.S. Open record of 276 within his sights. He stood on the tee at the par-5 18th knowing a birdie would give him 275. But he put thoughts of a record out of his mind, perhaps thinking about Arnie's humiliating U.S. Open loss just a year earlier.

With a commanding lead over Billy Casper (seven strokes with nine holes to play), Palmer seemed to have the title in his grasp – and Hogan's record within reach. Taking his eyes off the title to focus on the record proved a fatal mistake, as stellar play by Casper and careless mistakes by Palmer combined to produce a 72-hole tie between the two legends. The next day, Casper won the 18-hole playoff.

Nicklaus would not make the same mistakes. With characteristically shrewd course management, Nicklaus played it safe with a 1-iron off the 18th tee – and promptly hit into the right-hand rough. From there he chunked an 8-iron back into the fairway, well short of the water he was making sure to avoid. Left with a 230-yard uphill approach, he again chose a 1-iron, this time knocking it safely on the green, 22-feet from the hole. Nicklaus, being Nicklaus, calmly rolled in the long birdie putt for 65 and a U.S. Open record 275 total.

It was Palmer's fourth U.S. Open runner-up finish to go with his single victory, his thrilling come-from-behind win at Cherry Hills in 1960. Though he would go on to record ten more top-10 finishes in majors, he would never win another major title.

Nicklaus spoke frankly after the tournament about his new U.S. Open scoring mark. "Records just come. Nobody should try to break a record," he said, in an apparent reference to Palmer's stumble the year before. "What you're here for is to win a golf tournament."

As it happens, the man whose record Jack broke on Sunday played in his final U.S. Open that week. By then the competitive playing days of Ben Hogan, 55, were long since past. His last real hurrah came in 1960 at Cherry Hills, when he narrowly missed winning his long-sought fifth U.S. Open title. The legendary "Hawk," however, still drew a lion's share of fan and media attention whenever he teed it up.

So it was no surprise that of the 150 golfers hitting their opening tee shots that Thursday at Baltusrol, Ben Hogan would attract one of the largest crowds. Among those watching as Hogan strode purposefully to the first tee was 29-year-old Carl Unis, the new assistant professional at Ozaukee Country Club in Mequon, Wisconsin. It was the last Open for Hogan, but the first for Unis, who would tee off two groups behind the Hawk.

"It was my first major, and I was in awe of everything that was going on," Unis recalls. "I got there at 9:00 in the morning – and I didn't tee off until 2:30! So I watched everybody hit balls, I practiced, I hit balls – just to burn up a lot of excess energy. Talk about being nervous – wow!

"I was practicing putting around 2:00, and they called Ben Hogan's name around ten-after. There were a lot of people just sitting around the green, and when he came out of the locker room and started to walk to the first tee everybody just stood up. It looked like 'J.C.' himself had arrived!"

Given the physical struggles that Hogan was enduring by then, and the convoluted path Unis had taken to Baltusrol, it's hard to say whose appearance in the 67th U.S. Open was more unlikely.

• • •

Thirty-year-old Rose Unis was small in stature but large in heart. She was *strong* – in both body and character. Giving birth to her first child had been hard on her, but the arrival of baby Elizabeth made it all worthwhile. Though he had really wanted a boy, Rose's husband, Collie, more than 20 years her senior, couldn't have been prouder.

Four years later, with a second child due to arrive soon, Collie decided to send his young wife and daughter back to her family's home in Cleveland, Ohio, to wait for the arrival of the Elizabeth's new sibling. There was plenty of family to look after her, and the hospitals were better than in remote, Depression-era Atlanta, Texas, where the family lived. Meanwhile, Collie would continue to work hard to support them in Texas, where he had worked his way from being a peddler with a horse-drawn wagon to the owner of a successful dry goods store.

What they did not foresee, however, was that Collie would never make it back to Ohio. While on a buying trip to Dallas, Rose's husband died suddenly of a cerebral hemorrhage – just a week before the arrival of the son he always wanted.

Back in Ohio, doctors and family members made the decision to withhold from Rose the news of her husband's death. They feared the stress would only add risk to the situation. And in those days, it was not uncommon to go weeks without hearing from a loved one traveling far away.

Nonetheless, Rose eagerly anticipated Collie's return following their baby's birth. And when time passed without his arrival, she grew worried. Finally, the family broke the news.

"'Oh, he's got a bad cold, some kind of a flu,' I guess they told her," says Elizabeth, known to family and friends as "Libby." "So finally when she did find out, it was very, very sad."

The news devastated Rose, but it made her more determined to take good care of her young children. Once she and baby Carl were strong enough, Rose moved back to Texas with the children to put things in order. It took about four years, Carl says, to get everything settled. And then they all moved back to Cleveland to be near Rose's family – and work in her parents' restaurant.

In Cleveland, Rose did her best to make sure her children were well provided for. Her father opened the restaurant early in the morning; Rose would come in before noon and work into the early hours. Located in a light industrial area in Cleveland – across the street from a large distribution center – the restaurant had a beer and wine license, making it a popular place for night-shift workers to grab a late meal and have a few drinks.

Rose worked hard – and so did everybody else.

"Mom gave me everything," Carl says today. "But she made me realize values by making me work for it. So there were many days in the kitchen, scrubbing pots and pans, and cleaning out the grease trap, and all those wonderful jobs you don't want to do as a kid.

"But when it came time to maybe get a new bike, Mom was the

first one to allow that to happen. She really taught me to understand the values in life."

Because their mother spent so many hours working, Carl spent a lot of time under the watchful eye of his older sister.

"I was always the one who had to look after him," Libby recalls. "We would go to movies on Sunday afternoons, my girlfriend Irene and I, who lived down the street. And I always had to have my little brother tag along!

"We would go into the storefronts, and look at things. And he, of course, was always fascinated by the things boys were interested in. And we, of course, were interested in the things girls were interested in: dolls, and clothes, and shoes. And so we'd go around the corner and kind of hide from him, but he always found us. It was fun. We'd tease him mercilessly!"

Libby characterizes the young Carl as a very busy boy, always into things, always looking for something new to do, for a new way to earn a few coins. He loved to fish and ride his bike. He dabbled in music, learning to play the drums and the accordion. And once he was old enough, he started delivering newspapers.

Even growing up without a dad, there was no shortage of father figures in the children's lives. Rose was the oldest of six siblings, so there were plenty of aunts and uncles around. One was Uncle Isaiah, who remained close to the family in Texas following his brother Collie's death.

"We called him 'Uncle I,'" Libby recalls. "He was as close to a father figure as I can remember, before we moved up north to be with my grandparents."

Carl also has vivid memories of "Mr. Cary," a family friend who shared the boy's love for fishing.

"He's the one who showed me how to fish, and tie hooks, and catch fish," he says. "And his wife would make the greatest brownies to take along when we'd go. Those brownies, they were unrivaled. But those are things you remember as a kid, you know?"

This, of course, was all before the golf bug bit. At the suggestion of his Uncle Jim, Carl started caddying at Ridgewood Country Club in Parma at the age of 11. Completely ignorant of the sport to that point – no one in his family played – it took a little while to figure out what the big deal was about the game he would grow to love.

In 1950, when Carl was 13, Ridgewood hosted the third leg of the inaugural Weathervane Tourney, a 144-hole "cross-country" LPGA event played in four 36-hole legs at four different sites over several weeks. The legendary Babe Zaharias won both the Cleveland leg and the 144-hole overall title – but Carl was indifferent.

"I had no clue what a golf tournament was," he says. "They had them all there. Babe Zaharias was there. But I didn't know from nothin' what I missed out on, to see all those gals play."

Three years later, the men's tour came to Ohio. A few years older and wiser – and beginning to fall in love with the game – Carl did not miss the chance to see the best in the world play in the Carling World Open, held at the Manakiki Country Club in nearby Willoughby Hills.

"That was my first encounter [with big-time golf], seeing Ed 'Porky' Oliver, Al Besselink, Sam Snead, and Lou Worsham – in one group. I took a bus to get out there, and had no clue what this was going to be. And I absolutely got bit. I saw these guys in tournament conditions and said, 'This is something that could be for me.'"

Carl had begun playing a few years earlier when a restaurant customer gave him an old set of clubs in a beat-up canvas bag. Caddying, of course, gave Carl the opportunity to play Ridgewood on Mondays with the other caddies, a valuable perk he took absolute advantage of.

"It'd be nothing to play 72 holes on Monday," he says. "We'd get there at 6:00 in the morning and we'd play until dark, sometimes until 10:00 at night."

In addition to caddying, he soon started working other jobs around the golf course. One of his first was shining shoes in the clubhouse, where polishing 200 or more pairs of shoes was just a good day's work on the weekend. From there he worked his way up to the halfway house, and eventually out to the golf course, performing general course maintenance such as cutting greens and raking traps. Any job that needed doing, he would do.

His first exposure to tournament golf as a player was in the city caddy tournament, open to caddies from all across the Cleveland area. The first year he played, at age 14, he limped in with a 102. But just three years later, in his final year of eligibility, he shot 76 and won.

"It was a great environment to grow up in, with some great people," Carl says. "Mr. Reese, the pro there ... he never had a lot to say to me. But when I won the caddy tournament, he walked all the way around the clubhouse, to where I shined shoes at the back, and congratulated me. I thought that was the height of my career, that he would acknowledge the fact that I won anything. And Mr. [Larry] Tiedman [a club member] told me I could use his golf shoes, his white bucks [in the caddy tournament].

"FootJoy white bucks," he says with lingering pride. "I'll never forget it. I still have a picture of it."

By then Carl was living in Parma with his Aunt Ann, so that he could attend the new high school there. Getting the best education possible was very important to his mother.

"She always said that what you put in your head, no one can take away from you," Libby says. "And she didn't want us to have to work as hard as she had to make a living. I guess she fancied that one of us would be a doctor or a lawyer or something. And then when I chose music performance, singing, and he chose golf competition, she said, 'Oh, I wanted my children to learn something! But they picked two of the most difficult careers that there are!' We used to laugh about that. But she was a very strong, loving, strict head of the family."

After he graduated, Carl received a golf scholarship to Ohio State University. He played on the freshman team, but that's as far as his college career progressed. By his own account only an "average" student in high school, he found the rigors of a major university to be a little more than he was ready to handle.

"I joined a fraternity my first year and needless to say that didn't work out so well," he says with a chuckle. "And the coach gave me a job out at the golf course, making sure that all the rental clubs were in good shape, and just doing general chores around the pro shop. I guess I wasn't organized enough to study. That was the hard part."

After leaving OSU he worked for Wilson Sporting Goods by day and attended Cleveland's John Carroll University by night. He had just begun a new career, in the insurance business, when the draft board called. Through the referral of an acquaintance at Ridgewood, who happened to be a colonel in the Army Reserves, Carl soon began a six-month stint in a reserve dental unit. After putting in his time, he got home just in time to win the club championship – before his unit got called back up. When he got back home again he went to work for another insurance company, and then for the Cleveland District Golf Association.

His golf game, meanwhile, continued to improve. In 1963 he reached the semi-finals of the Ohio State Amateur, and followed that performance with a victory in 1964. He was the first Public Links player to win the Ohio State Amateur, and to this day, that title remains one of his proudest golfing accomplishments. It's a title that neither Jack Nicklaus nor Tom Weiskopf – two more-famous native Ohioans to happen to play a little golf – ever won.

"[But] Arnold Palmer won it," Carl is quick to point out. "So I got my name on the same trophy with Arnold Palmer, even though he's from Pennsylvania. He won when he was stationed in Cleveland with the Coast Guard there."

Not long after, a friend asked him if he had ever considered turning professional. "I answered the question with a question and said, 'Have you ever considered sponsoring someone?' He said he'd never thought about it, but that he'd let me know in a couple weeks."

True to his word, his friend called back and said he had gotten a group of investors together to sponsor him – "and I was on my way to the tour." But first he had to qualify.

"I was one of the last individuals to get approved [to play on tour] the old way," Carl explains. "I had to play with three different local golf professionals on two different occasions, and they would grade me. [Then] they sent my qualifications into the tour board to get approval on a temporary basis."

He made it. But eighteen months later, Carl was back home, having failed to earn enough money to keep his playing privileges.

Back in those days, the tour was much different from the "all exempt tour" the top pros play on today. Most players had to qualify for the tournament every week. If you made the cut, you were exempt from qualifying for next week's event. But even that was no guarantee of a payday. The top 60 and ties made the cut, but only the top 45 finishers earned a check.

"I played in 36 events and made the cut in 18," Carl says. "But I never finished in the top 45, I was always in the bottom rung. I couldn't get over the hump.

"But it was an experience that you can't really explain, the experience of a lifetime. You couldn't learn it from a book, you had to be there, live and in living color, to know how to manage yourself under many, many different conditions."

Back in Ohio, with his spirits at a low ebb, a career at a local men's store loomed in his future. But then the phone rang again. This time it was Bernie Haas, a good friend and fellow professional, who urged him to get down to Tampa, Florida if he wanted to get his "Class A card," which would eventually make him eligible to become a club professional. It was not quite as enticing a thought as being a touring professional, but it sure would beat the men's store option.

The decision to go was what you now might call a "no-brainer." And it paid off quickly.

"While I was there, a fellow touring pro called me, who was getting a job in the Milwaukee, Wisconsin area, at the Ozaukee Country Club in Mequon. He asked me if I'd like to come up and work for him."

By then he'd already put in applications to several other clubs – including the famous Inverness Club in Toledo, Ohio, host of several U.S. Open championships. And he felt an obligation to follow up with those clubs first. He told his friend, Bobby Brue, to call him in a month, half-thinking he'd never hear from him again.

In the meantime, Carl got a call from an old college roommate, Mike Mural, who offered him a job teaching golf at a large department store, which provided some valuable coaching experience.

Eventually, Bobby did call back, just as he said he would, and offered Carl the Ozaukee Country Club job. Before he knew it he was up in Wisconsin learning quickly how to be an assistant golf professional. He had barely gotten his feet wet before things got really interesting.

"Bob came to me one day, in the latter part of April and said, 'Are you going to try to qualify for the U.S. Open?' I said 'Nah, I have no desire to do that, not the way I feel after losing my card and all that.' He said, 'Well, you better start practicing, because I signed you up for the local qualifying tournament at [nearby] Tripoli [Country Club]!'

"So I accepted his invitation, went over to play, and led the qualifier there," Carl says. "And nobody knew who Carl Unis was until after that. But the members at Ozaukee were really great, they were so nice and supportive."

The sectional qualifier was a few weeks later at Chicago Golf Club, the oldest golf course in the Midwest. A "very, very private club," Carl explains.

"So I went down the night before and got up early the next morning to go over the course. We played 36 holes, and I remember shooting 74 in the morning and then came back and shot 71 in the afternoon, and I was in second place to go to the U.S. Open!

"Unfortunately, Bobby didn't qualify – but I did. So as the hotshot assistant I headed out to Baltusrol Country Club in Springfield, New Jersey."

• • •

At Baltusrol, once he burned up all that nervous energy and got over his awe of Ben Hogan, Carl performed beyond anyone's expectations. His 298 (+18) total did not threaten any records, but his 74-72 start put him three shots inside the cut line. In the process, he also led the field in one very impressive category.

"That was the first year they took the long-drive average for the players all four rounds. And I had the long drive average at the U.S. Open, 285 yards – with the balata ball and the wooden head," he says proudly.

His T54 finish earned him a well-deserved $655 check as a keepsake. It was his first significant payday as a playing professional.

"My first U.S. Open and I made the cut!" he says. "Everybody back home [in Wisconsin] was so excited. So it was more telegrams, more of everything. It was just an exciting time in my life.

"And when I got back, people thought I must know something. I was on the lesson tee giving anywhere between 12 and 16 lessons a day."

The surprising performance not only raised his profile around his home club, it also grabbed the attention of others. Before long, Bobby Brue got a call from nearby Brynwood Country Club, asking permission to interview Carl for their vacant head professional job. He gave it, they called Carl, and soon he was offered the job.

It's unusual, Carl says, to rise through the ranks so quickly. "But I got my name in the paper a few times, because of the U.S. Open, and that got people talking about it, and word spreads. So I happened to be in the right place at the right time."

• • •

Forty-three years later, sitting down with Coach Carl for lunch at the Silver Spring House, I had no need to be convinced of his credentials. He had come with a strong recommendation, and a cursory internet "background check" had revealed that he had spent those intervening years generally making the world (Wisconsin in particular) a better, lower-scoring place for golfers of all abilities and ages. I saw that he had remained head professional at Brynwood for 23 years. And that he had served as executive director of the Golf Foundation of Wisconsin after that. That he had appeared in a series of golf instruction videos with Tom Pipines (a local sportscasting legend) on Channel 6 in the mid-1990s. And that teaching golf continued to be a driving passion in his life. He was clearly legitimate.

No, there would be no need for him to persuade *me* of anything. *I'm not worthy!* This would be a one-way pitch, for sure.

I was desperate, after all – a crazy man with an insane idea about learning to play golf left-handed for no good reason other than to write a book about it. At least, that's how it sometimes felt. And so I would need to spend the next 45 to 60 minutes madly attempting to hide my lunacy from the sane and distinguished golf professional sitting across from me.

As I told him my story and gave him my pitch, my Buffalo chicken wrap grew cold on my plate. As I continued to rant, I hoped that Coach Carl would notice my uneaten food and see just how passionate I was about this idea.

I told him everything. About my love of the game. How I've always hated to practice. I told him that I've always had a good short game but that my ball-striking has been very limited by my crappy, deeply ingrained swing. I tried very hard not to spit while I talked. I bragged about how I had once bowled a 300 game and won pool championships in college. I did this not to glorify myself but to convey the confidence I have in my physical ability to accomplish things when I really set my mind to them. I told him I was committed to letting him be 100 percent in charge of my golf game. Whatever he said, I would do.

I told him I didn't have a lot of money to invest in lessons but was looking for someone to "partner" with – someone who was willing to invest in me and my cockamamie scheme by offering free or reduced rate lessons in return for a share of the (eventual) book proceeds. I told him I was hoping he might look at this as a unique coaching challenge – as well as an opportunity to put some of his teaching into book form for posterity.

I told him I was prepared to commit a year of my life to this project and would give it everything I could for that stretch – within the context of maintaining a full-time job and not neglecting my family. That I was planning to give up right-handed golf *completely* for at least a year – and that my "best case" scenario was that the left-handed golf would go so well that there would be no need to ever return to the other side.

In the rare moments when I actually let *him* talk, he told me about his experience at Baltusrol and a little bit about his teaching philosophy. I took advantage of these opportunities to wolf down my now cold lunch.

Finally, I gave him some written materials, including some samples of my previous writings.

By the time we parted company in the parking lot we had talked for about 90 minutes (sorry, Boss!). It was like a great first date! I felt good about how things went and was eager find out if we had a future together. *Call me!*

When I got back to the office I immediately wrote a thank-you e-mail. I told him I enjoyed our meeting and hoped we could work something out. I also said my dream was to learn lefty golf well enough to be able to compete in senior tournaments as a lefty a few years down the road. He replied:

> Hi Mike,
> I too enjoyed our meeting, I will look over the material you gave me. I feel after our lunch discussion we can work something out together. I like your last paragraph about your DREAM. "Old proverb": *Let your dreams become a reality!*
> Have a great weekend,
> Carl

• • •

Now that I had a coach lined up, it was time to think more seriously about getting a set of left-handed clubs. The problem is … I have a problem with golf equipment. And not the kind of problem where I can't stop buying stuff. More of the opposite, in fact. It pains me to part with my hard-earned dollars to keep up with all the latest "revolutions" in golf technology. When will the technological revolution end!? I surrender already!

People who know me – most notably, my wife – will tell you that I'm pretty cheap. Though I prefer to say "frugal." "Fiscally conservative." Or "tighter than John Daly's Lap-Band." How about, "family rich, golf poor"? Golf is high on my list of passions but fairly low on the financial priority scale. I prefer to put my limited golf budget toward greens fees, par-3 rounds with my son, and pre-round donuts rather than new stuff.

And when I'm honest with myself, that's at the heart of my love/hate relationship with equipment. If I had unlimited resources I would probably be a golf club junkie. But I don't, so instead I find myself mildly resentful of the ongoing equipment advances.

When I was a naive teenage golf nut poring over the pages of *Golf Digest*, there were lots of gadgets and gizmos advertised in the back that claimed to add yards to your tee shots and cut strokes from your score. I remember once pointing this out to my dad, who replied, "Well, according to these ads, if you used this, this, this, and this, you'd hit the ball 400 yards and shoot 60 every time. And I don't think that's going to happen." My dad was in advertising, and he knew not to take every claim literally. It was a lesson I took to heart. (He also taught me the value of hard work. Thanks for trying, Dad!)

In those days, there were good clubs and not-as-good clubs – but I never felt I was at a significant disadvantage when competing with my older Walter Hagen irons and Johnny Miller woods. When I splurged and bought myself a set of Wilson Staff woods as a high-school graduation gift to myself (Chargers RULE! Class of '81! Wooooo!!!), I didn't necessarily expect them to improve my game. I bought them partly for the prestige of owning fine clubs (I admit) and also because it seemed like a good investment (it was). I fully expected to play them for a lifetime, or at least until they wore out.

Things started changing in 1991 with the introduction of Callaway's Big Bertha driver. With a relatively tiny head (by today's standards), measuring just 190cc in volume, it was the first salvo in the modern equipment wars – and perhaps the first driver to offer a true advantage over more traditional clubs. Before long, drivers were topping out at a balloonish 460cc (now the legal limit) with price tags in the hundreds of dollars – for one club! I paid about $140 ($335 in

2010 dollars) in 1981 for my set of four Staff woods: Driver, 3-, 4-, and 5-woods (set of four puffball knit headcovers not included).

In 2010, the big new thing in golf shops was the TaylorMade R11 driver. This technological monstrosity features adjustable loft, face angle, and center of gravity, along with dual climate controls for player and caddie. I made that last bit up, of course, but it *should* have that for the whopping asking price of 400 smackers!

What would Old Tom Morris think? But then I remind myself that Old Tom himself was once all but disowned by his St. Andrews mentor and employer, Allan Robertson, for having the *audacity* to start using a gutta percha golf ball rather than the standard and time-tested "feathery" model in popular use at that time. Never mind that the new balls traveled much farther, were far more durable, and were much easier to make – at a tiny fraction of the cost of a feathery. (Now *there's* a golf technology revolution I could get behind!) Not one to change easily with the times, Robertson gave the new technology a catchy nickname; he called it "the filth."

Of course, Robertson's livelihood at that time depended on his skill as a feathery maker. So at its heart it really came down to a question of economic self-interest. Doesn't it always?

So I approached the club-buying process with some trepidation, fearful of what I might have to spend. As fate would have it, I made an important discovery on my first foray into the left-handed marketplace.

The most common complaint you'll hear from left-handed golfers is about limited club selection. It's not that clubs are not available (though in the old days they were much harder to find), but your choices are very limited. Try it sometime – take a look around your local pro shop or sporting goods store and see how many left-handed sets are available. Shopping online offers more choices, but trying them out is problematic. People don't usually like to buy golf clubs without at least being able to hold them in their hands before making a purchase decision. And you'd be surprised how often the words "right-hand only" pop up when you try to put a left-handed set in your virtual shopping cart.

But there's a flip side to this phenomenon. If you're not picky about the clubs you're buying – and/or don't mind buying clubs that might be outdated by a couple of years – there are tremendous bargains to be had.

The day before I had that first meeting with Coach Carl, my wife was out for the evening (shopping, or knitting, or drag-racing with her greaser friends down by the airport, I can't quite remember) – so I threw Jack in the car and took him to a big-name sporting goods store known for a large golf department. Let's call it "Richard's." My intention was to buy some practice balls. But of course, while I was there I wanted to, you know, just look around a little. What I found amazed me. And I took it as a sign from God.

There, hanging on the wall amongst all the new, shiny, and expensive right-handed brand-name iron sets, was a set of left-handed Slazenger "Raw Distance" irons: 5-PW plus 3i and 4i hybrids. The "list price" said $299.95*. The sign on the wall said, "Clearance: $89.93." And the sign below that one said, "Take an extra 25% off all clearance golf clubs." Doing the math real quick in my head that came out to … six dollars and 80 cents! No, wait … 68 dollars! Still a great deal! Seven dollars less, in fact, than I paid for those used Hagen irons in 1978.

(*I don't believe anyone ever pays "list price" at this particular store. In fact, I later saw a disclaimer on their website stating that the list price was for "comparison purposes only" and that no sales may have ever been made at that price.)

These were not top-of-the-line clubs, but they were nicer than the right-handed clubs I had in my bag at the time. And possibly – given the advancements in club technology – nicer than any irons I've ever owned! Was this too good to be true?

In true cheapskate fashion I hemmed and hawed at great length while mulling over this potential purchase, repeating the earlier scene at the pro shop with the $20 putter. I looked at the irons. I picked one up and held it in my hands (with my new lefty grip). I put it back. I walked away. (Where's Jack? I had no idea. Probably putting … or learning to shoplift.) I looked at other stuff. I went back to the irons. Lather, rinse, repeat. My mind was going a mile a minute.

I noticed that there were other bargain-bin lefty clubs – woods and drivers – on other racks. And all the *really* cheap stuff was left-handed. Believe it or not, they actually had a left-handed driver for sale for *five dollars*! Obviously, it was not a high-quality club. But it was *five dollars*!!

How can this be? I wondered, turning my attention back to the irons. It flew in the face of everything I'd heard about buying left-handed clubs. But I realized a couple of things: One, that fall was definitely the right time of year to find close-out sale items; and two, that it made sense that stores might get desperate to get rid of their surplus lefty clubs.

Finally, I pulled the trigger and told the guy I'd take the irons. These may or may not be the clubs I'd want to use long-term, but how could I go wrong with them as starter clubs? I still didn't know if I would even need them until spring, but if I waited, the chances of finding anywhere near close to such a deal at the dawn of golf season would be pretty much zero.

I resisted buying any woods (I refuse to say "metal woods" or "3-metal" or any other such nonsense, by the way, so just get used to it!), however, both because I didn't want to be tempted to hit the Big Dog before I was ready and because ... I don't know, it would have seemed like I was pushing my luck somehow. But I did go back a couple of weeks later and bought some Walter Hagen (now a house brand at "Richard's") woods: driver, 3-wood, and 5-wood – for the ridiculously absurd price of $40. Not per-club, mind you – *total*. The driver was $19.93, and the woods were $9.93 each. If you believe the list price, I had saved somewhere north of 90%. And, unlike my c. 1981 Wilson Staff woods, the deal even included three headcovers (with no puff balls).

(It should be noted, by the way – if only so no one takes me for a *complete* idiot – that the Walter Hagen clubs are fitted with high-quality Aldila shafts. I later confirmed via the interwebs that the shafts alone in these clubs run at least $60 apiece.)

My amazing bargain club purchases inspired me to make the most of the remaining nice weather – and figure out an inexpensive and convenient way to practice over the winter. Chipping and putting in my basement works fine, but there's no way to take a full swing with the low ceilings – otherwise I would set up some sort of hitting bay. And for some strange reason the living room was off-limits. The Currie Park Golf Dome, where I would be taking my lessons, is a great facility, but it's pretty expensive, upwards of $20 per hour. I'd much rather pay by the bucket and take my time. Plus, it's at least 20 minutes away, making it an impractical everyday option.

Fortunately, I had already talked to my bosses about setting something up at work. The GS Design "world headquarters" in Glendale, Wisconsin, is a fabulous facility. My bosses, Marc and Jeff, who started the company in 1986, have always strived to make it a fun place to work. As the company has grown over the years, they've built the offices (really just converted warehouse space) into a veritable office wonderland. It's very roomy, including some storage space in the back. When I described my project to Jeff, I asked him if I could use that back storage room. I envisioned hanging a blanket from the wall and hitting practice balls into it from a piece of carpeting – only during lunch hour and after-hours, of course. He said sure, that would be fine – though he appreciated it when I told him it would not be a "permanent" set-up, that I could put it up and take it down easily as needed.

One night after work I went back to the office and set up my new hitting bay. It turned out great! It even had a serendipitous built-in ball return, in the form of a slight incline leading to the door. After the balls hit the blanket, they dropped down, and rolled right back to my feet.

The only glitch I encountered was that the blanket I was using was not quite heavy enough to absorb the full impact of the practice balls – they were hitting the overhead door behind the blanket with a pretty good "clunk" and bouncing back pretty hard. But that was easily remedied by sliding a couple of plastic cups behind the top corners of the blanket to hold it out a little farther from the wall.

I decided my new facility needed a name, so I dubbed it the "Bob Charles/Phil Mickelson Indoor Backhanded Practice Facility" – or the "Lefty Dome" for short.

By then, Coach Carl had called back. We worked out a deal and scheduled my first lesson for that Saturday morning, November 13. In the meantime I continued my independent training regimen.

And boy, was I making progress! I was chipping little yellow balls into a little wicker basket with great proficiency in my basement. I was whacking more little yellow balls into the dusty old bedspread with a resounding *thwack*! at the Lefty Dome. And I was putting like a madman with my cheap, ridiculous-looking Odyssey knockoff mail-order left-handed putter. I was way ahead of schedule and eagerly looking forward to showing Coach Carl what a great *investment* he was making in me.

Saturday morning arrived and I felt more than ready. The only real question in my mind was … what to wear?

Should I wear shorts? Golf pants? Are blue jeans OK? Should I wear my golf shoes? Would I feel stupid if I wore them and no one else there was wearing them? Would I feel like a dork if everybody *else* wore golf shoes and I was in sneakers? Ultimately, I settled on khaki pants, my favorite Steve Stricker/Greater Milwaukee Open golf shirt (c. 1991), and *no* golf shoes – but I put them in my golf bag just in case.

The weather outside was horrible – cold and raining hard. But inside the Golf Dome it was warm and dry – for the most part. Water dripped here and there through small holes in the dome's outer shell. "I didn't think I'd need to pack rain gear for an indoor lesson!" I said to Coach Carl when he arrived.

We exchanged pleasantries and he asked me how I was doing. "Well, I'm a little nervous," I said. "How do you think I feel!?" he replied. I realized it's probably a standard line, but also a sincere one. I imagine many first-time students express nervousness, and it wouldn't surprise me if Coach Carl were a little anxious, too. He wants to do a good job, after all, and there are a lot of unknowns heading into a new teaching situation.

At that point, *I* certainly had no idea what to expect. Was he going to ask to see me swing a club right-handed? I had packed my right-handed 7-iron just in case. But the answer was no. Would he start me off with some putting? No. But the first part of the lesson was definitely evaluative. He began by just having me show him what I've got. *All right, here goes!*

We spent the next ten minutes or so with him watching me hit a variety of shots. Observation and analysis, it occurred to me, is an extremely important part of teaching golf – especially in the early stages. I didn't hit anything near a full swing, of course. But I showed off my skill in hitting a variety of little chips and half-swing pitches. Surely I must be impressing him!

"Wow, Mike, you're doing great! You've made great progress in three weeks on your own! I think you're going to be a very good left-handed golfer in a very short period of time. Have you given any thought to the senior tour yet? Needless to say, I'm *very* impressed!"

That was the voice in my head – Coach Carl's voice – as I *imagined* how that first lesson might go. Yes, I had gotten a little cocky, a little overconfident, a little ahead of myself – in just three weeks. Visions of grandeur danced through my head. But ... surely *no one* had ever made such amazing progress in just a few short weeks as

I have!

Instead, I got: "Hmm … let's fix that grip."

And that was just for starters!

CHAPTER 4
Major Breakthrough

"It is better to hit the ball from the wrong side and hit it right
than to hit it from the right side and hit it wrong."

—Sir Bob Charles

An eight-stroke victory – in a major professional golf championship.
The British Open (or Open Championship, if you prefer), no less: the
oldest major championship in the world. Very Tiger Woods or Rory
McIlroy-like, right? Or how about Young Tom Morris-ish, in honor
of Old Tom's precocious son winning the title by a whopping 12
strokes in 1870. Just 19 years old at the time, it was already his *third
straight* Open title.

Granted, Bob Charles didn't beat the *field* by eight, just his single
opponent in a 36-hole playoff. But still … you might think that's
what people would remember about Charles's 1963 British Open
triumph at Royal Lytham and St. Anne's. Or why it's so historic.

But no, Bob's triumph still resonates for a different reason,
something he doesn't really have any control over. It's remembered
because it was the first time a left-handed golfer ever won a "major"
golf tournament – professional or amateur. If you've been paying
attention, you know by now that Mr. Charles is not *really* left-handed.
Which is why *I* so badly wanted to speak with him.

For a man of his stature and accomplishment, the man now
known as *Sir* Bob Charles was surprisingly easy to reach. And
surprisingly willing to spend some time on the phone with an aspiring
writer. Perhaps it should not be surprising, however, as Sir Bob has
always been known as one of the true gentlemen of the game. A man
as famous for how he carries himself as for how he played.

The son of a schoolmaster in the mountainous Wairarapa district of New Zealand, Charles came by his "backward" ways quite naturally. Both his father, Ivor, and his mother, Phyllis, were left-handed golfers. So it was only natural that young Bob started swinging lefty.

"I'm just doing something that comes naturally," Sir Bob told me. "It's instinctive for me to grip with one hand, to pick things up, grip anything with my right hand. But when it comes to putting two hands on anything, I automatically put the left hand below the right hand.

"For example, if I pick up a rifle, I put the left hand below the right hand. If I pick up a pool cue, I put the left hand below the right hand. A spade, an axe, everything I do with two hands, I put the left below the right."

A left-handed golf swing, he explained, is just like a right-hander hitting a two-handed backhand in tennis – something I discovered for myself later on.

"I'm a right-handed tennis player with one hand," he said, "but to get a little extra with the backhand, I put the left below the right and use a double-handed backhand."

When it came to golf, his mother, curiously, started out as a right-hander, but switched to lefty (though he didn't say why). His father, on the other hand, an avid and skilled all-around sportsman, shared his same tendency toward backhandedness.

"My father was a very good sportsman, and had a good eye, [a good] instinct for ball games. And he was just playing what was natural for him. He played cricket, he was a good cricketer: he bowled right-handed, batted left. If you use baseball as an example, he and I both would have been right-handed pitchers and left-handed batters."

He said he can't remember ever *not* having a golf club in his hand, having started with the game at age 3 or 4. Using several hand-me-down cut-down clubs, he honed his skills by hitting a tennis ball all over the family's yard (hopefully he never broke anyone's nose!). Golf wasn't the only sport that captured his fancy, however; rugby and cricket offered stiff competition for his attention. So it took a while to realize that golf was where his truest talents lay. His first tournament experience came at age 16, when he and his mother narrowly lost a mixed foursome event on the final hole in the championship match. And it was only then that his father deemed Bob worthy of having his own set of clubs.

Finally able to swing away with his very own left-handed sticks, it took young Bob just four years to make his mark in the golfing world at-large. In 1954, as an 18-year-old amateur, he became the youngest winner of the New Zealand Open. Among those he bested were noted Australian professionals Peter Thomson and Bruce Crampton.

After finishing high school, Bob opted against continuing his formal education, as he "wasn't keen on studying." Instead he took a banking job. And for the next six years he remained the most accomplished golfer-banker New Zealand has ever known.

During this time, in 1957, he took advantage of the opportunity of a lifetime by accepting an invitation from New Zealand cricketing legend Ian Cromb – a wealthy friend of the family – to join him on a whirlwind world tour.

"I'm 21 and he was 52 at the time, and we're playing a round of golf together at the Christchurch Golf Club," Bob recalled. "And on the 14th hole he says to me, 'I'm going away for six months, around the United States and then on to Europe. How would you like to join me?'

"And I said, 'That's fantastic!'"

Who *wouldn't* jump at such a chance?

Cromb's wife was invited, too – which was fortunate considering the couple were essentially newlyweds. If it was at all awkward for Mrs. Cromb to have a young golfing phenom tagging along on what might have been considered an extended honeymoon, she didn't let on – at least not publicly.

In preparation for the journey, Bob wrote a letter to Clifford Roberts, one of the proprietors of a little golf club in Georgia known as Augusta National. It may seem quite audacious to write the business partner of the legendary Bobby Jones requesting an invitation to The Masters. Today, it would be nearly incomprehensible. But things were simpler in those days.

"He gave me a nice reply to the affirmative," Bob said.

"You see, their philosophy is The Masters is an international event. They like to have participants from all over the world, and they'd never had a New Zealander play in The Masters before. So I think that was probably a big factor in my getting the invitation."

The Masters wasn't the only tournament on Charles's itinerary. He also planned to try to qualify for the Phoenix Open in Arizona and the St. Petersburg Open in Florida. These were professional tournaments on what was then known as the "winter tour."

Leaving New Zealand the first week of January 1958, the trio spent a week in Hawaii before continuing on to the U.S. mainland. While there, of course, he played a few rounds of golf – with *borrowed* clubs.

"I didn't take any golf clubs on the trip with me," he explained. "I was planning to get a set of golf clubs through the Dunlop representative [in San Francisco], Howard Kinsey, who was a great tennis player. He played in the days of Kramer." (That would be Jack, not Cosmo.)

Ian Cromb, you see, had connections. One was Mr. Howard, who not only set Bob up with equipment, he also hosted them all at the "Crosby Clambake," a.k.a. the Bing Crosby National Pro-Am at Pebble Beach, "where I watched Billy Casper beat Bob Rosberg," Bob recalled.

"From there we went back to San Francisco and bought a six-year-old Hudson Wasp for $250. And Howard organized some equipment for me. In those days Dunlop didn't make any golf clubs. So I got a bag from them and balls. And we talked to the Wilson people and wound up with a set of Wilson golf clubs: Top-Notch [brand]. So now I had a set of clubs and I could play!"

Picture if you will a small paper cut-out of a Hudson Wasp. Now visualize it bouncing across a map of the southwestern United States, tracing a dotted red line from San Francisco to Los Angeles (including Disneyland and Knott's Berry Farm) to Palm Springs (where they watched the Thunderbird Invitational, before it became the Bob Hope Classic) and then to Phoenix. In the qualifying round for the Phoenix Open, Bob survived a sudden death playoff for a spot in the tournament. Though he failed to make the 36-hole cut, just qualifying for his first U.S. professional tournament was quite an accomplishment.

From Phoenix, the Wasp and its occupants made their way to Houston, where they took in the action at the Houston Open. Bob didn't play, but the opportunity to see the course first-hand would come in handy five years later. Then it was on to Florida and the St.

Petersburg Open, where Bob played well enough to earn low amateur honors.

"Of course, no money, but I got a nice gold watch as the leading amateur," he recalls.

After that they drove down to Miami, where they gave the Wasp a rest and flew down to the Caribbean for a few days to take in some cricket. Then it was back to Miami to drive up to Augusta for The Masters, "the biggest of them all," as Bob described it to me.

"I didn't make the cut, I have no idea what the score was. I probably shot high 70s," Bob recalled. "But I did play a practice round with Gene Sarazen."

(Sarazen, of course, is a Masters legend. One of only five men to win all four modern major championships in his career, he put The Masters (originally named the Augusta National Invitational) on the map in 1935 by holing a 235-yard 4-wood shot on the par-5 15th hole of the final round for a "double-eagle" 2. "The shot heard 'round the world" vaulted him into a tie with Craig Wood, whom he would defeat in a 36-hole playoff the next day. He is also credited with inventing the modern sand wedge.)

And that was it for the United States – for a while. After unloading the Wasp in New York for $50, Bob and the Crombs boarded a plane for London. While in Great Britain, Bob was able to play in a number of prestigious amateur events, including the British Amateur Championship at St. Andrews. At the birthplace of modern golf, he made it through to the quarter-finals before losing.

From St. Andrews they traveled on to Royal Lytham and St. Annes in Lancashire, where Bob would attempt to qualify for the British Open – or, as it's known more formally in Europe, the Open Championship.

"I don't know what I scored, or whether I even qualified, it's a bit hazy all that stuff," he told me. "But that was the year Peter Thomson beat Dave Thomas in a 36-hole playoff.

"After the Open, in July, my golf was virtually over and that was the end of the trip."

As we were wrapping up our conversation, I was able to go online and dig up the scores he couldn't quite recall from the 1958 Masters and British Open.

"Bob," I said to him (I think I called him "Mr. Charles" during our first interview and "Bob" during the second), "you shot 71, 79 in the British Open and finished in a tie for 60th." (Only the top 40, out of 96 entrants, made the cut that year.)

This result seemed to surprise him. "You said '71-79'?" he asked. "That 71 must have been ...."

He didn't seem quite able to finish his thought, so I jumped in and said, "It must have been a *thrill*."

"Yes, it must have been," he said with a smile I could sense from the other side of the globe.

"And in The Masters you shot 77-80," I continued. "And you beat Gene Sarazen! He had 81-78."

"So you're looking that up on the internet, are you?" he said with a touch of wonder. "Oh my goodness. I don't know if you could look up who Joe Carr beat in the final of the British Amateur that year?"

Of course I could! "In the 1958 British Amateur, Joe Carr defeated Alan Thirlwell," I told him.

"Oh, Alan beat me in the quarter-final!"

It was a thrill of my own to lead this golfing legend and fine gentleman down Memory Lane like that.

For a 22-year-old New Zealand banker, the trip was the thrill of a lifetime – and a great peek into the world of the touring golf professional.

"It opened my eyes to a few things," Bob said. "One is traveling. You've got to enjoy the traveling. And you've got to love the game, obviously. It also gave me the opportunity of playing in two majors – three if you want to call the British Amateur a major. Playing in major tournaments gave me the opportunity of playing with the best players in the world, and gave me the opportunity to play on the best golf courses in the world."

Essentially, it was the trip that made Bob decide he wanted to play professional golf for a living. He remained an amateur for two more years, competing in a number of prestigious amateur events. Later in 1958, he represented New Zealand in the inaugural Eisenhower World Team Championship at St. Andrews, where his Kiwi team narrowly lost to Australia and the U.S. after leading going into the final round. The following year, he represented New Zealand at a team event in South Africa. And in 1960, he saw a young Jack Nicklaus take the individual title while leading the U.S. team to a decisive victory in the 1960 Eisenhower event at Merion in

Philadelphia.

A month later, in October, he turned professional, deciding that he'd "better concentrate on either banking or golf." Hmmm ... tough choice, that one.

On the New Zealand Tour, he won the 1960 Queens Park Open and the 1961 New Zealand PGA before venturing to Europe, where he won twice and was the fourth-leading money winner in 1962. His winnings? A whopping $10,080 – which probably felt like quite a lot at the time. Still, knowing that greener pastures lay across the pond, he went back to America and joined the PGA Tour in 1963.

But a couple other fairly significant things happened first. For one, before coming to America he flew to South Africa to marry Verity Aldridge (a friend of Gary Player's wife), whom he had been wooing since he visited there in 1960. And second – in an event that lives large in left-handed golfing history – he played in the U.S. Left-Handers Open Championship at DeSoto Lakes Country Club in Florida, where he demolished the field by a whopping 17 strokes. And if you think, "Well, that was just against left-handers – how strong could the field have been?" – consider that in doing so he broke a long-standing course record.

Still, outside the world of left-handers, Bob's entrance onto the American Tour went largely unnoticed. Except by one particularly influential individual.

Mark McCormack is best known as the first "super agent" in sports. His first – and for some time *only* – client was Arnold Palmer, who he helped turn into the biggest name in all of sports. Eventually, his company became known as IMG, International Management Group, which today is widely considered the most powerful agency in sports. By 1962, McCormack's stable had expanded to include not just Palmer, but also Gary Player and Jack Nicklaus, known in later years as "the Big Three." So it was no small thing that McCormack also saw something great in the young Bob Charles.

As McCormack writes in the Foreword to Charles's 1965 book, *Left-handed Golf*:

> Except for golfers in New Zealand, Australia and South Africa, no one really knew very much about this impassive young man. He had thoroughly destroyed the DeSoto Lakes Country Club .... This spectacular victory ... should have catapulted him

into prominence in the United States. For some reason, no great significance was attached to his victory and the usual statement made by the average golf fan was: "He must be pretty good for a left-hander." ...

I must confess that before meeting Bob and seeing him play I might have had somewhat the same attitude. However, his feat at DeSoto Lakes was absolutely incredible to me as I had competed on that golf course in past years and knew it to be tremendously difficult. On that basis, before seeing him play, I suspected that he had to be more than a "pretty fair left-hander" and that his accomplishment was much more than a few "hot" rounds.

After meeting Bob in South Africa and watching him play two tournaments, I immediately accepted the request to become his attorney and business manager throughout the world.

McCormack noticed something special in Bob Charles. And it didn't take long before other Americans noticed, as well. McCormack continued:

Beginning with the California tournaments in 1963, many persons were curious about this left-hander from New Zealand, and I could see that most of them did not take me seriously when I stated unequivocally that he would be the first left-hander to win an American PGA tournament. People laughed when I said he had an excellent chance of winning one of the four "major" tournaments as well. Some so-called experts even intimated that I was probably a little bit out of my mind.

By May, McCormack had been proven right on the first prediction, when Bob captured the Houston Open. Two months later, his more audacious claim came true when Bob returned to Royal Lytham & St. Annes for the 1963 Open Championship.

The oldest golf tournament in the world, the British Open/Open Championship was once the *only* golf tournament in the world. Or the only one of any consequence. Though the first iteration, staged in 1860 at Scotland's Prestwick Golf Club (not at St. Andrews as is often thought), featured only eight golfers, it gradually gained in scope and scale, attracting the finest golfers in the world. By the time Young Tom claimed his third title in 1870, the field had swelled to a whopping 17 golfers. (The field would not top 50 golfers until 1885; or reach 100 until 1901.) That third victory changed the course of history, as Young Tom, having won three times in a row, claimed the Championship Belt for keeps. Thanks in part to some squabbling among the sponsoring clubs about who should pay for a replacement, no tournament was staged in 1871.

The tournament resumed in 1872. A new agreement not only allowed for clubs besides Prestwick to host, it also introduced the now-famous silver Claret Jug to replace the Championship Belt. This time, however, no provision was made for anyone to keep it permanently. Fittingly, the first presentation of the Claret Jug went to none other than Young Tom Morris. (But he didn't actually receive it because the Jug, though commissioned, had not yet been crafted at the time of the tournament.)

By the mid-20th Century, however, the Open Championship had faded in stature as the United States became the hub around which the golfing world revolved. With a few notable exceptions, the game's best players – that is to say, America's best players – could not be bothered to make the trip across the pond. The trip was too expensive, the travel was too arduous, and the purse was too small.

One of those notable exceptions was Ben Hogan's epic triumph at Carnoustie. Encouraged – even *pressured* – by friends and supporters to play in the game's oldest championship at least once in his life, Hogan traveled to Scotland in 1953 and won the event in his only appearance. In the process, he impressed the Scots with his precision play and stoic demeanor. The "Wee Ice Mon" they dubbed him, with a mix of awe and affection (Hogan was only 5' 7" tall). Along with his Masters and U.S. Open titles, it was his third major win of the season in three attempts.

But Hogan's three-legged Slam, which earned him a New York City ticker-tape parade, failed to spark an Open renaissance. It was not until Arnold Palmer made his first appearance in 1960 that the original major began to regain some of its historic luster. The King had already won The Masters and the U.S. Open that year, and first gave birth to the notion of a "modern Grand Slam" by suggesting that adding wins in the British Open and the PGA Championship that year would rival Bobby Jones's 1930 feat of winning both Opens and both Amateurs in the same year. Unfortunately for his legions of fans, Palmer came up just short, finishing second at St. Andrews, one stroke behind winner Kel Nagle. But when he won the event the next *two* years, the Open Championship was firmly re-entrenched as a "major" championship.

Charles, having won at Houston just a month previously, arrived full of confidence, ready to take on the world's best – even though he's the first to admit that the competition wasn't as stout then as it is today.

"Let's put it in context," he said. "We're going back how many years? Well, 47 years, aren't we? The best players of the day were there. Nicklaus was there, Palmer was there, [Gary] Player was there, Peter Thomson was there, Kel Nagle ... they were the leading players of the day. In effect, those five players were probably the only ones I had to beat."

In fact, despite Charles's modesty, that 1963 field was considered quite strong. Past champions included Palmer, gunning for his third straight triumph; Australian Thomson was trying for his fifth overall; and Gary Player and Kel Nagle, each with an eye on a second Open Championship title. Perhaps even more notable – in hindsight – 23-year-old Jack Nicklaus wanted badly to win his first Open title, having been somewhat unimpressive (finishing in a tie for 32nd) in his debut the year before.

To put things in further historical perspective, by the time they finished their playing careers, those five players combined to win 40 major professional championships – not even counting senior events. Nicklaus, of course, famously won 18 (the mark Tiger Woods most wanted to reach), Player nine, Palmer seven, and Thomson five (all in The Open), with Nagle bringing up the rear with his lone Open title. So there was plenty of firepower, even if it was mostly concentrated near the top.

"Nowadays, of course, things are quite different," he continued. "What I'm saying is, the quality was there but there was no great depth to the field. Whereas today, instead of just five players, you've got 50 [top] players to beat.

"You with me? Good."

But it was unheralded Phil Rogers, a short and stocky former U.S. Marine, who made a statement early, shooting 67-68 (five under par on the par-70 layout) to take a healthy halfway lead. A third round 73, however, brought him back to the pack while Charles fired an impressive 66 to take the top spot after three rounds. Meanwhile, playing solid if not spectacular golf, Nicklaus shot 71-68-70 to stay two shots back of Charles. Heading into the final round, it was pretty much a four-man race, with Charles at three under par (-3), Thomson at -2, and Rodgers and Nicklaus at -1.

(A couple of quick notes on history: For one, it's odd to imagine that in 1963, the British Open was played Wednesday through Friday, with 36 holes scheduled on the final day. So it was all over – except in the case of a playoff – by the weekend. Unimaginable in today's TV-driven media coverage. Also, it was not yet commonplace to use "relation to par" when reporting scores. The *Sports Illustrated* article about the tournament, for instance, includes barely a reference to the scores being over- or under-par. This practice, however, would soon become predominant as televised golf grew in leaps and bounds during the 1960s.)

Late in the fourth round, Nicklaus had the tournament well within his grasp. Playing two groups ahead of Charles and Rodgers, he held a two-stroke lead standing on the 71st tee. A costly bogey on 17, however, shaved that lead to one. And it was here that Royal Lytham's notoriously quiet fans might well have influenced the outcome. Knowing the situation was extremely tight, Nicklaus stood on the 18th tee, waiting to hear a cheer if Charles and/or Rodgers birdied the 16th hole. When he heard nothing, he assumed he was still in the lead and needed only a par to maintain a one-stroke clubhouse lead. In fact, they had *both* birdied 16 to pull even. When Nicklaus bogeyed 18, it spelled the end of his chances.

There's no way to tell how Nicklaus's mindset may have influenced how he played 18. But it's not a stretch to think that playing "defense" in search of a par instead of aggressively for birdie could have made the 23-year-old tentative, and influenced the outcome. In fact, it's something he now points to as a learning experience. In a June 2012 *Golf Digest* article, Nicklaus lists his bogey-bogey finish as one of his career regrets. With the benefit of hindsight, however, he says it likely helped him in the long run.

"I was probably better off not winning, again, because of the learning experience," he said. "Those bogeys were useful for me in my career."

But Rodgers and Charles weren't thinking about any of that.

They still had golf to play, with the tournament still on the line. On the 18th, a relatively short par-4 with both the fairway and green well-guarded by bunkers, Rodgers found himself facing a 15-foot birdie putt to win the tournament – Charles had four feet remaining for par. After leaving his first putt a nervous two-feet short, Rodgers tapped in – barely. Then he slapped his tweed cap over the hole (something of a trademark move) and made a show of walking rubber-leggedly around the green in a display of literal comic relief. The hi-jinks did not faze the stoic Charles, who calmly knocked in his par putt to force a playoff.

It was an exciting end to regulation play, but not at all the one golf fans had expected. Palmer, the odds-on favorite (British bookmakers listed him at 2-1 to win, an irrationally exuberant figure) was never a factor after opening with a disappointing, to put it mildly, 76. He finished in a relatively devastating tie for 26th, a whopping 17 strokes back. Player, another pre-tournament favorite, rallied from an opening 75 to finish tied for 7th, a (slightly) more respectable 10 strokes behind. And Nagle's third-round 73 took him out of contention, though he finished with a solid 71 to place solo fourth, six strokes back at +2.

In the 36-hole playoff the next day, tall, thin, and stoic Charles made relatively short work of short, stocky, and flashy Rodgers. By lunch he had built a three-stroke lead; two holes into the afternoon round he was up by five. On the 21st hole of the playoff, number 3, a long par-4 with railroad tracks down the right-hand side, Charles gave Rodgers an opening when he hooked his drive out of bounds. Rodgers pulled within one after making a few putts of his own, but on number 8 Charles broke his opponent's spirit for good. After Rodgers sank an unlikely 50-foot birdie putt on the eighth – and predictably made a spectacle of himself in celebration – Charles sank a 30-footer of his own. Without so much as cracking a smile, he then turned on his heel and headed straight for the 9th tee, leaving his caddie to retrieve the ball and perhaps offer a wry smile to the crestfallen Rodgers.

After that, it was all over but the non-shouting. Charles continued to make putt after putt en route to a solid 71, while Rodgers wilted to a 76 under the barrage of Charles's red-hot flat stick.

"The 36-hole [playoff] final with Phil Rodgers was a little bit of an endurance contest, as you can imagine, playing 72 holes in two days," Sir Bob told me. "And I think I was the fitter of the two. But then, Phil Rogers would never consider himself to be one of the fittest people in the world!

"And my putting continued through the final. I think I won by, what was it, seven shots?"

It was eight, of course – with every stroke of the difference accounted for on the putting surface. If all that counted was hitting the green in as few strokes as possible, Rodgers would have edged Charles that day by a stroke. But thanks to a nine-stroke (56 to 65) putting advantage, the lanky New Zealander won in a blowout.

Drive for show, putt for dough – you bet!

Charles would go down in history as one of the great putters of the game – as well as one of the most modest, as evidenced by this story told by his good friend Tony Jacklin, in an essay he wrote prior to inducting Charles into the World Golf Hall of Fame:

> I remember being in Memphis once. I had finished my round and was back at the hotel, sitting beside the swimming pool with my wife. Bob walked by and I asked him how he had played. He said, "I putted quite well today." I thought, what in the world does that mean coming from him? So I asked, and he said, "I never missed anything under 30 feet." I was like, well, say no more. He shot 63 that day. ... His prowess with the putter really benefited him when he went to the Champions Tour. He made mincemeat of everyone.

What was the key to his success? Well, one thing Charles had going for him on the greens at Lytham & St. Annes was "cross-dominance"; he played left-handed while his dominant eye was his right. Having his stronger eye closer to the line of play was something Charles feels gave him a distinct advantage.

"When I'm lining up a putt, I'm looking at the hole and the ball with my strong right eye," he explained. "So, I've got a theory ... if you're left-eyed you should be a right-handed putter; if you're right-eyed you should be a left-handed putter."

And here's another thing I found intriguing, something I didn't get a chance to ask him about. I've always been fascinated by how "wristy" putting strokes were in those days. Arnold Palmer is a prime example. Back then he would stand hunched over close to the ball, with his hands tucked in close to his body, almost seeming to brace his elbows into his mid-section. He would then strike the ball with the putter almost entirely using his wrists. Nothing at all like today's "modern" putting strokes, in which the wrists and elbows remain locked, and the stroke is made primarily by rocking the shoulders.

But I ran across this description of Charles's putting stroke on the official Open Championship website (www.theopen.com), in a summary of the 1963 tournament:

> Locking arms, hands and putter into one solid unit he rocked his shoulders back and forwards in a classic pendulum action that was devastating.

Could it be that part of Sir Bob's putting brilliance was due to his "futuristic" stroke? Whatever the reason, Charles dominated the short grass that day in England to win his first major victory. He had officially "arrived."

"It opened a lot of doors for me," he said. "And, of course, winning a major, it's meaningful even to this day. Much more meaningful than winning a half-dozen Houston Opens!"

Yet despite what seemed like the start of something big, the 1963 Open Championship was the first and only major Charles would win. Not to say that was the end of his success, however. Bob went on to win some 40 professional titles around the world, including six on the PGA Tour. He also had a number of subsequent close calls in majors, including second at the Open Championship in 1968 and '69, second at the PGA Championship in 1968, and third at the U.S. Open in 1964 and 1970.

To be clear, he did all that *before* he turned 50. Because perhaps Charles's most enduring legacy is the outstanding success he enjoyed on the U.S. Senior Tour (now called the Champions Tour), where he won a whopping 23 times from 1987 to 1996. That doesn't even include the two Senior British Open titles he won, in 1989 and '93.

He is also credited with being the oldest golfer to make the cut on one of the world's professional golf tours. As a young man of 71, Bob finished 23rd in the 2007 New Zealand Open – more than half a century after he won the tournament as an 18-year-old amateur. And, though his performance was ultimately upstaged by Tom Watson's near-miraculous runner-up finish in 2009 (at age 59), Charles is also the oldest to make the cut at the Open Championship, when he finished 71st at age 60 in 1996 – once again at Royal Lytham & St. Annes.

"To what do you attribute such amazing longevity?" I asked. "Good health," he replied. Being friends with Gary Player certainly didn't hurt in that regard, Player being pro golf's original fitness freak, long before Tiger Woods made working out commonplace on tour.

Charles was elected to the World Golf Hall of Fame in 2008 – the first left-handed player to receive the honor. In 1999 he received an even higher distinction, becoming known as "Sir Bob Charles" upon his appointment as "Knight Companion of the New Zealand Order of Merit" (though I could find no information regarding the number of left-handers that may have preceded him).

Today he lives with his wife Verity on the New Zealand farm they purchased in 1972, at age 36 – "envisioning an early retirement from golf," he said. But the game was just too good to him to abandon. He's officially retired from competition now, but not from playing. He's thankful for continued good health and a long, successful, career – and life. In 2011, he told a New Zealand television station:

> I wouldn't change anything, I've been very fortunate. I've got a great marriage, 48 years married. Two children, four grandchildren – unfortunately they live in the northern hemisphere, but I do get to see them fairly regularly. My health has been good, I've been fortunate in that respect. A lot of my contemporaries have had ill health, which has cut short their careers. But I'm still – perhaps not as flexible – but I'm still as fit and healthy as I was in my 20s. I guess I attribute that to good genes. My parents, they managed to get to 96 and 91. So I suppose that's the next thing to aim for, is to try to reach 100! I never made 100 in cricket, actually. But [if] all [continues] going well with my good genes and good health, I might get to 100 [years]. I just hope I'm mentally sane enough to enjoy making a century!

And though he doesn't mind being so well-known for having broken golf's dexterity barrier, he's not crazy about being known as a "left-hander."

"I'm a *backhander*," he said. "I play a double-handed backhand. I stand on the *right* side of the ball, I hit the ball on the *right* side of the clubface, and I'm hitting to my *right*, while wearing a *right*-hand glove."

It couldn't be more clear. Right?

CHAPTER 5
Ready or Not

"I fear not the man who has practiced
10,000 kicks once, but I fear the man who has
practiced one kick 10,000 times."

—Bruce Lee

As I began my quest, it probably didn't help matters that I was a little beat up right from the start. For one thing, I was still recovering from a soccer coaching accident. Yes, that's right. I hurt myself coaching soccer. More precisely, I hurt myself *learning* to coach soccer, at a clinic.

From an early age, Jack seemed to take quite a liking to the game those crazy Europeans call "football" for no apparent reason. We practiced in the backyard quite a bit, and signed up for the local micro-soccer program as soon as he was old enough. After we finally got him on a real team at age 7, we got an e-mail from the league saying that if they couldn't find one more coach, the league would have to contract – so I reluctantly volunteered.

Even though I knew next to nothing about soccer, I was head coach for two years – which proved to be both much harder and much more rewarding than anticipated. It was a source of both joy and stress, the latter of which mostly resulted from insecurity. I lacked confidence that I knew what I was doing, and also worried that the *parents* lacked confidence in me, and that I was perhaps cheating the kids out of learning as much about soccer as they should be.

So after the first season I signed up to take a coaching refresher course. Problem is, a big part of learning to coach soccer involves

THE WRONG SIDE OF THE BALL

actually *playing* it. They didn't just show us the drills they wanted us to learn, they made us do them.

Did I mention already that my competitive streak is a little wider than it ought to be? Especially for a 47-year-old non-soccer player who doesn't have a history of keeping himself in shape. So I went after the ball a little too hard during one of the drills, extended my right leg a little too far, came down awkwardly, hyper-extended my knee, toppled over, and hit the ground hard.

At first I feared the worst. Years ago I had torn a knee ligament playing softball – in much the same way I had just fallen. But this time, my right hamstring took the brunt of the blow. To add insult to injury, it all happened right at the end of the drill. The whistle blew just as I fell, everyone headed back to the main area, and I suddenly found myself alone on the ground clutching my leg in pain. It felt like when Bart broke his leg on *The Simpsons* and Milhouse said, "Hey, he's really hurt! Let's get out of here!"

It wasn't long, however, before one of the instructors saw me lying there and came to my aid. In a few minutes I was resting on a bench with an ice pack strapped to my butt. It did not appear I would be missed in any way.

I'm not sure how I made it home; I probably shouldn't have driven myself, but I did. Men are stubborn that way. A visit to the doctor the next day revealed that I had suffered a bad hamstring pull, but nothing worse. A few days later, however, after the leg pain subsided, I realized I must have hit the ground pretty hard, because I seemed to have some pretty good bruising in my chest and rib cage. And this, more than the hamstring, is what would linger and cause me a few problems as I began swinging a golf club every day.

It was clear already that conditioning might become a bigger factor than I realized – so I resolved to make exercise and fitness a priority in my quest. (Key word: *resolved.*)

The discomfort did not slow me down too much, so I continued to make ample use of my lunch hours and after-work time (as long as the light held out) to hit the practice area at Brown Deer. Our stretch of beautiful fall weather continued: Indian Summer temperatures, bright sunshine, and of course some spectacular fall color. Autumn in southeastern Wisconsin can be quite beautiful. People like to complain about the winters we have, but I truly enjoy having four distinct seasons. Our springs can be pretty cold and wet, but our summers are generally wonderful (not as hot and humid as down in Central Illinois) and autumn even better. I even enjoy winter, as long as it snows. "If it's going to be cold, it might as well snow!" I always say. Otherwise it's just cold, grey, brown, and useless.

As I pushed onward, I started noticing weird little things about playing left-handed. Like how awkward it felt to clean a left-handed club! Through all my years of wiping off my clubs, I never once thought about which hand did what, or how to bring the club face into contact with the damp towel. But now everything felt backwards and hard. What have I gotten myself into!?

More seriously, some weird little aches and pains started to show up. It wasn't just my chest, which was still a little sore from that dark day on the soccer field. My right thumb was starting to hurt – and I had no idea why. But it was significant enough to cause some worry. I also noticed that my back would feel sore after a long session on the putting green. Early on, my thighs even ached a little from standing in a putting position for an extended period of time. Really?

Doubts about the project began to flash in and out of my brain. Most of the time I was pretty excited about it – but not everyone I told about it seemed convinced it was a good idea. Far from it, in fact. My friend Rob, the one guy I thought would be the most supportive, regularly expressed doubts: He doubted I could learn to play golf left-handed with any level of proficiency, and he doubted the process would be interesting enough to make a good book. But he was a great sounding board and our discussions (mostly via e-mail) were very useful in thinking things through.

"I was thinking about the whole left-handed thing," he wrote me one day. "To me hitting right-handed feels natural, as I can control the breaking of the wrists more with my right hand. And it feels like the power is coming from the right as well, but I understand you're saying you'd get more power from the right hand if you hit left-handed? Don't you need your dominant hand to help control the swing path and break your wrists?"

"I know exactly what you're saying," I replied. "But how do you know that it doesn't just *feel* natural because you're used to it? My theory (and it's only a theory) is that guys like us [who haven't had a lot of instruction] use our right hands more than we're really supposed to because it's more natural to use our right hands more. Then we become used to it and it feels right.

"But this is all an experiment," I continued. "I'm not setting out to prove anything, I'm setting out to see if it can work. I suspect there are advantages and disadvantages to both approaches. It could well be that when all is said and done I conclude that nothing was really gained [by switching to lefty]."

Even Elizabeth – though she was always *extremely* supportive – expressed doubts. At dinner one night she pointed out that it could take a *long* time to get any good: "Just think how long it's taken you to get where you are now – practically your whole life!"

Yes, I said, you're right. But part of what I'm exploring here, I explained patiently, is how much of what I already "know" about golf will carry over. In that sense, I'm not *completely* starting over. I have a lifetime of experience that's not going to just vanish.

That said, her comment did raise some doubt in my mind in one regard: I catch myself assuming that my *good* habits (along with all my touch and feel) would carry over, but my *bad* ones wouldn't. But there was no guarantee of that at all. What if the opposite happened – the good stuff stayed on the right-hand side while all my bad stuff (like my temperament!) crossed over effortlessly!?

There was only one way to find out, of course. And now I was committed.

And despite that initial moment of disappointment – when Coach Carl nearly shattered all my dreams by telling me I did not have a perfect grip right out of the gate (I nearly cried!) – that first lesson was amazing. To say it was eye-opening would be understating the obvious. What I discovered was how little I really knew about the golf swing. I guess this didn't come as too much of a shock – a big part of my project's appeal, after all, is the attempt to re-learn everything the right way. Still, I was taken slightly aback by how screwed-up some of my fundamentals turned out to be. Some of the things I thought I was doing right were actually working against me.

Let's start, as he did, with that grip.

I had gotten at least a couple of things right, thank goodness. My research revealed that as a right-hander, I was holding the club too much in the palm of my hand. I should instead be holding it more with my fingers – a revelation confirmed by Coach Carl during that first lesson. And he showed me how to check to make sure the grip of the club is positioned snugly *underneath* the pad (on the pinky side) of my right hand.

"You're pretty good with where you want this heel pad," he told me. "And a good checkpoint for that is going to be if you can take your thumb and index finger off the club, and you can lift that club straight up [using just your three other fingers]."

On my left hand (and remember, this will be reversed for you right-handed readers!) he showed me how my two *middle* fingers provide the bulk of the gripping power. The pinky basically goes along for the ride, tucked into the gap between the middle and index fingers of my right hand. Meanwhile, my left thumb and forefinger stay relaxed on the shaft. My left thumb, in fact, should not go on the shaft at all; rather, Coach said, it should lay to the right side of the grip.

(Right-handers – are you starting to get a sense of how confusing it can be to lefties trying to "transpose" standard right-handed instruction? To simplify, I'll start using the terms *top hand*, to refer to the hand nearest the body, on the end of club shaft, and *low hand* to refer to the hand nearer the clubhead.)

I realized that this is a very different concept from what I routinely put into practice with my right-handed (RH) swing. Historically, I've always gripped the club very tightly with my right thumb and forefinger … I mean, the thumb and forefinger of my *low hand*. I used that hand to provide power *and* to steer the clubhead through the ball – with lots of tension in my hands. Based solely on what I now knew was a more proper grip, it became clear that it was wrong to let my dominant hand dominate my swing.

But the main mistake with my new left-handed (LH) grip was with the ring finger and pinky of my low hand (my left, your right – probably). Rather than tucking the pinky into that gap and keeping my ring finger on the grip, I was letting both of those fingers creep up onto my top hand and "go along for the ride." So instead of having a good hold of the club with the two middle fingers of my low hand, my thumb, index, and middle fingers were left to do the yeoman's work of gripping the grip.

As far as the position of my hands on the club was concerned, we started with a pretty "neutral" hand position – that is, with my two palms facing each other, more or less parallel to the target line.

Once we got the grip straightened out he had me hit a few more soft shots, just half-swings, and then moved on to my address position. Again, he made a simple suggestion to fix a major flaw.

"Relax your shoulders and drop your hands," he said. "Everything is way too tense."

All my life I had addressed the ball in a very rigid position, with my elbows locked (or nearly so) and my arms extended away from my body. If you were to look at me from behind the target line, you would not see much of an angle between my arms and the shaft of the club. This is something I've always done rather instinctively – I can't recall ever giving it much thought. It always just *felt* like the right thing to do.

But not according to Coach Carl.

"Take your normal stance, relax your arms and shoulders, and just let your hands and arms drop naturally toward the ground," he instructed. "Now, see where your hands are? That's where you should be holding the club."

"Really?" I said, probably with a bit of skepticism in my voice. It wasn't that I didn't trust his judgment – it just felt so different from what I was used to. It felt so much more … *passive*. How could I possibly generate any power from such a relaxed position?

But in the weeks following that first lesson I started to pay very close attention to how the pros do it. And sure enough, almost all of them let their arms drop almost vertically from their shoulders when addressing the ball. I've been watching golf on TV – lots of it – since I was a kid. How could I have never noticed this before?

I suppose it probably had something to do with the fact that I have never once, in all those years, seen myself swing a golf club. Maybe if I had, I would have noticed how far I extended my arms. But no more!

Then he talked about the importance of *tempo*, and how my ability to develop a proper and consistent rhythm would be one of the keys to my success.

"Think of your golf swing as a *pendulum*," he said. "Think about letting the club *swing through* the ball; not about trying to *hit* at it."

In fact, just about everything he had me do that first lesson was geared toward *reducing tension* in my set-up and swing. He moved my feet a little bit closer together – into a less aggressive, more *relaxed* position. He also had me level my shoulders; another bad carryover from my RH swing was pushing my hands toward the target by tilting my shoulders.

"Just relax," he said, over and over again. "It's all about

eliminating tension."

By the time we were done I was so relaxed I was just about ready to fall asleep! But that would have been impossible, because my brain was absolutely buzzing with new information.

We also spent a fair amount of time just talking – about the mental side of golf, the importance of fitness and stretching, and how golf is "a game of contradictions." One of the most important things to remember, he said, is that "less effort equals more results; and more effort equals less results." It's counterintuitive, but it goes a long way toward explaining why two of the biggest hitters in the game (from my generation) are guys who look like their putting the least amount of effort into their swings: Fred Couples and Ernie Els.

We also talked more about the project in general. I confirmed that I was planning to play *only* left-handed golf, even in practice, for the duration.

"Well, that's good," he replied, "because it's a totally different feel. A lot of the things you're going to be doing are going to be foreign to your body, because your muscles aren't used to reacting that way."

This reminded me of what Rob had said, about how unnatural it feels to swing left-handed.

I scoff at Rob's scoffing, but he raised a fair question: Can I really teach my body something completely new at the (relatively) advanced age of 47? Is it true that you can't teach an old dog new tricks?

And this reminded me of a comment from another doubter, my friend Bill from church, an older man who's been something of a mentor to me (for life, not golf). Over lunch one day, he shared a story of a conversation he once had with a woman from China. She had no accent, he said – and the woman's husband explained that it was because she came to the U.S. as a girl of about 10. Before you reach puberty, he said, your brain is much more adaptive and flexible, and able to learn new things much more readily. His point was, essentially: You're way past puberty, Mike – so don't get your hopes up!

Come on, really!? Talk about unscientific, anecdotal evidence. There are plenty of stories of golf pros who didn't take up the game until relatively later in life. Perhaps the most successful is Larry Nelson, who didn't play golf until age 21. He was introduced to golf by an Army buddy after coming home from Vietnam in 1968, broke 100 his first time out of the gate, and was breaking 70 in less than a year. In 1973, just five years later, he qualified for the PGA Tour, where he would claim ten victories during his career, including three majors (the PGA Championship in 1981 and '87; and the U.S. Open in 1983). He also won 19 times on the Champions Tour.

More recently there's Y.E. Yang, who famously beat Tiger Woods down the stretch in the 2009 PGA Championship. He didn't start to play golf until age 19. Yes, I know – 19 or even 21 is not the same as 47! But my goal is not to beat Tiger in a major championship, either. Breaking 90 left-handed would do nicely.

Speaking of goals, one of mine was to avoid setting one – other than to give it 109 percent (110 just feels out of reach) and see what happens. But it was difficult not to think of a target score. In October, very early in the process (before I had even ordered a wedge!), I wrote in my journal: "Somewhere in my head I think I ought to be breaking 100 by next summer. Maybe breaking 90 by fall. I don't know what I'm basing that on, but that seems doable to me for some reason."

Yeah, well, we'll just see about that! Is 47 too old to start this process?

To help answer that question, I arranged to speak with Dr. Bobby Hart, a retired professor of motor learning from the University of Wisconsin–Milwaukee (UW-M), former coach, and avid golfer. She had been one of my wife's professors while she was in school (Elizabeth has a Master's degree in Human Kinetics from UW-M). We met for breakfast. I had French toast.

The first thing she did was confirm that this would be harder to do as an adult. My 47-year-old brain, she explained, lacks the "neuroplasticity" it had in my youth – which is basically the same as calling me an "old dog" and telling me not to expect to learn any new tricks any time soon. More of my dreams – dashed!

And then there's the whole left-handed thing. Because I'm not just an old dog learning something new. I'm learning to do something familiar using my opposite hand. She told me about research being done with stroke victims, those who lose much of the use of one or the other side of their body. It's called "constraint-induced therapy," she explained. In order to help restore motor function in their "bad" arm, for instance, patients are restrained from using their "good" arm at all. This forces them to use the bad arm much more than they otherwise would be inclined to – which in turn forces the brain to start building new neuropathways where the old ones have been damaged.

"The results are mixed, however, because most strokes occur in older adults," Dr. Hart explained. "But there have been some experiments done with very young stroke patients."

In those studies, when their good hand or leg is restrained, the children "improve their skill with their affected limb quite dramatically." But again, the key difference is that these patients – and their brains – are much younger.

"The neuroplasticity of the child is much greater. But I think that the potential for the older adult learner is that you would have to really severely restrict function in order to change, basically, the brain-wiring – which is what's really going on."

"So what you're saying is … I should strap my right-hand down in order to train my left hand to work better?" I replied.

"Well, I think for you it's what you suggested, that you may have to give up playing golf right-handed pretty completely."

Eureka! So I was right – at least about *something:* that I should stop playing golf right-handed. It was nice to have that idea confirmed by a real-life scientist. Maybe my brain is still a little more neuroplastic after all! Or maybe it's true what they say about blind squirrels and nuts.

But … I already know how to play golf – sort of. Won't that make it easier for me to learn these "new" skills on the left-hand side? Or will all those bad habits I have outweigh whatever good feelings or habits I'm able to carry over?

"I think the good habits have an advantage," Dr. Hart replied. "There's a loosely understood phenomenon called 'reminiscence.' You know your first day out in the spring, and you get up there and you hit this shot, and it's like where did that come from? It's beautiful, let's have another!"

"Yes, yes, I *do* know that feeling!" I said. "It happens to me all the time. In fact, I've often said that my first round of the year is usually one of my best. Well, maybe the first nine – or the first three holes, anyway. It tends to go downhill fast after that."

"That's reminiscence," she said. "The strong *good* habit has been reinforced more than the many *variations* of that. A metaphor would be a path across the vacant lot. You take that straight shot a lot, so you wear it down. Then you can go lots of other ways when you're wrong, but the paths don't get reinforced quite so many times."

And it's the same with the pathways in your brain – I get it! Hmm ... well, that presumes I do it *right* more often than I do it wrong. But it seems to make sense, and it lines up with my experience. It also lines up with what I've read about the mental aspects of golf (which we'll discuss more in Chapter 9), regarding the body's tendency to do what your brain is visualizing – for better or worse.

But I keep going back to the *age* thing. How big a factor is that going to be?

"I think it's pretty big," she said. "You can look at it on a number of levels. Regarding the mental aspects: If you're focused and disciplined and clear in your goals, there's probably an advantage to all of your experience that will help. But the fact that you're not as strong, you're not as flexible, you're not as quick, you're not as neurally flexible in your brain ... I think those things are clearly disadvantages."

Gee, thanks, Doc! What are you going to tell me next, that my mother doesn't love me as much as she used to? (Actually, I think that's true. I used to think I was my mom's favorite, but ever since I got *married*, I've had the distinct impression that she loves her daughter-in-law more!)

All-in-all it wasn't a particularly encouraging discussion. But I wasn't really expecting her to dispel my concerns – I was expecting her to *confirm* them. Which she did, quite clearly: This is not going to be easy!

But she did give me at least one nice positive thought to hang onto. She explained that when she was a tennis coach, she would sometimes experiment by teaching her beginning students *backhand* first.

"I'm pretty convinced that worked better," she said. "Because that natural motion of opening, of extension [in a backhand stroke], is easier than coming across the body. But people don't *feel* more comfortable that way. We're much more comfortable with the muscles on the front of our body than the muscles on the back of our body, I believe. There are a whole lot of 'frequent use' kind of issues there. So people didn't like that. But I'm pretty convinced that it was good for them [to learn backhand first]."

So there's that — encouraging because a "backhanded" golf swing (as Bob Charles calls it) is so similar in some respects to a backhand stroke in tennis. And if Dr. Hart's tennis students could pick it up more easily than a forehand stroke, maybe — just maybe — that means there's hope for a broken-down old right-handed golfer to learn a backhanded golf swing.

And the French toast? Delicious.

Meanwhile, friends were still weighing in on what they thought of the book project. One of the early supporters was Mike "Scruffy" Neuses, a friend from high school, and part of the "White Lake Classic" gang we'll talk much more about later. He wrote in an e-mail:

> I still think [the book is] a GREAT idea and I'm glad you are pursuing it. Even if you don't make any $$$ on the book it will still be a worthwhile adventure. When I told Rob I thought it was a good idea he looked at me like I had 5 eyes. I think he was expecting me to pooh pooh the idea but I think it's a real winner. The hard part will be finishing the book. The finishing part will be the time consuming and drudgery part of the project — and you aren't known as a closer.

Even though he put a little smiley-face icon after it, I wasn't sure how to take the "closer" remark. I appreciated the support, of course — it meant a lot. But he had struck a small nerve. It's true that I've sometimes had trouble "finishing the job." And while it's true that … you know, I think I'll finish that thought later.

As lesson #2 approached, I continued to take stock of my little aches and pains. My hamstring wasn't an issue, but my side was still a little sore, as was my right thumb. But neither seemed to be affecting anything, so I pressed on.

It was now mid-November, but the gorgeous weather was still hanging on. I continued to sneak over to Brown Deer as often as possible, but I also was starting to make more use of the Lefty Dome at the office. Finding time to practice at lunchtime was usually pretty easy; but carving out larger chunks at other times of day was already proving challenging.

I was determined to stick to my commitment of putting family ahead of the book, so when Elizabeth called the Monday after the lesson asking if I wanted to get together for lunch, I said "sure" – even though I had been planning to practice. I'll just practice this evening instead, I thought to myself. Problem is, even after more than 10 years of marriage, Elizabeth still can't read my thoughts.

That evening, a friend of Jack's stayed for dinner. When it was time to take him home, I volunteered. I told Elizabeth I would drop him off and then head for the Lefty Dome. "Are you planning to take Jack?" she asked, sounding slightly irritated.

"No," I said carefully. "Why?"

"Because I was planning to go see my Dad tonight."

Hmm … seems as though she also thought I could read her thoughts?

Elizabeth's dad, Bill, 82, had been in a rehab facility following a recent hospital stay, and Elizabeth liked to visit him as often as possible. I was torn. I *really* wanted to practice! But I also felt very guilty about potentially making things more difficult for Elizabeth to see her dad. After a few uncomfortable moments she said, "You go. I'll take Jack along to see my dad."

"No, that's O.K.," I replied. "You go. I'll take Jack with me or stay home."

No, you go. No, you go. Back and forth it went, two would-be martyrs in a heroic stand-off. Finally I said, "Look, how about if I take Jack's friend home then head over to the office to hit balls. I won't stay very long. You take Jack to see your dad, and I'll come by in a little while. We'll all have a visit, then I'll take Jack home and then you can stay as long as you want."

Perfect. That's what we did and it worked out great. "Balance," says Mr. Myiagi in *The Karate Kid*. It's all about *balance*.

My 30-minute practice session that evening went pretty well. I hit mostly 9-irons, concentrating on rhythm and smoothness. Coach Carl had told me to slowly count "one-and-two" in my head as I swing to keep a smooth and steady tempo. But I decided instead I was going to say "Er-nie Els" – because I once heard (six-time major winner) Nick Faldo say about him during a golf telecast: "It's no wonder his tempo is so good, he's got the perfect name for it. Instead of saying 'one-and-two' as he swings he can say 'Er-nie Els'!"

It's kind of silly, but it works. And there's certainly no harm in putting thoughts of Ernie Els's fluid swing into your head while you practice.

I continued to practice indoors all week, trying to be ready for Lesson #2. I really wanted to show Coach I had made progress! But it continued to be hard for me to stay focused. I realized that for me, hitting balls for more than 30 – or maybe 45 – minutes can become counter-productive. If I lose my focus, I stop thinking about what I'm doing, and then I risk ingraining bad habits instead of good ones. So I resolved to practice for shorter periods of time, but more often.

Still, I also knew that *repetition* – as tedious as it sometimes seemed – was very important for me at this stage. My LH swing still did not feel that natural – and it would only become natural by repeating it over and over and over again. Coach Carl once told me that he spent an entire winter in Ohio swinging a club for an hour a day in his mother's bedroom (the only room in the house with high ceilings). Not hitting balls, mind you; just swinging a club. The following summer he won the Ohio State Amateur.

My tendency, however, was to hit a few good shots, think to myself, "O.K., I got it," and then move onto something new. But at my lesson that Saturday, Coach Carl gave me some words that would help remind me going forward how important it is to keep doing things over and over.

"An amateur practices until he gets it right," he told me, "but a professional practices until he can't get it wrong."

That's a big difference. And clearly, my attitude in life to that point had been very "amateurish." If I really wanted to get good at left-handed golf, I would need to adopt a more-professional approach.

Overall, that second lesson went very well. We started by revisiting a few things from the first lesson: grip, rhythm, set-up, balance, etc. He told me that one of the hardest things for a beginning golfer is just getting the ball *into the air* consistently, and that I'm already doing a very good job of that. A good sign. He said it's important to let the momentum of the swing do that work, but most people try to *push* the ball into the air instead of letting the club *lift* it.

"It's *swing* versus *hit*," he said. "Let the weight of the club lift the ball."

Overall, we seemed to be painting a picture of fluidity: a smooth, rhythmic motion that just happens to come in contact with a small white ball placed in its path. It's kind of like ... picture a limber Amish man swinging a scythe back and forth cutting wheat, not a muscle-bound circus roustabout pounding a tent stake with a sledge hammer.

One thing I had to "un-learn" was the idea of what's called a "one-piece takeaway." This is a concept taught by many professionals, but that others, including Coach Carl, don't believe in. In a nutshell, it involves taking the club back with your shoulders, arms, and hands staying in "one piece," without breaking your wrists until near the top of the backswing. The wrists then remain cocked on the downswing until just before impact.

The countering viewpoint, which Coach Carl teaches, is that the takeaway should more closely mirror the downswing – that your wrists start to break (or, more correctly, *rotate*) as soon as you begin taking the club back.

This was not a difficult adjustment – largely, I think, because everything was new on the LH side anyway. It was a new motion, but I was doing it on a new side, so there was no bad habit to break.

Another new concept was how to properly engage my lower body in the swing – which is not something I did well as a right-hander. When you watch professionals on TV swing a golf club, they all finish in roughly the same position: with their arms and club in the air, their hips rotated so their belt buckle faces the target line, their back foot rotated with the toe on the ground, the heel lifted high, and the sole facing away from the target.

As a right-hander, my swing was all arms and swaying hips, with little to no rotation and virtually no leg- or foot-work. But Coach showed me how to push toward the target line with my back knee, so that on my follow-through the natural momentum resulting from a good rotation would cause my heel to come up naturally. If everything works together properly, the result is a nice "pose" position on the finish – "As Seen on TV."

But the tendency I would continue to fight was to lift my heel as an afterthought. I would swing the club and then lift my heel, pushing my knee away from my body. The right way is to drive my back knee down the target line (toward my front knee), letting the natural momentum of my rotation pull my heel up off the ground.

That is, that "heel up" position should happen naturally as a *result* of a good full turn.

Mostly we worked on tempo and rhythm. And balance. And eliminating tension – all the same stuff we worked on the previous week. At one point I told Coach I felt like I had about five swing thoughts in my head, fighting with each other.

He replied by saying, "OK, let's go back to the three thoughts [that I told you earlier]. First of all is *set-up*. Second is our *balance*. Next is our *motion*. Once you can get the first two out of the way, all you want to think about is the club *swinging*."

Relax, relax, relax. Tempo, tempo, tempo. Rhythm, rhythm, rhythm. Easier said than done, right?!

Somewhere toward the middle of the lesson, things were going really well and I started to get excited – even a bit "giddy," as I wrote in my journal. Trouble is, that sense of excitement tends to work against my relaxation and makes me want to swing harder. And then things fall apart. I explained to Coach that this happens to me frequently on the course.

"You don't have a franchise on that!" he replied.

We wrapped things up with a discussion about not "separating" my hands from the swing. What he means by that is making sure my shoulders, arms, and hands all function as a unit. "Big muscles move small muscles," he reminded me. And when I try separate may hands by focusing on using them to *hit* the ball instead of swinging through it, I start having problems.

"I feel like I made good progress today!" I said.

"Oh, you did. You're doing great," he replied. "Outstanding."

I grinned. It's always nice to end on a high note.

Back at home, excitement was building for the upcoming Thanksgiving holiday. And by "excitement" I mean tension and drama. Elizabeth's brother John had been staying in our spare room in the basement while he figured out some things with his wife. But on Sunday, *my* brother, who goes by "Fritz" (he won't acknowledge his real first name), flew in from California to stay with us a few days before we all drive down to Illinois to visit my mom, my sister, and her family for Thanksgiving.

But John, fearing he had overstayed his welcome already, bailed out before Fritz arrived. We were not sure where he went, but he didn't go home. We were kind of worried and it sucked. (I'm happy to report John and his wife Kathy eventually worked things out.)

Meanwhile, the idea of spending a week with my brother was making me tense. It's not that we don't get along, but we're very different. In nearly every conceivable way. It's hard to find things we can talk about without arguing. As kids we fought about the stupidest things – like whether *Rocky* or *Star Wars* was the superior movie. These days, movies are about the only thing we *can* talk about. One Thanksgiving we discovered we can't even talk about e-books; that is, whether they will ever completely replace paper books. Somehow, the discussion got heated, and in about three seconds built into a brief flurry of shouting – followed by an abrupt and awkward silence. It was awful. Everyone was in the room, and no one knew quite what to say. It was Jack, bless his sweet little heart, who broke the tension a few moments later: "Wow, I've never seen *that* happen before!" In retrospect, it seems pretty hilarious.

The point is, it was a chaotic time at home, which didn't leave me well prepared for lesson #3 the following weekend. As I wrote in my journal, it was "kinda ugly! Started out great but then absolutely lost it! It was weird, frustrating, discouraging."

For one thing, I was still struggling with the idea that my hands should not control my swing. My old swing was all about my hands. But Coach Carl was teaching me that my hands should be primarily *passive*. That is, they should *primarily* be acting as a hinge as my body, shoulders, and arms do the swinging. It was a tough idea to absorb.

"But how do I *aim* the clubhead if not with my hands?" I wondered. With my old swing I had a strong sense of my hands guiding the clubhead through the ball, in the right direction and with the clubface at the right angle (not that it necessarily worked that well!). But with the new, LH swing, I felt I had no control at all in that regard.

But Coach explained that it's all in the repeatability. If I line up properly, with everything positioned properly, and the clubface square to the target line, then swing through the ball with a repeatable motion, I will be able to trust that the clubface will return to the same position at impact.

It seemed foreign to me, but I had vowed to trust Coach Carl, so that's what I was going to do.

(Upon reflection, I think this is an example of something that would not have worked if I had just tried to "fix" my RH swing. It would have been harder to trust the new idea, because there certainly would have been a period where my shots got worse before they got better. And I'm not at all confident I would have had the patience to stick with it until I saw results. It would have been too frustrating to go out and play – the minute things started going south I would have reverted to old habits.)

For a while, it was working great! I started hitting some really nice shots, and I swear I heard Coach Carl chuckle once or twice in appreciation. And then it all went to pot. Information overload, I think was the culprit. I started thinking too much, about too many things – and probably again started to swing too hard. Suddenly I started shanking everything – hitting the ball on the heel/shaft of the clubface, sending it shooting off at a sharp angle away from me. It's an embarrassing miss, and a tough thing to stop once you start.

I went from totally grooving it to feeling totally lost in the blink of an eye. As my frustration grew, my brain went into overdrive and the tension in my swing went through the roof. The result was shank after shank after shank. I was just about ready to cry.

Finally, Coach Carl told me to shut it down. It was almost time to quit anyway, and I think sometimes it's best just to cut your losses and try again later.

I knew this was all part of the process, that there would be "days like this." But it felt like my first real setback. I shook Coach's hand, thanked him, packed up my clubs, put on my coat and walked out into the dreary December day with my head down and my confidence in pieces.

CHAPTER 6
Life, Death, and Living the Dream

"This, too, shall pass."

—Ancient Proverb

"Jack I have some very bad news to tell you," I said. "Grandpa died."

Jack's sweet little face took on a confused, pained expression as his eyes welled with tears. "He *died*?"

"Yes, I'm afraid so," I said. And then Jack cried … and cried, and cried.

I was taken somewhat aback by his reaction. Jack usually takes things in stride. Not to say he's unemotional. Sometimes he gets very angry, but that's different. When something goes wrong, he's usually very good at just rolling with it. He's mellow that way. And though I knew he loved his grandpa, I was caught off guard by how hard he took the news.

Not that his death was a surprise. Grandpa Bill had been dealing with a variety of health issues, including diabetes, heart failure, kidney problems … the list goes on. Recently he had been on dialysis – and kicked and screamed at the very idea of having to go through the treatment. Especially since they had to transport him off-site, away from the rehab facility, to administer it.

Finally, it seemed like he just stopped fighting. He was ready. Elizabeth was with him when he died, and she said that at the end he was praying to Jesus to take him.

All in all, Jack held up pretty well – and so did Elizabeth. It was a beautiful funeral, with military honors, including a color guard and a uniformed Naval officer presenting the flag that covered the casket to Janet, Bill's widow (Elizabeth's step-mother). It was a bitter cold

January day, so the mourners stayed inside while I and the other pallbearers carried the casket out to the waiting hearse. As we slid Grandpa Bill inside, I looked over and saw Jack and his mom standing inside the glass door of the church. He was clutching his blanket (which he still carried occasionally under stress) and crying again. Elizabeth was standing behind him with her hand on his shoulder. And she was crying, too.

Grandpa Bill's death was one of those big "life events" that help you keep things in perspective. And our grieving was complicated by the fact that the funeral took place on Elizabeth's birthday – which just happens to be one day before Jack's. So it was a weird period of time for our family.

And of course it meant I took a little bit of a break from left-handed golf. The Christmas holidays had already compromised my lesson schedule a bit, putting three weeks between lessons #4 and #5 instead of the usual two. Then there was another three-week gap because of Bill's death. Practice time was compromised as well, so things slowed down. But I still was thinking about it quite a bit.

One thing I had been struggling to get a handle on (so to speak) was the whole "hands" thing. I was trying to make it make sense in my mind that my hands could be so passive. I just didn't see how you could get any power that way. Rob, who I bounced everything off of, had similar doubts.

But then I had an epiphany of sorts, when Jack and I watched the show "Punkin Chunkin'" on the Discovery Channel. That's the event up in New England where teams compete to shoot or fling pumpkins as far as they can, using either air cannons or any number of different types of catapults and contraptions. One category was for *trebuchet* catapults, an ancient weapon that uses a large counterweight to hurl heavy objects from a sling at the end of a rope. (Go ahead, Google it. I'll wait.)

As you can see in the picture or video you found online, a trebuchet is basically a large lever. On the short end is a heavy weight, sometimes just a bucket full of rocks. On the long end a rope is attached, with a small pouch at the end, where the projectile (pumpkin) goes. The physics are pretty simple: As the firing sequence commences, the weighted end is raised, while the rope is laid out on a track underneath the machine. When the weight is dropped, the swing arm is lifted into the air, pulling the rope along behind it. As this rotation continues, the pouch/projectile swings in a wide arc at the end of the rope, accelerating all the way. As it reaches the top the pouch falls away and the pumpkin goes chunkin' into the wild blue yonder. Using nothing but gravity and leverage, the best trebuchets can fling a pumpkin nearly half a mile.

Timing is important, of course. If the length of the rope, the length of the swingarm, and the size of the counterweight aren't "tuned" properly, the pumpkin might fly straight up into the air or get thrown straight down into the ground.

What does this all have to do with left-handed golf? Hang in there, it's coming.

Jack and I were both fascinated by all this. In the subsequent weeks, Jack tried on various occasions to fashion his own catapult out of yardsticks, Lego blocks, masking tape, gunpowder (wait … not gunpowder), and whatever else he could find around the house. One model had a string at the end like a trebuchet, and in trying to help Jack "tune" it properly, I realized a trebuchet could be a model for a golf swing – and solve the mystery of the passive hands.

It's quite simple, really. Think of my clubhead as the pouch/projectile, the shaft as the rope, and my arms as the swingarm. The leverage/force provided by the counterweight is instead provided by the rotation of my body, the "big muscles." My backswing is akin to raising the counterweight. As my body releases its rotation, my arms swing through the ball, pulling the clubshaft (rope) behind it. If the timing is right, centrifugal force accelerates the clubhead through impact, sending the golf ball into the wild blue yonder, upwards of half a mile.

Well, okay, maybe just a quarter mile – if you're Bubba Watson, whose longest official drive on the PGA Tour in 2010 measured 422 yards, just 18 yards short of a quarter mile.

Eureka! I had found it! Was this the key to a major breakthrough in my left-handed progress? No, not necessarily. But it did give me a new way to think about things, and helped me have more trust in this new method. And in golf, trust in your swing is *always* a good thing.

It was about this time that the official trash talk started for the White Lake Classic. All the participants were very curious about how my quest would affect my approach to the tournament. "Zim, are you really going to play left-handed at White Lake? How will that affect the handicap system!?" The handicap part was a big unknown. But I was definitely committed to playing lefty. In fact, I made competing respectably at White Lake left-handed a major goal. A final exam of sorts. But how many handicap strokes I would get was still wide open.

Early on, Scruffy told me he thought that if I committed to playing lefty at the 2011 WLC that I should get 20 handicap strokes, same as Keith. (I'm normally one of the "scratch" players.) The others agreed; at the time, this seemed reasonable. And I could have held them to that! But the last thing I wanted to do was win handily just by having too many handicap strokes. So I told them we would have to wait and see.

As word spread about my project among friends and co-workers, I started hearing everybody's weird left-handedness stories. A lot of people told me things like, "I do everything left-handed except throw a baseball." Or, "I throw and write left-handed, but I kick better with my right foot. Is it possible to be left-handed and right-footed?"

Lisa, our receptionist at work, was a very interesting mix. She told me that although she's "left-handed," she does a lot of things right-handed, such as bowl, play golf, and eat. She thinks it's because she was taught to do a lot of things by right-handed people. For instance, she has memories of being a very small child and trying to eat with her left hand – only to have an older brother or sister "correct" her by putting the spoon or fork in her right hand, instead.

More interesting still, she said that when she paints, she does detail work with her left hand, but makes broad strokes using her right.

It seemed like every lefty I talked to does at least something using their right hand. I heard enough to make me wonder if there really even is such a thing as being "left-handed."

In fact, it turned out that my anecdotal evidence is very much in line with what research shows: that "right-handed" people tend to be *very* right-handed, but people who identify as lefties usually use both hands to varying degrees. There are very few *pure* lefties.

One well-known metric involves a list of ten common, everyday things you do with one hand. Things like writing, or opening a can of soda, or turning a doorknob. The survey asks participants to identify which hand they *most often* use to do those things. About 80 percent of respondents indicated they do nine or all 10 things with the right-hand. Another 5 percent or so do eight things right-handed. Conversely, just over five percent perform nine or all 10 tasks with their *left* hand. About 1.5 percent do eight things left-handed.

For purposes of categorization, you could say that 85 percent of people are at least 80% right-handed and about 6.5 percent are at least 80% left-handed, with the remaining 8.5 percent falling somewhere in between.

Does that make those people "ambidextrous"? Not really. Though there are plenty of people who use that label to describe themselves, testing shows that these people still naturally favor one hand over the other. They may do different tasks with different hands, but doesn't really make them "ambidextrous," which is defined as being able to do things equally well with either hand.

What does that all mean? For my purposes, not much; simply that it's harder to positively identify true "left-handers" who play golf right-handed – because left-handedness is largely a matter of degree. So, for the purposes of this examination, if a golfer *writes* with his left hand, he's "left-handed." So there.

And now, back to the golf ...

Over the course of the next several months, Coach Carl built me a new swing piece by piece. And I began to realize just how seriously screwed-up my life-long, home-built, right-handed swing really was.

My old swing was all about *lateral* – side-to-side – movement. A proper swing, it was hammered into me, is all about rotation. As I righty, I didn't rotate my shoulders much at all, which probably goes a long way toward explaining my dramatic out-to-in swing path. I swung a golf club more like an axe, and cut across the ball sharply through impact. This produced the dramatic spin that sent my drives (and most other shots) curving wildly to the right.

It also explained why a big, tall guy like me was never able to generate more power. I was not taking advantage of the natural leverage my height gave me, instead trying to just *swing harder* to get more distance. Oh, sure, I could belt one out there pretty good now and then – especially when the strong southerly breezes over the Central Illinois hardpan prevailed on a north-bound hole. But I had to catch it just right, and I was usually falling over pretty good by the time all was said and done.

Thirty years later, this "rotation" thing was such a revelation it made me wonder how a lifelong passionate golfer like me had never figured it out before. Sure, taking a few lessons would have helped, but as much golf as I watched on TV and as many golf magazines as I read, you'd think it would have soaked in. Maybe I was subconsciously *rejecting* the idea of rotating more, because that would have meant … you know, hard work.

In any case, I was glad I didn't have to *correct* my terrible lateral motion. I didn't have to fight the ghosts of my old habits as I learned to rotate properly. I was starting from scratch in a very real way, and it seemed like this would be a big advantage in my quest.

One of the visuals Coach Carl had me use was to imagine myself turning my body inside a barrel. This would not have been possible with my old swing – I would have banged against the barrel's sides. But the image helped me understand that I should be coiling my body like a spring as I brought the club back — and then uncoiling on the downswing and follow-through.

Another big help was "Let your right [front] shoulder be your motor." Coach told me to think of my right shoulder as the prime initiator of my rotation. As I start the club back, think about bringing my right shoulder underneath my chin to create a better turn. He also showed me how it's helpful to keep my chin up in order to create some space for my shoulder to rotate farther. I asked if that's the same reason Jack Nicklaus cocked his head back a little bit. "Exactly," he said.

As I started hitting the ball a little better each week, we worked our way down from pitching wedges and 9-irons to a 7-iron. I don't know why that jump from 9 to 7 made such a big difference, but it did. I guess just that little bit of extra club length makes it more difficult to keep the club on the right path with the clubface square. Or maybe it's just because the decreased loft magnifies my mistakes.

Whatever the reason, I was alarmed to see that my 7-iron shots, even the good ones, seemed to have a little bit of a tail on them, a slight right-to-left movement, a bit of a fade. Can you tell I'm trying not to use the word "slice"!? Seeing the ball move in that direction was instantly discouraging, because one of my primary objectives for the new swing was not to have to deal with a slice anymore.

But Coach said not to worry about it. He said that the fade was not a swing-path issue, but the result of not getting the clubhead quite square at impact. It should go away as my rotation keeps improving. Well, okay … if you insist. But I was not convinced.

He also had me focus on keeping my weight on the balls of my feet. I have a tendency to lean into the shot sometimes, which is what causes the shanking I had experienced in earlier lessons. This became less of a problem over time, but the dreaded "hosel rockets" still made a few ugly appearances from time to time.

The big bright spot of Lesson #4 was Jack, who tagged along for the first time. He was a bit of a distraction occasionally, but he clearly had a good time and kept things entertaining. As I had hoped, Coach took a few minutes to work with him, showing him how to use an interlocking grip. Up to that point I had always let Jack keep his baseball grip, telling him only to "keep your hands together" whenever I noticed them drifting apart. He likes doing things his own way, and generally resists the coaching I give him. So it was nice to see him take Coach Carl's instruction to heart.

The only problem with having Jack along is that it's expensive! It ended up costing me $46 just for dome time for the both of us. Not something I can get in the habit of doing every time. But it was well worth it at least this once.

Which is another great thing about the Lefty Dome – it's free! So in between lessons I continued to hit balls in the back room at work.

The downside is that I'm really self-conscious about practicing when others are around – even in the next room. And whenever I hit a shank in the Lefty Dome, the ball goes shooting off into the corner, bounces off some aluminum ladders, and makes a terrible racket.

It's also hard on my elbows. I never did break down and buy a real hitting mat, so I just used a piece of carpet, which doesn't provide a lot of shock absorption on the concrete floor. Sometimes I would double it up, which made for a softer impact, but also made it harder for me to tell when I was hitting behind the ball. So I usually used just the single layer. As a result, I developed a mild but persistent case of tendonitis in my elbows. Not bad enough to interfere with anything, just bad enough to be annoying. So I pressed on.

As I continued to work on swinging in a barrel, one idea that really started to sink in – and was consistent with the trebuchet metaphor – was that strength isn't nearly as important in golf as flexibility. This was confirmed by comments from Golf Channel analyst Brandel Chamblee about Tiger Woods's latest struggles.

"In my opinion, Tiger ruined the greatest swing and the greatest physique in golf history," Chamblee wrote. "Tiger's body was perfect for golf. He was lean, sinewy, quick. He's turned himself into an NFL linebacker – but why? In golf, you don't have to lift a car over your head. You swing an 11-ounce club."

Well, that's a relief. I know I'm not going to be able to lift a car any time soon. But then, I'm not sure that "lean, sinewy, quick" is within my grasp, either.

Nonetheless, I got better and better at coiling up my stiff, 47-year-old body into something resembling a proper golf swing. Progress continued, enough to keeping my confidence soaring and plummeting with regularity. After a good lesson or practice session, I felt like a world beater. After a bad one, a worthless hacker who had no business taking on such a silly pipe dream.

Often, the results would vary wildly during a single lesson. And I recognized a pattern I had often seen on the golf course (as a righty): I would start off really well, then gradually get worse as play continued. And I recognized the same cause: I started relaxed, with low expectations, just thinking about swinging easy and making good contact. Then, as I got warmed up and hit good shots, I would get confident and start to swing a little harder, and faster, which of course threw off the nice rhythm I started out with. Then I would start to panic, which added tension to my swing, which made things still worse. Things would snowball, and then next thing you know I'd be hacking and duffing and slicing and shanking and sweating and muttering under my breath and not having any fun at all.

That's when Coach would tell me (again) that rotation was key and remind me about the barrel and my right shoulder-motor.

Still, the idea of hitting the ball by *rotating* my body would take a little getting used to. Even considering that I was swinging from the opposite side, it felt unnatural. Hitting the ball by rolling my forearms through impact rather than snapping my wrists like I was swatting a fly was another new concept. But I was starting to get it and hitting some pretty shots now and then.

And I found out by accident that Coach Carl was actually pretty impressed with my progress. After I explained to him I was concerned about my wrists from hitting off the carpet in the Lefty

THE WRONG SIDE OF THE BALL

Dome, he went over to ask the proprietor of the *real* Golf Dome about buying a used hitting mat. I didn't think to turn off the microphone I had him wear during our lessons, so I later overheard the conversation he had with one of the guys at the counter. It went something like this:

> Counter Guy: Do you have lessons today?
> Coach Carl: Yeah, I got this guy here. I'm converting a right-hander to a left-hander, this is about his fourth lesson. Watch this move ...
> Counter Guy: He's a lefty?
> Carl: No, he's a righty. But he's enamored by the fact that ...
> Counter Guy: Nice set-up
> Coach Carl: ... he always wanted to play left-handed, and he's writing a book.
> Counter Guy: Impressive. Well ... he doesn't look totally awkward doing it, that's for sure!
> Coach Carl: [chuckles] No!
> Counter Guy: How long has he been trying this?
> Coach Carl: He's only been at it about a month. [Actually several months.]
> Counter Guy: Smooth!
> Coach Carl: Yeah, we've been working on that.
> Counter Guy: That's pretty impressive.
> Coach Carl: Yeah.

Talk about a confidence booster!

On the negative side of the ledger, I could tell Coach Carl was less-than-impressed by my fitness regimen. Not that he grilled me on it, but during our discussions that day I mentioned that I wasn't really keeping up with my stretching. I also gave myself a fresh dose of guilt about my practice habits, which weren't quite meeting the goals I'd set. And when our lesson was over, he asked me if I was going to hit more balls or if I was done with the stall. I told him I needed to get home – which was true. But as I left I scolded myself for not being more eager to keep working. Especially considering I had hit fewer balls that day than in a usual lesson.

But the dome is expensive! And I had other stuff to tend to at home. Just another example of the opposing forces at work inside my

MIKE ZIMMERMAN

soul: Just how much was I willing to sacrifice to give this project the effort it deserves? And just how much effort *does* it deserve? It was a constant battle.

One part of the solution, of course, was to work Jack into the project as often as possible. So when the golf show rolled into town in March, I took Friday afternoon off to take him. I wasn't sure how much it would hold his interest – it wasn't as "interactive" as he would probably like – but he did pretty well. He was mostly interested in entering drawings – there were lots of opportunities to fill out a card for a chance to win things. He had his eye on a new car.

I wasn't wild about the idea, because I didn't want to get on a lot of mailing lists. But I told him he could enter as many drawings as he wanted, as long as he filled out the cards himself. This slowed his pace considerably, but ultimately it proved to be a profitable strategy.

Afterward, we went over to the Golf Dome to hit a few balls and try out the new "dual wedge" I had bought Jack at the show. It was lighter and more lofted than his current pitching wedge, and seemed like it would be a good addition to his arsenal. His prowess with it at the Dome proved it to be a good purchase.

As successful as Jack's session was, however, mine was nothing short of disastrous. I had arrived full of confidence and started out strong, but suddenly couldn't make any kind of consistent contact. I couldn't stop shanking. It pains me to admit this, but I hit one so far on the heel of the club that it actually hit the *back* of the shaft, came straight back toward me and hit my right foot. An uber-shank! Perhaps the first one in the history of golf – at least as far as I knew. I tried everything I could think of to fix it, but nothing worked.

But before I could quit out of frustration, I had to quit due to pain. Something had given way in my left rib cage. It got worse very quickly, until I couldn't swing without a stabbing pain in my left side. It continued to get worse after we left, and by that evening I was very uncomfortable. I could tell it wasn't something that would go away overnight, so I called Coach Carl and canceled my lesson for the next morning.

As bad as the physical pain was, the discouragement was worse. Just when I felt like I was really making some progress, I was sidelined by an injury. For who knows how long?

It was somewhat comforting, however, to think about how this would affect the "story" of my left-handed quest. There had been

104

stretches in recent weeks when my confidence soared – to the point where I occasionally worried that it would be "too easy" to get good at left-handed golf. That the challenge of it wouldn't be significant enough to make a good book.

In fact, I had even fantasized about qualifying for the Champions Tour as a left-handed golfer after I turned 50. I had it all figured out. Not just the Champions Tour part, but the series of best-sellers I would write along the way.

My first book, of course, would be the one you're reading now, covering the first year of my quest. The second book (working title: *Senioritis*) would be about my quest to qualify for the tour. Then the third book, *Senior Moments*, would cover my adventures and misadventures as a struggling rookie with an interesting back story.

I even shared this plan with Elizabeth – and later with Coach Carl, who had the grace to tell me that would be a great goal to work toward.

But yeah, perhaps my head was getting a little big. On the other hand, where would Robert Landers have been if he hadn't dreamed big back in the 1990s? He certainly wouldn't have been playing professional golf. The 51-year-old Landers became an instant legend in 1995 when he seemingly stepped off his Texas dairy farm and right onto the Senior Tour – in sneakers, no less. He didn't start playing golf seriously until age 28, and then honed his homemade swing hitting balls in his cow pasture. "His sudden, slashing whacks at the ball bring to mind a man trying to kill a cornered rat," wrote Austin Murphy for *Sports Illustrated*. (I wonder what he would have written about *my* old swing?)

Yet somehow, some way, the man fans simply called "the farmer" made his way through qualifying to become a member of the Senior Tour. He didn't last there very long: two seasons with a top finish of T14 in the 1996 Kroger Senior Classic. He made just under $164,000 in 57 events those two seasons (plus one in 1997), so he didn't get rich. But what a ride that must have been! And what an inspiration he is for schleps like me, who dream of following in the footsteps left by his manure-encrusted sneakers.

But maybe the injury would be a good reality check. And dreams don't get closer by ignoring nagging injuries. So I reluctantly benched myself for what I thought might be a week – but turned into more than a month.

As I rested and rehabbed my injury, I learned that basketball legend Charles Barkley was working on the same quest that I was – though for entirely different reasons. "Sir Charles" had become famous in golfing circles for developing what you might call the "full-swing yips." Whenever he tried to hit a golf ball, his body would spasm and lurch in really bizarre ways. Often his swing would stop cold about halfway into his downswing, and he would draw the club back a little bit before continuing downward with the ugliest lunge toward the ball you've ever seen. It was both excruciating and hilarious to watch.

What made it all so bizarre is that Barkley used to be a decent golfer. And then this mental affliction grabbed hold of him and would not let go.

He became so infamous for it that the Golf Channel launched a show in which Hank Haney, Tiger's coach at the time, would set out to fix Barkley's swing over the course of 13 episodes. Long story short, it kinda-sorta worked, for a while, kinda-sorta. Haney got Barkley swinging the club okay again, but only in certain situations. He could hit it fine on the range, most of the time, and for short stretches on the course. But he always seemed to resort to old habits after a few holes.

After Haney couldn't fix him, Barkley got so desperate he decided to try to re-learn the game left-handed – quietly, and without fanfare. I couldn't find much mention of it online, but I did come across one YouTube video of him taking a left-handed swing. To put it mildly, he wasn't too successful.

I dreamed of being able to interview Barkley for the book – and for a few brief shining moments, as the result of a truly bizarre chance encounter, I thought I might get my opportunity.

At my "day job" I do a lot of work for a prominent major American motorcycle manufacturer, and frequently get the opportunity write articles that involve riding those motorcycles in beautiful locations. And so it was in June I found myself ascending Mount Laguna, outside San Diego, on a motorcycle. At the journey's outset, I stopped to buy a map and crossed paths with a really tall guy riding an extra-tall, bright yellow bicycle. Outside the store, he saw me looking at my map and asked if I needed help. "No thanks, I'm good," I said, barely looking up.

That wasn't the last I saw of him. All the way up the mountain, he kept passing me. Not that he was riding his bike faster than my motorcycle, but I kept stopping to take pictures, and he kept chugging steadily up the steep grade. It was impressive, to say the least. Every time he'd pass me I'd give him a little wave, and he'd nod in return.

Finally, at the little store at the top of the mountain, just as I was getting ready to leave, the freakishly tall bicycle man pulled to a stop. He parked his bike, and just as we were about to cross paths, a bolt of recognition hit me: "Are you Bill Walton?" I blurted out. "Yep," he said simply.

No way! I mean … like, really? What are the odds, this is too cool!

I'm normally not a big celebrity guy, but I decided to hang around for a few minutes and see what happened. After a moment he sat down outside with some fruit and a couple cans of V-8. It was a weekday afternoon, so there was virtually no one else there. But as he sat and refueled his body he chatted easily with a few other gawkers, so I eased my way into the conversation. With uncharacteristic boldness I asked him, "Say, you probably know Charles Barkley, don't you?"

"Yes, I know him well," he said.

So I explained to him what I was up to and why Sir Charles was of interest to me. He looked me right in the eye and said, "Call Greg Hughes. Tell him I told you to call."

Mr. Hughes, Mr. Walton said, was Mr. Barkley's representative. He gave me his phone number, and then he gave me his *own* cell number and e-mail address and said if I had any trouble reaching Greg Hughes to get in touch with him.

I was completely floored. All I really knew about Bill Walton was that he was an amazing basketball player whose pro career was cut short by injury (you could see it in the way his ankles bent when he walked). He was also a basketball announcer with a habit of angering players with his bluntness. But to me he could not have been nicer.

Unfortunately, the end of the story is not as inspiring as the beginning. Though I did succeed in contacting Greg Hughes, Sir Charles ultimately rebuffed the opportunity to talk to a no-name wanna-be writer about his left-handed golf exploits.

Oh, well. It never hurts to ask – as I keep telling myself.

A few weeks after the golf show, Jack got a call from Morningstar Golf Course in Waukesha, a far Milwaukee suburb. He had won a round of golf for four!

This presented me with a slight moral dilemma. I had promised Jack that we would play golf at a "real" golf course (one with par 4s and sand traps) sometime during the upcoming season. But Morningstar – a somewhat upscale, semi-private course – was way out of his league. Heck, it's a little bit out of *my* league! Still, Jack had won the prize, not me. So it wouldn't be right for me to just commandeer the free passes.

Fortunately, Jack didn't really have any interest in playing Morningstar, so we worked out a deal. I would buy him the new Wii game disc he had been wanting and take him to a different "real" golf course – one more his size – some other time and I would use the golf passes. He was thrilled with the deal and jumped at the opportunity. I only felt a little bit guilty, because it seemed like the deal was tilted pretty heavily in my favor. Those were pretty valuable passes! But Jack was happy, and I was happy. Win-win.

Part of the reason I wanted them so badly was because they presented the perfect opportunity to turn my first official round of left-handed golf into an *event*. So I called Rob, Mike, and Keith, and we set up a round of golf at Morningstar for Friday, June 3.

All I had to do now was get better. My ribs, I mean. And get better. My *game*, I mean. And maybe learn to hit something longer than a 7-iron.

CHAPTER 7
Summer of My Discontent

"If he stands out there on the practice tee till he's 90, he's not going to improve. He's going to get worse and worse, because he's going to get his bad habits more and more deeply ingrained."

—Ben Hogan (in *Five Lessons*)

As nervous and excited as I was about my first left-handed round of golf, I made it a point to arrive early for our morning tee time at Morningstar. I wanted to have plenty of time to warm up properly, stretch, hit some balls, do a little putting, and try to bring myself down into a reasonably calm and effective mental state. So I was the first to arrive.

Somewhat surprisingly, Keith, who is always running late, was second on the scene. Later, after Keith and I spent some time catching up on the putting green, Mike and Rob pulled up in Mike's car. Rob opened the door almost before the car came to a full stop and stepped out quickly … to the sound of Mike's jabbering inside.

Mike and Rob are both great guys, but they're about as different in temperament as you can get. Mike, who has somehow become a big-shot financial analyst in downtown Chicago, is a big guy, with a personality to match. He enjoys lively conversation. More precisely, he likes to *stir the pot*, and seems to enjoy making his friends squirm a little bit. It's all very good-natured, but a little bit can go a long way – especially with Rob.

By contrast, Rob is very non-confrontational. He doesn't like making waves, and is maybe the most easy-going guy I've ever met. We sometimes call him "The Glacier," both for his always-cool demeanor and his sometimes overly deliberate ways. The "Glacier" name, as I recall, was hatched one night while we waited interminably for him to hit a shot at the pool table. Either way, it fits. And fortunately, his glacial pace does not manifest itself on the golf course. (Keith is another story.)

Apparently, some sort of political discussion had broken out in the car. Suffice it to say that by the time they arrived at the course, Rob was more than ready to put an end to the conversation.

It was a good thing Keith was there for Mike to pick things up with. When those two get together ... whoo-boy! Mike and Keith have been best friends for a long time, but there doesn't seem to be any subject under the sun that they can't find a way to disagree about. Arguing is sport to them, and it often can be pretty entertaining to watch. Once, they bickered for 15 minutes about how long it took to drive from Keith's apartment to Mike's house. A full hour, Mike maintained. No way, 40 minutes tops, Keith countered. Back and forth they went, covering the same ground over and over, until finally Mike said, "How do you even know? It's not like you ever come over anymore!"

Without missing a beat, Keith shot back, "Mike, it's not like I can just *pop over* anytime, it takes me *an hour* to get there!" And what made it so dang funny was that he didn't even realize he had just blatantly contradicted himself until we called him on it.

Once Mike and Keith arrived it was time to head over to the practice tee. Normally, I don't like to hit a lot of balls to warm up; as previously noted, my performance tends to deteriorate as we go along, and I don't want to waste any of my good shots on the range! But I wanted to hit enough to get loose – and to get back in the feel of hitting off grass instead of a practice mats (or thin piece of carpet on a concrete floor).

To say I was pleased with my warm-up would be to say that Tiger Woods was pleased with the outcome of the 2000 U.S. Open (he won by 15 shots). My rib injury had healed nicely, and I hit nearly every shot well, from my opening wedges all the way down to the few hybrids I hit. "Okay, have you seen enough?" I asked rhetorically, suggesting I had perhaps already proved the worthiness of my quest by hitting a few good irons on the practice tee.

As even the pros know, however, practice performance does not guarantee on-course success. In fact, sometimes it has no bearing at all. I knew that everything would change once I stepped onto the first tee for real.

We weren't quite there yet, however. First we had to make the important decision of who would ride with whom in each cart. And we also had to wait for Keith to make a last-minute run to his car to get … we never did figure out what, but it almost made us late (typical Keith!). The cart decision was easy this time, however; I insisted on being with Rob, all the better to feed off his icy-cool demeanor and keep myself calm. And let Mike and Keith argue in peace about which is better: springy clothes pins or the other kind.

Once Keith came running back from his car, the party moved to the tee on hole #1, a tricky little par-5 with a split fairway. We made a big to-do out of my opening tee-shot, and captured it on video for posterity. (Search for "This One Counts!" and MikeZim883 on YouTube to view.) After announcing that I was "very nervous," I made a loose and twirly swing and pulled my first official lefty drive (with a 5-wood) low and to the right. It clipped a tree branch slightly but then faded back just enough to end up a few feet from the fairway, probably no more than 180 yards out.

It was a little depressing how much it looked like a mirror image of one of my bad right-handed drives. But I was off the tee, in play, and on my way.

From there I hacked it around until I got within 8-iron range, then promptly hit a baby shank to the left of the green, lying 5. I had a good lie, but in an effort not to duff it I powered the ball all the way back across the green into the right fringe. From there I hit a good chip and sank the putt for an opening 8. A triple-bogey. Not what I was hoping for, but it could have been worse.

The second hole, a short par-4 with a sharp dogleg left, went a little better, but not a lot. A bad drive put me a long ways back in the right rough; a decent recovery put me back in the fairway, about 150 yards short of the green. I pulled out a 6-iron and took a nice, easy swing. I made good contact, but pulled it into light rough just off the green. Again I powered the chip past the hole (but still on the green), made a weak attempt at my bogey putt, and tapped in for a double-bogey 6.

Number 3 was a short par-3, just 116 yards from the white tees. I hit a 9-iron fairly solidly, but didn't quite get the clubface squared through impact. It flared a bit to the left, into an unpleasant lie in the left rough. I hit a good chip, leaving about five feet for my very first left-handed par! But I pulled the putt badly to the right (it still sounds weird to talk about *pulling* a shot to the *right*), and felt fortunate to make the two-foot comebacker for my bogey.

Triple-bogey, double-bogey, bogey ... I was definitely trending in the right direction. But don't ask me how Rob, Mike, or Keith were doing, because I had no idea!

On hole #4 it all came together. I stroked a perfect hybrid right down the center of the fairway, with not a trace of slice. It didn't have much on it, but it was a sight to behold. Seldom has a 180-yard tee shot been so celebrated. Fortunately, the tees were far forward that day, so I was left with only about 100 yards on the tiny par-4. I hit a nice solid wedge to what looked like the center of the green. When we reached the putting surface, however, I saw that I still had some work left, with some tricky undulations between my ball and the hole. My approach putt was a little aggressive (again), but I nailed the five-foot comebacker for par.

It as a hole of "firsts": First fairway hit, first GIR (green in regulation), first par – a good hole! My confidence began to grow.

Things got even better on #5, as I just missed a legitimate birdie opportunity on the 135-yard par-3. Unfortunately, I'm sure I had begun to think too much about score. On the first tee, I was thinking only about trying to make a good swing (and not embarrassing myself). By the time I sized up that birdie putt, I was thinking about how awesome it would be start my round with a triple-bogey, then a double, then a bogey, then a par, and then ... a birdie! Heck, I was probably thinking about making the Champions Tour again!

While it felt at the time like I was standing at the brink of newfound left-handed glory, it was in reality more like the beginning of the end. Despite my best intentions to stay calm, take it a shot at a time, and not worry about shooting any kind of score, I was furiously doing the math in my head, trying to figure out what I'd have to do over the next 13 holes to ... oh, I don't know, break 80 or something. My imagination was getting out of control, preparing to toss a few rocks into my path on the road to glory.

Meanwhile, without a lot of fanfare, Rob had quietly chipped in for birdie. I barely noticed.

After missing another par putt on #6, things got a little ugly again on the beautiful 7th, a long par-5 from an elevated tee. I touched it all on the way to the green: fairway, rough, sand, everything but water. Two chips and two putts later I had built another snowman: triple-bogey 8.

By then my nerves were probably starting to show, as Rob and I had a little conversation about "objectives." The goal, he helped me remember, was not to shoot a particular score, but "to try to test my golf game, a shot at a time, on a real course under real conditions." Try not to think about the *results*, or the total score I was shooting, and not even the scores on each individual hole.

Yeah, yeah ... sure, sure, whatever. Let's see, I'm at 10 over par through seven, so to come in under 50 for the front I can only lose three more strokes to par on 8 and 9. Bogey, double-bogey – that's doable!

Thanks for the pep talk, Rob. Are Mike and Keith still here?

Number 8 was a short but scary par-4 with a very narrow fairway. Trees to the left; sand and scrub to the right. I was fortunate my weak hybrid stayed on the left edge of the fairway. I followed my weak tee shot with a chunked second shot. But it stayed in the fairway and put me in good position for a nice easy wedge into the green. I hit the approach solid but too firm, all the way through a very deep green. My long putt from the fringe went a good six or seven feet past the hole. If nothing else, at least I was staying aggressive on my putts! Whoops ... spoke too soon. My bogey attempt was right on line, but a few inches too short. Double-bogey.

The highlight of #9 was a classic "Neuses Drive" from Mike. Scruffy's a big guy. In high-school, he played linebacker at a solid 5-11, 200 pounds. Since then, his fluctuating weight has been a source of amusement for the rest of us. Over the years, we've compared him to the Skipper (with Keith as his "Little Buddy"), Homer Simpson, and, more recently, the governor of New Jersey. Meanwhile, his golf game has been as erratic as his body fat percentage. But one thing hasn't changed: When he catches his driver just right, he *crushes* it. It could go anywhere, but it goes.

On this occasion, he hit it far *and* straight, leaving the ball about 20 yards short of the green on the short par-4.

For my part, I hit an ugly little 3-wood into the left rough. From a side-hill lie I managed to hack an 8-iron to within about 100 yards of the green, followed by a "good miss" miss to about 12 feet below the hole. Two putts later, I carded another routine bogey.

Add it all up and it came to 49 strokes for the front nine.

Hmmm ... wasn't my goal to break 100? Well, I seemed to be right on pace! Not bad, especially considering the rocky triple-bogey, double-bogey start.

Meanwhile, Rob had quietly carded a very fine 38. Thirty-eight!? How did *that* happen? I knew he was playing well, but I had no idea it was *that* well. I felt bad for not paying more attention to Rob's round, but hey – didn't Ben Hogan once fail to notice his playing partner's ace because he was so focused on his own birdie? That's what the legend says, anyway. And if I can't be more Hogan-like with my swing, maybe I could at least emulate his legendarily callous disregard for his playing companions.

Over a quick snack between nines, opinions were offered on my initial showing. "Your mechanics look good," Scruffy weighed in, "but you seem to be lacking in power." Fair enough, coming from the author of that prodigious drive on #9. "And you seem to be keeping your head down, which is good," he added, invoking perhaps the oldest swing cliché in the book.

Keith felt compelled to comment on my mental state. "I noticed that there is an element of serenity about you," he said. "It's almost like you're absorbing it from your surroundings – or maybe one of the players with you. Would it be Scruffy?"

Of course, he was actually implying that Rob's natural calmness was rubbing off on me, perhaps literally. "You see, when Rob and I get together," I explained, "his level of serenity goes down, and mine goes up!"

But the truth is I was feeling my base-level anxiety *increase* as we moved toward the 10th tee. A familiar pattern was recurring. I had played the last six holes in just seven over par – which under the circumstances should have boosted my confidence. But instead I started feeling the pressure to keep the good play going.

It's really quite remarkable how mental golf really is. Even pro golfers have trouble keeping their foot on the accelerator when things are going well. You'll hear the phrase "he's not afraid to go low" – meaning he doesn't freak out and start to back off when he has a great round going. It's a rarer quality than you might think, and one of the things that helps separate great (or potentially great) golfers from the so-called "journeymen."

(In the second round of the 2014 Masters, Marc Leishman turned a birdie-birdie-birdie start and a share of the lead (at -5) into a

79 and a missed cut! Many factors were likely involved in his epic collapse, but a bit of panic at finding himself in the lead was surely one of them.)

In my case, it's not so much about keeping my foot on the gas as keeping the car on the road! I've had my share of epic meltdowns. There was that time in a high school golf tournament I shot 38-48. Another time, playing individually in the U of I Open at the Orange course, I opened par-birdie-birdie and briefly imagined myself leading the tournament! It was downhill from there on the way to a very disappointing 94. (In those days I was shooting pretty consistently in the low 80s.)

So I guess it shouldn't be too surprising that my back nine was less stellar than my front. But I did manage to keep the car on the road and shoot a not-embarrassing 53 for a semi-respectable 102.

The most memorable part of the back nine was giving everyone else a chance to hit a left-handed shot on the 18th tee. It was fun to watch how awkward everybody looked. Mike and Keith (Mike especially) struggled just to make contact – or even figure out how to hold the club. Keith, after about five practice swings (his usual allotment), clanked an iron off the hosel maybe 25 yards down the hill. Mike actually whiffed a couple with the driver before topping one straight into the ground. I don't think the ball even made it off the tee area.

Rob, however, even though he pulled it right, actually made pretty good contact – which was weirdly discouraging. It was one of those (many) moments that made me second-guess everything, if only momentarily. If Rob can hit it that well the first time, shouldn't I be better by now, after all this work? But it's also one of those things I can't dwell on.

The best part – as is so often the case with golf – was hanging out afterward: reliving and scrutinizing key shots; eating big juicy burgers and downing a couple cold ones; and giving each other tons of crap. I don't get to hang out with Mike, Rob, and Keith all together that often, but when I do, it's always a fun time.

So after I got over the "what might have been" factor, I was pretty pleased with my 102. Breaking 100 seemed like a long shot going in, and 102 would have been deemed a "success" before we teed off. And I actually beat Mike and Keith! So I guess I can't complain about that.

One thing I realized is that it's a lot harder to go through my little pre-shot "checklist" on the course than on the range. Partly because I don't want to take too long, and also because the heightened tension makes it easy to forget. I can really see how practice will make a huge difference in this regard. The more it becomes second nature, the easier it will be to incorporate without excessive thought.

It's also because in a fun, casual round like that, I don't want to become all withdrawn in an effort to concentrate. That's very easy for me to do – to get all "inside myself" and too serious, and start to ignore the social aspects of the game. That is, I can turn into a bit of a dick on the golf course when I'm trying too hard. It worked for Hogan, but I don't really want to go down that road.

On the other hand, staying relaxed and loose, without excessive golf thoughts in your head, can often be a *huge* help. But really only if you've already got your swing grooved pretty well.

Take D.A. Points, who won the Pebble Beach Pro-Am with Bill Murray in 2011. They were laughing and joking the whole time, and it no doubt helped them both (Points won the individual pro title; he and Murray won the team pro-am portion) to take their minds off the pressure and just play. I'll be glad to get to that point, but so far I needed to stay pretty focused on what I was doing to hit the ball well.

One frustration was the continued presence of a nagging slice. I noticed that I sliced/faded the ball a little more after I started hitting off the grass, as opposed to the mats in the Golf Dome. On the grass, I would occasionally dig my club into the dirt, which sometimes hurt my wrists. So I may have been guarding against doing that a little bit. Also, on the course, it's easy to fall into the mindset of trying not to hit bad shots, rather than really focusing on making a good swing. So I think I swung a little tentatively for those two reasons, which allows bad habits to creep in. Hopefully they would be corrected with time and practice.

All in all, it was a promising start to the "real" golf season. My first as a lefty.

As the summer wore on, however, it became ever more difficult to devote the same attention to the lefty golf project. Jack decided to play Little League baseball for the first time, which conflicted with his soccer activities. But that was not his biggest challenge.

Jack had not previously expressed any interest in playing Little League. But after playing some baseball the previous summer with his friend Ajay, he decided to try it. Trouble was, he was joining as a 9-year-old, in the 9-and-10-year-old division, with many boys who have been playing organized baseball since they were 7 or younger. Half of them were older than he.

Complicating things further was that this was the first age division where the kids did their own pitching (as opposed to machine- or parent-pitch). So the quality was pretty poor. Jack not only had to learn to hit a pitched baseball, he had to pick out strikes from balls – and harmless balls from potential bean balls (which came flying at him all too often). This did not make for the best learning environment.

Jack's attention span – or lack thereof – was also an issue. Even though he's a decent fielder and has a pretty good arm, they never let him play anything other than right field. Getting him to stay engaged was nearly impossible.

In this league, everybody bats, whether they're in the field that inning or not. So he'd generally get at least three plate appearances each game. But to Jack, the time in between was interminable.

After the first game I asked him how he thought it went. After a moment, he said, "Well … I didn't expect there to be so much *waiting.*"

He improved at the plate as the season went on, but in the first few games he struck out every time. I'm not sure he ever even made contact – unless you count the ball making contact with *him.* The first time that happened it bounced off his helmet, which sent him scurrying, unfazed, down to first base with a big smile on his face. The second time his hand took the blow, a painful experience that resulted in tears and, no doubt, a drop in courage and confidence.

By mid-season, however, a breakthrough. Jack started reaching base nearly every time … by never taking the bat off his shoulder. He figured out that the pitching was so bad, that if he just never swung, he would walk most every time. I was really torn. He was suddenly enjoying the game much more, running the bases and occasionally scoring a run. He even once scored the tying run in the bottom of the last in a close contest. His teammates mobbed him in the dugout and we both smiled widely.

But here's the thing: My son was being rewarded *for not trying!* I thought of the Homer Simpson quote: "You tried your best and you failed. The lesson is, never try." Is this what my son was learning?! Not trying is something that comes all too naturally to him (I think he gets it from me), so the last thing I wanted to do was encourage that. But he was having so much more fun ….

For better or worse, the problem seemed to take care of itself toward the end of the season. Jack started to swing the bat more often, making contact here and there, and even getting the occasional hit. Well, more likely reaching base on an error, but why get technical?

It wasn't enough to convince him that baseball is his game, however. It turned out to be the only season of Little League he ever played. (Though he did discover softball two summers later, which he loves.)

Like me, I think Jack is ultimately better suited to individual sports. Like golf! Or tennis, which Jack has also taken an interest in.

It was during a hard-fought tennis "match" with Jack about this time that I made a key realization: A two-handed backhand stroke for a right-handed player is a lot like a left-handed golf stroke. Just like Bob Charles said! The same motion that imparts top-spin on the tennis ball squares the clubface in the golf swing. I had always struggled with hitting a top-spin backhand in tennis, but equating these two motions made it come together somehow. Suddenly, I was pounding top-spin backhand winners down the line at Jack. He had no chance! Well, not really. Jack is still very much a beginner, and my backhand improved marginally, not dramatically. I even wondered if hitting top-spin backhands against a wall over and over would help ingrain that motion. I never got around to testing it, but it was a good thought to file away for future reference.

After the Morningstar round, my back was a little stiff and sore, so it wasn't until the following Thursday that I returned to the practice tee. The back issue was starting to concern me a little, which is interesting, because it was about this time that Tiger Woods was having some back issues of his own. He was still mired in the post-scandal slump, and it was becoming clear that his body might become an obstacle in his quest to break Jack Nicklaus's all-time record of 18 major professional championships.

In fact, Nicklaus made some interesting comments about Tiger's injury issues at the Memorial Tournament (Jack's tournament) that same weekend:

> I think Tiger's swing, and I think a lot of the swings of today, are far more violent at the ball than some of the old swings. Some of the old swings were far more rhythmic. I don't think a lot of the swings today are as rhythmic as the old swings. I don't think the game is the same game from that standpoint. The game today is far more an upper body game, and we used to play more from the ground up.

Injuries were never a big issue for Nicklaus, and he thinks this is an important reason why not. Interesting food for thought moving forward, for sure.

But it wasn't just a sore back that kept me from keeping up with practice. Life was getting pretty hectic, and time was feeling more precious. I said from the beginning that I wouldn't let the lefty project interfere with family life, but now it was getting more difficult. Things were getting busy at work, too. And it didn't help that I had temporarily lost my Lefty Dome space. A bunch of "stuff" had accumulated there – I was setting up in a store room, after all – and I didn't feel right asking if it could be moved elsewhere. So I was out of luck for a while.

In spite of these challenges, I was preparing to debut my left-handed golf game in front of regular people (rather than my closest friends) at our church's annual men's golf outing. It would be a scramble, at a fine golf course, in front of people who knew that I was a pretty good golfer, but hadn't necessarily seen me play. The problem is, almost nobody knew what I was up to with the book project. And it proved surprisingly difficult to explain *why* I was doing it.

I wrote in my journal that the church outing was "frustrating and discouraging." Not just because I didn't play as well as I would have liked, but because I really felt "on display." It felt like every eye was watching every swing, evaluating – make that *judging* – me and my project with close scrutiny. The reality is that nobody cared nearly as much as I imagined they did. But that thought, in turn, bubbled up feelings of futility. What's the point of doing all this if nobody cares?

From the journal:

[But] truly *original* ideas are often greeted with a lot of skepticism, right? At least that's what I keep telling myself! I also have to keep reminding myself that it's a process. But my back and the lack of practice time lately are *very* frustrating. Because the point is to give this 100% effort for a year. I don't want to be left thinking, "But what if I had practiced more?" But then, again, I've already acknowledged in the intro that 100% effort will be very difficult – for many reasons. So ... "it all becomes part of the story" (and God is in control).

The following weekend Jack and I met Rob and his son Nate at Raymond Heights, a par-3 course near Racine, about halfway between our respective homes. We've played together before, and it's interesting to watch the boys in comparison to their fathers. Jack is as laid-back as you can get on a golf course, kinda like Rob. Nate, on the other hand, tries *really* hard and gets upset when things don't go well, kinda like me. It's like somehow some little piece of DNA, the one that controls golf course temperament, got switched between the two boys.

Even though it was a fun outing, I'm afraid I showed more than my share of frustration on the course. Rob said I "looked stiff"; I think my back was bothering me more than I realized or let on. And the lack of practice was starting to have an effect. I think when you're at the beginning stages like that, it's easier to backslide when you don't practice. It's *not* like riding a bike. My good habits are not well ingrained yet, and they deteriorate quickly without repetition.

The following week I had a little better session on the range, noting that I actually *drew* (hit with a slight hook) a couple of 7-iron shots. But a prevailing feeling of frustration was starting to set in. I wrote in my journal:

Whenever I drive past a golf course, especially on a beautiful day like today, I get this "stirring" inside. I imagine most golfers do. You see the course, and it draws you – you want to go play it. You envy the golfers you see on the course and imagine/recount those good feelings you get from hitting a nice drive down a beautiful green fairway or a nice high iron shot onto the green.

What had worried me just a bit after the church golf outing was that I was so discouraged I think those feelings went away for a little bit. I looked at the golf course and remembered frustration rather than success. It was not a good feeling, and it didn't not "stir" me or draw me in, in any way. Very unfamiliar. I didn't like it.

But it reminded me of one of the questions I ask in the Intro, something to the effect of, "is it going to be 'no fun' to play bad golf for a while?" How frustrating will it be? Will I lose my love of the game? Up until very recently, the answer was that the joy of learning a new skill made up for the quality of the golf. As long as the learning curve was going up, it was fun. What changed at the church outing was that I felt for the first time like I had taken a step back. I wasn't hitting the ball nearly as well as I should be, as I knew I could, and it was "no fun at all"! And it really made me question things again. Of course, there were other factors involved – such as lack of practice and my ongoing back issues. But still – it started to feel "no fun" and that was scary.

But even yesterday's good day on the range, which kind of reminded me what it feels like to hit good shots again, seemed to bring back the good feelings. Driving past the course on the way to the range today I felt drawn in again. The good feelings returned. And I was frustrated not to have a chance to hit balls [the range was closed for some reason] – even as I chipped and putted for a while. So it was good to have that feeling again, and hopefully it will last. And even if the frustration does return, I'll at least have this experience to draw on to remind myself that it won't last forever. Keep moving forward!!

But just when my attitude started to improve a little bit, my back started to get worse. It was so sore it ruined my Fourth of July celebration. Jack and Elizabeth marched in the parade with the Cub Scouts, but it was all I could do to get in the car and drop them off. Afterward, they went to a pool party at a friend's house, but I stayed home – not just because my back hurt, but because I was in a sour mood about it. I also wanted to "save my strength" for the fireworks later.

I knew going into the project that my back might become an

issue, and the truth is I hadn't prepared for that as well as I should have. Now it was time to do something, to "fix it." So I made an appointment with Dr. Bernie, Coach Carl's chiropractor.

I got to see him right away, and just from that very first visit I started to feel a little more confident. He did not take any X-rays, but gave me a thorough examination and asked a lot of questions. He basically said, as I suspected, that I was "a little crooked down there," meaning in my lower back. He also scolded me for not doing more to strengthen my core if I'm going to be playing a lot of golf. He gave me a few spinal adjustments and a thorough lower-back massage, then assigned a number of stretches for me to do at home. I was surprised to learn that stretching your hamstrings is *very* important in keeping your back in good shape.

All in all, it was very encouraging just to be "doing something" about the back problems.

As this was going on, I was trying to arrange an exciting opportunity that had arisen. Rob's nephew John, a student at the University of Illinois, had won a raffle at the men's basketball banquet. The prize was a round of golf for him and a guest with Mike Small, the Illinois men's golf coach, and former Illini and NFL football player Fred Wakefield. John knew about my book project and, not really being a golfer himself, asked Rob if he thought I might like to use it. I imagine the original thought was that Rob would round out the foursome, but when it proved inconvenient for Rob's schedule, he said it would be fine for me to choose someone else.

Making it all the more intriguing was that the round would be played at Lincolnshire Fields Country Club in Champaign, where we played our high school golf back in the day. What an opportunity! I was thrilled at the idea of playing that course again. The question was, with whom?

I first asked Tom Scaggs, who jumped at the chance. But then he had to cancel after breaking his collarbone in an ATV accident. At some point, Rob suggested (I think as a joke) that I could invite Mike Hagan, my old golf team nemesis. I laughed at the suggestion, but the more I thought about it the more I thought it might make great material for the book, to reconnect with "Hagan" and talk about those days. I tracked him down and invited him, but he said he would not be available to join me. Oh, well. He might have just ended up breaking a club across my leg again.

Then it dawned on me I should ask John if *he* knew anybody who'd like to fill the empty spot. Duh. He did, his friend Landon, who turned out to be a pretty good golfer.

After considerable difficulty setting it up, the round was scheduled for Friday, July 22. Problem was, I hadn't really been playing, and was still working on trying to get my back in shape. At a chiropractor appointment that week, I told Dr. Bernie what I had planned for Friday, and asked if he thought I'd be ready. He said, "Well, you gotta do it!" I took that to mean that "ready" is a relative term, and that he'd give his blessing for me playing even if I was still feeling sore.

On Wednesday I got a massage at our health club, using a gift certificate Elizabeth had given me for my birthday. I wanted to be ready for Lincolnshire, and figured that was a good time to cash it in. Truth is, I was still hurting, and wasn't at all confident that Friday would go well.

That same night, I got an e-mail from Coach Small with some bad news: he had injured *his* back and wouldn't be able to play with us. He was preparing to play in a PGA Tour event the following week, and didn't want to take any chances on being ready to go. He was very nice about it and clearly felt bad, asking if I wanted to reschedule, or ...? But it had been so difficult to find a date that worked. And he said he'd be happy to still have lunch with us and maybe give us a few pointers before the round with Fred. So that's what we did.

Coach Small and Fred could not have been nicer, both are great guys. Fred picked up the lunch tab, and the Coach told us to charge all our drinks to him on the course – which we needed a lot of, because the temperature was over 100 degrees that day! In fact, it was so hot that my mom thought I shouldn't even play, feeling it was too dangerous. In an e-mail to Elizabeth she wrote, "Well, I hope he at least has the good sense to take a cart!" Aw, come on, Mom! You raised me. You know I'm "the responsible one"! (But I know it's all because she loves me.)

It was, in fact, a pretty brutal day on the course. But we *were* in carts, and it was a real treat to play Lincolnshire again. At times, it was hard to recognize. It's one of those course that winds among houses. When I played it 30 years ago, some of it was still empty lots

– and there wasn't much in the way of trees. Now there are houses and trees everywhere. And still with lots of out-of-bounds and water lining the holes.

I wish I could say I played as well as the course looked. But it was a struggle all day. I shot 59 on the front nine – terrible! But things got even worse on the back. At the turn I went into the bathroom to freshen up, and became alarmed by how red my face looked. I feared I was getting sunburned, so I applied more sunscreen. But I later realized it was mostly just my body shedding all of its excess heat through my face. That's just how I roll. Back when I used to play basketball, people would sometimes say to me, "Are you okay? Your face is *really* red!"

I was hot, stiff, sore, frustrated, and discouraged -- but having a nice time! Golf-wise, things hit rock-bottom on the 12th hole, a short but narrow par-5, with water on the right and O.B. (houses) on the left. After visiting more than one backyard, I carded an ugly 11. My worst score yet as a lefty – and the first double-digit score I can remember recording since I was … I don't know, maybe 13 years old.

But it had a freeing effect. I effectively gave up after that, which, as it usually does, helped me play a little better. I scored a par on the next hole – my first of the day – and cheered loudly watching Landon roll in what we estimated to be an 80-foot birdie putt. The longest holed putt I've ever witnessed. It was a truly exciting moment.

Fred and Landon were great the whole time – I just hope my frustration didn't make me a bad golfing companion. I confess this has happened before, and I don't always recognize it while it's going on.

On the 17th hole, a short par-3 over water, Fred and Landon each tried a left-handed tee shot. Fred's was horrible. He looked completely awkward and topped it badly. But Landon's lefty swing actually looked pretty good – and he made decent contact. And then I had that same little feeling of panic I had after Rob hit his lefty drive: *It's supposed to be harder than that!* Why did Landon look so good hitting that ball lefty for the first time? Is it because he's younger? Or more athletic? More naturally ambidextrous? If he can hit it that well on the first try, I should be hitting it *much* better after 10 months of hard work. Right?

It didn't help that on the 18th tee they persuaded me to try a right-handed drive. Part of me didn't want to, because I didn't want to break my "vow" about not playing right-handed. But it didn't feel sporting to decline, and I was curious to see how it would go. So I borrowed Landon's driver (Fred's had an extra-long shaft; he's a *big* guy!), lined up, and swung away. It felt very awkward and off-balance, and I never really saw the ball, losing it quickly in the late-afternoon sun. But I heard Fred and Landon both say, "Oooooh." Turns out, it was a pretty good shot: middle of the fairway, short of the sand traps. Not much distance, but solid. My best drive of the day.

Again, this only served to discourage me, to make me question again, at least for the moment, why I was doing all this. I was playing such bad golf left-handed – and apparently, even my awkward, off-balance right-handed swings produce better results than my lefty ones!

After the round, Fred invited us to hang around to have a couple beers, which we happily did. It was one of those moments. My golf had been horrible, but the company was great, and in the end it was another valuable learning experience. I was glad to have done it, but I was *really* glad to be done. I was ready to put it behind me and move on.

Back in Milwaukee, things continued to stagnate. I wasn't practicing as much as I should, and I was playing even less. Because of my back issues, I had gone about six weeks without taking a lesson. I was even neglecting my journal, something I had been extremely diligent about previously. Dark thoughts were setting in more frequently. I started thinking about extending my one-year "deadline." With all the setbacks I've had, wouldn't it make sense to give myself more time? But one of my fears at the outset was the project turning into a never-ending quest. I set the deadline for a reason: to avoid taking more time than necessary away from my family.

So I decided to keep plugging away with an eye on the White Lake Classic as the finish line. Sure, I may end up playing golf lefty long after that, but it made sense to make that be the end of the official book project. No matter what.

My spirits were at a low ebb. Thank God (and I mean that quite literally) we were about to discover the joys of Fort Wilderness.

CHAPTER 8
Back in the Swing of It

"To play golf well you must feel tranquil and at peace,
with nothing to lose and everything to gain."

—Harry Vardon

It's hard to overstate what an amazing time we had during our week of Christian "family camp" at Fort Wilderness — or what an effect it had on my mental and spiritual well-being — or to know where to begin. So perhaps it's best to begin at the beginning.

Our trip up north actually started badly, with a delayed departure (which is expected) and some car trouble (which certainly was not). When we were *finally* packed up and ready to get going, the car wouldn't start. Apparently, just leaving the doors open a little too long while we loaded was enough to wear down our failing battery. Not good. But after some futzing around with it, and a brief consultation with a knowledgeable neighbor, we got on our way — discontent in the knowledge that our battery problems were likely not behind us.

The result was that we arrived *after* the end of the official check-in period. Not really a big deal, as we called ahead, and they were extremely understanding and accommodating. In fact, there was a small "welcoming committee" of a half-dozen or so volunteers (college-age kids) waiting for us at the gate when we finally pulled in. We got checked in with no problem (though with not much time to spare before dinner) and led to our campsite by another friendly volunteer … just as it started to rain.

Setting up a campsite in the rain is never any fun; it's worse when you're running late. And even more so when the campsite isn't at all what your wife expected. She had pictured a secluded spot surrounded by trees, fully anticipating that we (and she in particular) would spend much of the week "getting away" from people and just relaxing around our tent. Instead our site – the last one to be set up, of course – was barely distinguishable among the mass of tents and pop-up trailers that were set up among the trees.

Between the stress from car problems and being late and the rain and now the unmet expectations, Elizabeth, who had been doing a slow burn much of the day, was now ready to go all Mt. Vesuvius on anybody within spewing distance. In fact, she was so disappointed in the campsite (on top of the other things) that she was just about ready to get back in the car and go find a hotel someplace. But she didn't. Instead, she responded by taking total control of the situation, barking out orders (Jack and I meekly complied) and getting the tent set up in record time.

Not an ideal way to get things done, but it worked.

By then, however, we were late for dinner, which is served family style in the dining hall. It was already underway when we walked in, no doubt looking a little frazzled, wet, and bedraggled. But literally within seconds someone waved us over to join them at their table. Turns out, it was another family from the Milwaukee area, also with a 9-year-old son named Jack. Go figure! The kids were seated at the next table, so Jack joined them while we joined the grown-ups. The food and company were both amazing … and the tension immediately started to melt away.

We soon discovered that the first question everybody there asks you is, "How long have you been coming here?" Some families had been coming for ten years or more – even longer when you count the multi-generational continuity (Fort Wilderness was founded in 1956). And when we answered that it was our first time, we were treated like long-lost friends. It was truly unbelievable.

It didn't take us long to realize that the "communal" setting of the campsites was probably by design. The intention is not for campers to "get away" from people while they're there, but to become a part of a week-long community. There were kids Jack's age everywhere, and he had already made a number of new friends by bedtime. Twenty-four hours later, Jack had proclaimed his first full day at Fort to be "the best day *ever!*"

For Jack, the big draw was the unprecedented amount of

freedom he had. Because it was such a safe environment, we were able to just turn him loose on his bike (we all brought our bikes) for long periods of time and say, for instance, "Be back at the tent at 4:00." We gave him a watch to wear, and it was a great exercise in responsibility to see if he could keep track of the time. For the most part, he did very well.

For Elizabeth and me, a week away from the everyday pressures of life was priceless. And even though I hadn't necessarily been looking forward to "going to church" every day, the morning worship services turned out to be a fantastic way to begin each day. It didn't hurt, of course, that Stuart Briscoe, a prominent Milwaukee area preacher, one of our favorites, was the speaker for the week.

Oh … it was also Jack's first opportunity to spend quality time doing some "serious" fishing. Just about every spare moment he could find he spent dangling his hook, baited with a tiny piece of beef jerky, into the water's edge near our campsite. Ask him how many fish he caught during the week and he will be quick to tell you the exact number. I believe the final tally was 33 – all little pan fish – though I'm sure that number includes a few that were caught more than once. He also placed second in the carpetball tournament, despite his initial disappointment at being placed at the very bottom of an age group that included 13-year-olds!

By the time we packed up the van at the end of the week (with a new battery), it was very difficult to leave. There was a lot of hugging, exchanging of contact information, and inquiries regarding not *if* we'd becoming back next year (that much seemed presumed), but whether we'd be returning for the same week. "We'll sure try!" was our answer.

And though I had actually packed a few golf balls and a couple of clubs in order to avoid going a whole week without practice, I never touched them. In retrospect, I'm sure this was for the best as I arrived back home feeling extremely refreshed and eager to get back to the practice tee.

After Fort Wilderness, all I had left on the golfing calendar were lessons, practice, and the White Lake Classic – as well as a yet-to-be-scheduled playing lesson with Coach Carl, something I was really looking forward to.

The final push began with my first lesson in nearly eight weeks.

Eight weeks! Hard to believe it had been that long. But my back was finally feeling better and my spirits were buoyed by Fort Wilderness (well, really by God – credit where credit is due). So I was ready to go.

My lessons by that point were primarily review, working on cementing stuff we'd already worked on, without introducing much new. But that first lesson after Fort (as the cool kids abbreviate it) was the first time we'd really worked on my short game. All my Brown Deer practicing had not really translated into success on the course. I'd been playing 9-hole rounds with Bill, a friend from church, at a course called Mee-Kwon at the crack of dawn, and had been hitting the ball pretty well. But I was throwing away a lot of shots around the green. I shared that with Coach Carl at that first lesson (after the long layoff), so that's what we worked on.

He identified that I'd been moving my lower body too much when I chipped. Keeping it still seemed to help a lot. He also warned me against trying to "manufacture" a shot; that is, trying too hard to make the ball behave in a certain way, rather than just making a smooth, natural swing through the ball. I still didn't have nearly as much "feel" on a left-handed chip shot as I used to on the right side, so it made sense to keep things simple.

Overall, it was a pretty good lesson. I hit a lot of good shots, and Coach Carl mostly just watched and made comments. He talked about staying in balance, making a good turn, rotating around my chest, not dropping my chest, and keeping my weight on the inside of my left foot. Nothing revolutionary, just a reminder of the fundamentals we'd worked on.

I was really starting to get very confident with the shorter clubs. It was feeling very natural to hit 9-irons and wedges. I felt like I could stand up there and hit nice easy shots just over the 100-yard sign all day. But I still struggled when I worked up to a 7-iron or longer. The ball started to curve a little more, right to left, and it was harder to make good contact. It didn't seem like it should be any more difficult, but it was. It was like the 9-iron mental picture I had in my head just didn't *quite* translate to the longer clubs. Coach Carl always emphasized that it should be the same swing with the longer clubs as with the short ones. I could tell my brain that, but I had a hard time making my body believe it. Hopefully something would eventually *click* with the longer clubs and I'd have a little breakthrough.

I was also starting to spend less time on the practice tee and more time on the course. I hate getting up early, but if I teed off by about 6:00 a.m. at Mee-Kwon I could squeeze in nine holes and still make it to work by 8:00 (or a little after). Sometimes I would play alone, other times with Bill, but I would always walk – both to keep costs down and to help justify my time expenditure by getting a little exercise. And also because I consider walking part of a "pure" golf experience, the way the game was meant to be played.

I really enjoyed these rounds, though it would have been nice not to have to play through the dew. I got to know the back nine really well; it's a little easier than the front, and easier to walk because it's flatter. Overall, the course is quite beautiful. It's hilly, with a good number of trees (but not too many), and the greens are in very good shape for a public municipal course. It's not very long, but the challenging greens, very difficult to read among the hills, help keep it from being too easy.

My first couple of rounds there produced scores in the low 50s, but I improved steadily and was soon working my way toward bogey golf – and, by extension, shooting half of a sub-90 round.

After shooting 49 one morning I had this e-mail exchange with Rob:

> ME: In other, less-exciting news [Rob had just told me his family was getting a dog], I shot 49 this morning. The last four nines I've played (all on the same 9) were 52, 51, 50, 49 -- so I guess that's progress. But each one has still felt vaguely unsatisfying. But I guess that's golf, right? Today's round was actually pretty solid, but I had two bad holes coming in, I triple-bogeyed the 6th and 9th. The 6th was bad, but could've been worse. I top-shanked (double-whammy) my tee shot about 35 yards to the right, had to take a drop, and still had 125 yards to the green. Hit a reasonable shot from there onto the fringe, but three-putted from there for six. (The greens on this course are incredibly tricky to read sometimes, on this particular hole I swear my first putt broke uphill!)
>
> I think what still seems a little frustrating is that my good shots aren't really getting any better, but I'm hitting fewer bad shots. My best 3-wood still only goes about 200 yards, tops, often more like 180 -- on a "good" shot. I can imagine

playing bogey golf this way, but it wouldn't be very exciting. Kind of "Andy golf" if you know what I mean. Just plop it out into the fairway. Plop my approach a little short. Plop it onto the green and two-putt for bogey. Plop, plop, plop.

On the last hole I think I just got a little anxious -- I had 46 or 47 in my sights. Bad tee shot. Fluffed recovery into the fairway bunker. Fluffy bunker shot to 100 yards. Good 9 iron to the back fringe. And then another bad misread for a 3-putt (from the fringe) triple. Frustrating. (Ya still with me!!?) :)

ROB: I read a chapter from [Harvey] Penick's book the other day that surprised me, about the improvements coming in large stroke breakthroughs. He said most golfers don't improve as you have, a stroke at a time, they make a breakthrough and drop 5 strokes. I think you've talked about this before. I wonder what the change would be that would lead to a breakthrough to get you to the mid 40s? Maybe more snap on the long irons/drives to get you more distance? Or maybe just more consistency to avoid the bad shots leading to a triple.

You sound more like a Phil [Mickelson] golfer than a Ben Hogan golfer. Didn't Ben say boring is good?

ME: If "boring" means hitting fairways and greens and two-putting for par, I'm all for that. But right now it means wimpy small ball golf and playing for bogeys. That's fine for now, and it's kind of what I have my sights set on for the WLC. Reducing the bad shots is the primary goal right now. But I'm also holding out hope for that breakthrough you describe, where I can start thinking about getting more distance and hitting more greens in regulation.

That's why the par-3 triple was so frustrating, because on the par 3s I know I can hit the green in regulation and ought to be able to a good percentage of the time. The par-3s are my "scoring holes" right now, which is kind of opposite of what seems normal, where you look at par-5s to score. Right now, the par-5s feel like its just more opportunities to hit a bad shot in there somewhere!

Kind of weird. Like, the one par-5 on this nine (it's a par 35) is quite short, like 485 yards double dogleg (but it's uphill after the drive). Today I hit a decent 3-wood and a decent 5-wood, but was still like 160 yards out, in the rough. I played a 6-iron, hit it just a little fluffy, and left it just short of the green. Chipped up to about 10 or 12 feet and two-putted for bogey. Bogey is good for me on that hole, but it's hard to feel satisfied. (I've gotten an 8 on that hole more than once.)

I'm a little bit torn on how to approach the next five weeks, before the WLC. Right now I'm kind of looking at it as taking the game and the shots I have right now and making the best of it. I'm not even going to try to hit driver. My goal is to shoot 90 at White Lake, and I think that's within reach. I worry a little that if I strive for that five-stroke breakthrough I might upset what I have going for me right now. But I'm not sure if that even really makes sense. That is, what would I really be doing differently with a different "strategy"? (Other than maybe trying to hit driver.) I think the big difference is to play more vs. spending more time on the range. But then, I really should be doing both. It would probably benefit me tremendously to spend some time on the range just working on the longer clubs. I have a lesson tomorrow, so I'll talk to [Coach Carl] about it then.

I have a hunch he's going to tell me I'm over-thinking it. :)

The 18th hole at Mee-Kwon, in fact, had stopped me more than once. Deceptively difficult, it's a short par-4 with a sharp dogleg left around trees and a big sand trap with a steep uphill climb to the green. As a right-hander with a slice, it drove me nuts, because there wasn't much I could do to keep my ball from running through the right-sloping fairway, long and/or to the right. The smart shot probably would have been to hit an iron into the turn, but that leaves a long, uphill second shot. It was much more tempting (and fun) to try to cut the dogleg over the trees. But I can't ever remember doing that successfully. I'd end up either in the trees on the left or, if I pushed it right at all, in the rough and trees to the right of the fairway.

As a lefty, on the other hand, it seemed tailor-made for me and my slight fade. And yet – probably because I was trying too hard to hit that perfect shot – and no doubt feeling the pressure of trying to finish off a good nine – I never seemed to be able to pull it off. I typically ended up in the sand trap or, just like before, down the hill to the right facing a long, uphill approach from the rough. No good. But overall, the results at Mee-Kwon were getting better, and I was encouraged.

The frustrating part, as I had shared with Rob, was realizing that my "good golf" as a lefty was really unspectacular. Occasionally I would hit a green in regulation and two-putt for par. That's about the best I could hope for. The potential downside was still very high. If I got into any trouble, it was a lot harder to get back out. As a right-handed golfer, a double-bogey was *usually* the worst I would do. As a lefty, a triple-bogey or worse could come at any time. Shooting a decent score felt like walking a tightrope: One loose shot could ruin my score in a hurry. And, despite my efforts to feel otherwise, I still cared way too much about my score.

All the while I was starting to think a lot about "the big day": the upcoming White Lake Classic. I shared this with Coach Carl at my next lesson, and he said it sounded like I was definitely putting too much pressure on myself. The trick is how do I *not* do this? I've been trying to play better under pressure (or to not put unnecessary pressure on myself) my whole life.

I knew Coach was right, but I also think he didn't really understand how much this tournament, not to mention this whole project, meant to me. The "deadline," artificial as it was, existed for a reason. I wanted to have a good idea of whether it's going to "work" by the time the season ended. But it was been getting harder to think that way.

Truth is, if this weren't the case I'd probably have been taking it a lot easier, resting my back (which had been acting up again), instead of trying to push myself toward White Lake. Maybe that was the wrong approach, but I was determined to go for it. I was also trying to remember to pray about it, and ask God to show me the best approach. But I feared I was too wrapped up in myself to listen well for what He might be saying.

Nevertheless, the quest continued. And the clock was ticking.

My last regular lesson was September 17, just about two weeks before White Lake. It went really well; I was hitting shot after shot right on the button. Coach Carl seemed impressed, which is always nice – good for my ego! I think much of the success was related to my back feeling good; that seemed to be a key factor lately. Coach said my rotation looked a lot better and that I seemed to be swinging more freely, with a little more "snap." That was very good to hear, as lack of distance continued to be one of my chief concerns. And I have to say, things were starting to feel really natural. It was getting harder and harder to imagine, or remember, what it felt like to swing righty.

As the lesson went on, however, things started to deteriorate. It was frustrating how often this happened. But I knew it wasn't a "left-handed issue," so I didn't worry about it too much.

Jack came along on this lesson, which is always a treat. Coach Carl worked with him for about ten minutes while I was warming up. He said he was impressed with Jack's natural ability and that he has a lot of potential. I said, "Yeah, the problem is he's too much like his old man! It's difficult to get him to work hard at anything." But I was certainly proud to hear it. I'm sure I beamed.

Afterward we played some mini-golf and took a few laps on the go-karts. Jack said it was "an awesome day," which is always nice to hear. And it makes everything else feel unimportant.

Those good feelings carried over into my next practice round – at least, to 8/9ths of it. Afterward, I sent this report to Coach Carl:

> Thinking back to yesterday's nine holes, where things started great and then gradually deteriorated as the round went on (a pattern with me – it even happens during my lessons), what jumps out is how relaxed I was when I started. Walking down the fairway at 6:30 in the morning on a beautiful day, before the sun had even officially risen, I was so happy and content just to be out there! I was totally focused on making good swings and enjoying myself. And it showed in the results: I made tap-in bogeys on the first two holes. I hit four good shots (two on each hole) to get close to the first two greens, and hit two good chips. If I had read the speed of the greens a little better I would have had tap-in pars. If I'd read my first putts a little better, I still might have had two pars.
>
> As it was, I had two very solid bogeys -- and started thinking about a score. (Bad!!) From there it started to go downhill, very gradually. Not horribly (until the last hole), but just enough for a little frustration to set in by about the fifth hole. Still, I held it together, got a break (a bladed 6-iron to about 10 feet on a par 3), and still had a chance standing on the 18th tee to shoot a 44 or 45. That's where it fell apart.

One thing I'm very encouraged about, however, is my ability to "create" a shot now and then. The club feels comfortable enough in my hand that I can start to do some of the "non-standard" things I used to be able to do as a righty. For instance, on #13 I had a downhill lie on the back of a fairway sand trap, in fluffy rough just past the lip. The ball was a little above my feet. I was able to choke up on a 7-iron, hit down on it a little and run it up the fairway pretty far. I wasn't trying to get it to the green, just advance it enough to have a half-wedge left, which I did.

And on number 17 -- do you know Mee-Kwon? 17 is a fairly straightforward par 4, longish, approaching 400 yards from the white tees, with a big fairway trap on the right and a big, old, nearly dead tree guarding/blocking the right side of the green. In two shots I found myself in the right rough, about 75 yards out, with that big tree in my way. There was room to go around it to the right, but I had to keep it low. So I punched a 9-iron with the intent of bumping up it onto the green. I pulled it off exactly as I envisioned it!! Beyond my hopes, actually. It stopped about 7 feet from the pin. (I missed the par putt, of course, which I'm sure only added to the tension and pressure I was feeling on the 18th tee.)

Anyway, all in all I'm feeling very encouraged. Need to work on those relaxation techniques, though. The challenge is that I'm so *excited* right now about how things are going, what with the big "White Lake Classic" (my "major") barely two weeks away! :)

I apparently stopped short of telling him exactly what happened next. Again, the last hole was my downfall. I stood on the 18th tee at 40 strokes, with a good chance to shoot 45, or half a 90. But I shanked a drive, hit 3-wood into the trees, left my third in the rough, and flopped a wedge to the very front of a very large green with the pin at the very back. Four putts later I carded a snowman for an extremely disappointing 48. Again, the pressure of closing out a good round seemed to get to me.

Still, there were lots of positives to focus on as I continued my march to the WLC. And my back seemed to be holding up pretty well.

During those last few weeks I really enjoyed working on my

putting at Brown Deer over the lunch hour. For some reason, it was always more enjoyable than hitting balls. Maybe because it's easier to not over-pressurize things. A bad day putting is less discouraging than a bad day on the range. It's also easier to feel good about not putting any unnecessary wear and tear on my back (or other body parts). Plus, it's very common to read that most amateur golfers don't spend nearly enough time practicing their putting, even though the green is where they likely waste the most strokes. So it was easy to justify the time spent there in terms of helping my game.

As usual, the challenge was keeping it interesting. So I was always looking for drills or little games I could do to stay focused. Touring pro Geoff Ogilvy suggests finding a four- or five-foot breaking putt, then trying to make it at three different speeds. Ram one straight into the hole, hit one at medium speed with moderate break, and then lag one slowly with a big break. He likes it for two reasons: One, because making a lot of short putts helps build confidence; and two, because it's a great way to develop a feel for the relationship between speed and break.

Another drill is an old classic: Pick a flat three- or four-foot putt and see how many in a row you can make it. Again, watching the ball go into the hole over and over is a great confidence builder. But it's surprisingly hard to stroke the ball perfectly over and over again. I think the most I ever made in a row was about 50.

And I still enjoyed playing my three-ball "18-hole" putting rounds. I eventually got to the point where I felt like my lefty putting was pretty nearly as good as my right-handed. But then, it always seemed like there was no reason I couldn't achieve this level with my putting. Achieving it with my full swings was another matter.

On days I hit balls at lunch instead of putting, I focused primarily on the driver and 3-wood, realizing how important it would be at White Lake to get off the tee consistently. I wouldn't need a lot of distance there, but I would need to be fairly straight. Shanks and tops would do me no good at all, and could easily get me into real trouble.

I was getting pretty consistent with my 3-wood, but was still fairly frustrated that it continued to fade, and I didn't seem to have any "snap" on the ball. It never went as far as it seemed like it should. And that ugly "top shank" continued to make an occasional appearance. But then one day I had a little breakthrough.

Finally, I hit one of those shots where everything just seemed to go right. Good, crisp contact. Nice trajectory. And a good, straight ball flight right down the middle. On that particular swing, I was keying on letting my hands and arms be more passive, to create more of that "whipping" action Jack and I observed in that punkin chunkin' trebuchet catapult. After many months, it was still counterintuitive *not* to use my hands to muscle the clubhead through the ball. But lo and behold, thinking *passive* thoughts produced one of the best lefty 3-woods I've ever hit.

Of course, it did not instantly make every shot that good. But I knew I was on to something that I could key on in the future.

Even so, the distance was still disappointing.

It was difficult, however, to make good comparisons with the distance I *used* to be able to produce. So many things had changed since I was in my "prime": club technology, my age, my back, and, of course, my *handedness*. I was pushing 50, but my clubs were the nicest I've ever had. All of my clubs had larger sweet spots than I've previously enjoyed.

That said, I started to wonder if the shafts on my woods were holding me back. They were rated "stiff." I've never paid much attention to those details, so when the woods I wanted to buy so cheaply had "S" shafts, I didn't think much of it. But now that I was more in tune with the idea of "whipping" a golf club, I could see how a stiff shaft might be limiting. Pros use them because their swing speeds are so high. Seniors use light or "whippy" shafts because they're swing speeds are low. I was not a senior quite yet, but I knew my swing speed was no longer on the high end of the scale, even if it ever was.

So I asked Coach Carl what he thought, and he said, yes, chances are the shafts were costing me some distance. I also asked him about loft – my driver was 9.5 degrees, on the low side. Again, good for pros, but for guys like me it just makes it that much harder to get the ball up in the air off the tee. He said 10.5 degrees would probably be better.

Yay! An excuse to go club shopping again! There wasn't much time left before White Lake, but I figured it couldn't hurt to try a switch right now. And it was already fall again – a good time to look for bargains on the clearance rack.

Sure enough, in fairly short order I found a TaylorMade Burner driver – with a Regular ("R") shaft and 10.5 degrees of loft – clearance priced at just $75. That's about one fourth of the original MSRP. It's a very high-end driver, but probably two years from being "the latest technology." I snatched it up and headed straight to the practice range.

I noticed a difference immediately. It felt the same to swing it, so there wasn't any real adjustment period, but the ball definitely jumped off the clubface with a little more pop. I even seemed to hit it a little straighter. Maybe the more flexible shaft was helping to get the club square through contact a little better. I was in love! And I immediately started thinking about new 3- and 5-woods.

Within a few days I found a very reasonably priced Cleveland 3-wood. Cleveland is not quite as high-end as TaylorMade, but it's a respected brand, a good club. I think I paid $40, again a fraction of the original price. The results were again promising. A little more distance, a little more snap on the ball. Success! They didn't have a matching 5-wood, but I found a used one on eBay for $30 that fit the bill.

It sounds silly, but I was thrilled! I was now super-excited about my clubs. I loved my irons, my woods, and my new putter (another late-summer purchase). It was the most proud I've ever been of a set of clubs ... well, since I bought those beautiful Wilson Staff woods so many years ago.

I also started thinking about using a different kind of golf ball. I used to think it didn't matter; I always just tried to find something cheap and durable. For years I bought Pinnacles, which I could sometimes find on sale for $10 a dozen. That's the kind of price I like to pay! They're "distance" balls, which means they're on the hard side and don't spin much.

But I discovered how much difference a ball *can* make a few years earlier when I won a dozen Titleist Pro-V1 balls – the kind so many pros use – at an outing. I tried them out at a White Lake practice round and spent the first 15 holes or so wondering why I was slicing it so much more than usual. It was really frustrating. Finally, Tom "Serbo" (pronounced SARE-bo) Lessaris said, "Well, you know those are high-spin balls, right?"

No, it never occurred to me that my slice would get worse with a higher-spin ball. I only thought about more backspin, and a little more "bite" on the green. Or that I might even hit it a little farther.

So I went back to my old reliable Pinnacle "Gold" balls. Hard as a rock, but long and straight.

But now that I was hitting it straighter (at least in theory), I started to notice how difficult it was to get the ball to check up on chip shots. It probably had something to do with having less feel as a lefty, but I think it also had to do with the hard ball. It was harder to generate backspin on chips and pitches and therefore harder to get the ball to stop quickly.

So I scoured the annual equipment "Hot List" on the *Golf Digest* website for information about low-priced golf balls. One stood out: The TopFlite "Gamer V1." It was rated as a medium spin with good distance for a very affordable price. I found this a little ironic, because when I was a kid, TopFlite was known only for distance and durability. It was one of the first "cut-proof" balls. You could hit it a long way, but lacked anything resembling touch and feel. In fact, Andy and I called them "rock balls," because that's what it felt like when you hit them.

But this new version performed as advertised. I'm not sure they cut any strokes off my game, but they did indeed feel softer. Even if it was primarily a placebo effect, they gave me a little added confidence around the green.

So I had the clubs. I had the balls (heh). And my lefty game was starting to show signs of promise. White Lake was almost here. All I had to do now was get my head together. Right?

Oy vey.

CHAPTER 9
Keeping My Head in the Game

"Competitive golf is played mainly on a five-and-a-half-inch course:
the space between your ears."

—Bobby Jones

It didn't hit me until I was standing on the 17th tee, just how well I was playing. I was two over par for the round, two under for the back nine: by far the best 16 holes I'd ever played. Until that moment, I was playing extremely relaxed golf.

It's funny how a few days in the hospital with blood clots in your lungs can take the pressure off.

Almost exactly seven days before, the pain in my chest came on very gradually, on my left side, near my rib cage. I noticed it mostly when I took a deep breath – I thought it was a pulled muscle. Or – I'd eaten a lot of tacos for dinner that night, so perhaps it was indigestion. I took some antacid, just in case.

It was Labor Day weekend 2009, and we had taken advantage of the long weekend to do some backyard camping with Jack. That night, I just couldn't get comfortable in the tent. It hurt worse when I was lying down, so after tossing and turning on the thin camping mattress for a while I got up to go sleep in the house. "Is it your chest?" Elizabeth asked with some concern (I'd mentioned the pain to her earlier). "No, no," I lied. "I just can't get comfortable out here."

But I couldn't get comfortable inside either, and by 3:00 a.m. I was starting to get worried. But it was *3:00 a.m.*, so I was very reluctant to wake anybody up over what I was still convinced was nothing. Yet, just to be safe (and knowing my loving wife would kill me if I had a heart attack without telling her), I called the medical hot-line number provided by our insurance company. A few minutes later I was trudging out to the backyard: "Honey, wake up, I need you to take me to the emergency room." We phoned a friend from church to look after the boy and got in the car.

Several hours later, at roughly the crack of dawn, we got the diagnosis. "Well, it's not a heart attack," the doctor said. *See, I knew it!* Then she continued: "But you have blood clots in your lungs. A pulmonary embolism."

What!!?? That can kill you, right? How can that be!?

She started asking me all kinds of questions. Have you been on any long plane rides recently? Have you had any recent surgeries or injuries? Has anyone in your family ever had this? No, no, and no. "What about sitting in a canoe for a couple hours," I asked (we had taken the canoe out the day before). "Does that count?" She shook her head. "It has to be for much longer, like six or eight hours, at least."

Over the next few hours, days, and weeks, I learned a lot about pulmonary embolism. What generally happens is, when you sit for long periods of time without moving, blood can pool behind your knees and start to clot. The clots then break off, travel through your bloodstream, through your heart, and then get stuck where the vessels leading to your lungs branch off and get very small. If the clots are big enough or there are enough of them, they can kill you. Genetic risk factors make you more susceptible, and certain diseases can cause them, as well.

Later, I remembered David Bloom, a respected NBC news correspondent who died from a pulmonary embolism in the early days of the war in Iraq. In his case, he spent day after day riding in a cramped military vehicle, even sleeping in it sometimes. Just a few days before he died, he consulted medical personnel complaining of cramping in his legs. They suspected blood clots, and urged him to seek immediate medical attention, but he ignored the advice. Soon he was dead, leaving behind a wife and three young daughters. (Blood tests later revealed that he was genetically at risk.)

I also thought of Ben Hogan, one of my golfing heroes. Most golf fans know about the near-deadly encounter he had with a Greyhound bus in early 1949. But not as many know that he almost died a second time, a result of blood clots he developed during his extended hospitalization. Between all the surgeries and all the time he spent confined to his bed, he was a prime candidate.

In 1949, of course, without all the technology we have today, a pulmonary embolism was even more serious. In Ben's case, doctors performed a radical surgery to save his life and his legs. To keep more clots from traveling to his heart and lungs, they tied off some of the major vessels in his legs. His circulation was very poor from then on, which made it painful to walk and was the major reason he had so much trouble getting around a golf course. The fact that he won six of his nine career major championships *after* the accident – including going three for three in '53 – is nothing short of astonishing.

Let me be clear: I was never close to death. The blood clots I had were not that serious – they merely could have been. The bigger issue became figuring out *why* I got the clots, and making sure it didn't happen again. I'm happy to report, following extensive testing, that they ruled out all the serious stuff that might have produced them. And later, we figured out that it's just *possible* that I got them from spending a sleepless night slouched down on the couch a few days previously. Go figure. In any case, my recovery, at least for now, is complete.

Besides finding a cause, my biggest concern during the three-day hospital stay was, "Will I be able to play in the White Lake Classic this weekend?" I'd only missed it once before, and had no intention of missing it again. Fortunately, the doctors cleared me to play just in time. Which brings me back to the 17th tee of the Stone Creek Golf Club in Urbana, Illinois (the White Lake Classic is not always played in White Lake).

Up until that moment, I had been playing stress-free all day. I was thrilled just to be there, which relaxed me, helped my focus, and freed me to putt aggressively on the recently aerated greens. As I lined up putts, I thought of Arnold Palmer and the balls-out putting style of his peak years. I didn't have a single three-putt all day – and I don't think I left any first putts short, ramming home the three-foot come-backers without fear.

The shot I faced at 17, a par-3, was one I'd been nailing all day, the perfect 7-iron distance to the pin, which was up front in the narrow portion of the green, guarded by bunkers left and right. But my pulse quickened once I started thinking about my score. I took a deep breath, addressed the ball, and swung. My contact was less than perfect, a little thin. But in a strange way, it was almost a relief to see my ball take one hop into the left front bunker. Something was bound to go wrong, and now I had gotten it out of the way. Even though par was still a good possibility, I could afford a bogey, I reasoned, my first of the back nine. I played the tricky sand shot about as well as I could, but missed the 15-foot putt. Bogey.

Not to stretch the Hogan analogy too thin, but I later realized that the Hawk himself once hit a bad shot in a clutch moment on the 17th hole – in the famous 1960 U.S. Open at Cherry Hills. Deciding, uncharacteristically, to play aggressively to a front pin over water on a 55-yard approach on the par-5, Hogan came up just short, drowning his chances to win what would have been a record fifth Open title (at nearly 48 years of age).

In fact, in my study of golf history, I've marveled at how many of the greats hit bad shots in clutch situations. Even Palmer. Even Nicklaus. Even Tiger. Not to mention guys like Mickelson, Norman, and Snead, three men who seemed to have blown more than their share of big tournaments. If nothing else, I was in good company -- and I still had a one hole to play and a chance for a career round.

I've replayed that 18th hole in my head many times. Playing away from trouble on the right, I aimed my 3-wood down the left side of the wide fairway. Perhaps with a touch of adrenaline, I made great contact, hit it dead straight (for a change), and ran it through the dogleg into thick rough. As I'd been doing all day, I decided to play conservatively (what would Hogan do?). Realizing I'd need at least a 5-iron to reach the green, I pulled a 6 from my bag just to make sure it got it out of the rough. I didn't. The club caught in the grass and the shot traveled maybe 30 yards, hopping just into the first cut, the shorter rough. This time, the ball was sitting up. The yardage was another perfect 7-iron, and I hit it pure. "Be the right club today!" I said in a moment of cockiness, thinking of Hal Sutton's famous words at the 2000 Players Championship, when he beat Tiger down the stretch. But it was too much. The ball hit the middle of the green, took a big bounce, and ran onto the back fringe.

From there I faced perhaps a 35-foot double-breaker, which I stroked well but misread. It settled about three feet left of the hole. No problem, make this for a 76. All day long I'd just been ignoring the little aeration holes (little holes they put in the greens, usually once a year in the fall, to keep the soil from getting too compacted). But this time there was one particular, bigger-than-usual hole right in my line. At the start of the round, my friends and I had declared that moving balls out of the holes would be allowed when we marked a ball on the green, but we made no mention of holes in your putting line.

Again, Cherry Hills comes to mind, where 20-year-old amateur Jack Nicklaus faced a similar dilemma. Contending for the U.S. Open lead on the back nine on Sunday, young Jack faced a two-footer with an unrepaired ball mark directly in his line. Jack was so young and unseasoned that he wasn't sure if he was allowed to repair it (he was). And he was too intimidated by his legendary playing partner (Hogan) to ask. So he putted away – and missed. The mental effect of the miss was bigger than the stroke it cost him, and Jack was not a factor after that. (It was probably not Nicklaus's only mental error of the day, as Hogan was later quoted as saying, "I played 36 holes today with a kid – this Jack Nicklaus – who could have won this Open by 10 shots if he'd known what he was doing.")

So instead of asking for relief, I hit it firm and hoped for the best. But the ball hit the little hole right in the middle and took a big hop to the left. I tapped in for double-bogey and a 77. Five over: a great round for me, perhaps tying my best-ever on a quality course. And I won the White Lake Classic title by four strokes. But it was not the 74 or 75 I had in my sights.

Clearly, it was one of those situations where if you'd told me before the round I was going to shoot 77 and win by four, I'd have jumped for joy. Yet, I'm still haunted by what might have been. Two-under on the back nine through seven holes! I've never shot *under* par for nine holes, and have never even come close since that day.

What was so different that afternoon? I didn't change anything in my swing, so it must have been mental. What little switch turned on – or off! – to enable me to play so well?

Does it really take a "near-death" experience to get me to play to my potential!?

I learned early on as a golfer that pressure changes everything. And also that pressure is relative. As a boy, I faced no greater golf anxiety than the taunts of my friend Andy back at the old Par-3 course. The fear of failure caused me to tighten up like Tiger Woods at tipping time. And as I've since learned from Coach Carl, tension is the enemy of an effective golf swing.

Later, the greatest pressure I faced on a golf course was at the White Lake Classic. Nothing meant more to me than trying to win the coveted trophy each year. And you can see the effects of pressure quite clearly by examining my "qualifying" round vs. competitive round (or my front nine vs. back nine) scores.

The White Lake festivities typically consist of two rounds of golf. The first is a practice, or qualifying round. A tradition has developed that the pairings and order of play for the competitive round is determined by the practice round. Whoever shoots the best net score (including handicap) gets to choose what position they want to tee off in, 1 through 6 (or 7 before Andy died). I don't think that it would be boastful to say that I often win the practice round – it's just a fact! And when I win I always, always pick the #1 spot.

I do this for a couple of reasons. First and foremost, I like the statement of confidence. I like, in essence, giving myself the honor right off the bat. (In golf, whoever scores best on the previous hole tees off first on the next. This is called having "the honor.") It's a way of forcing myself to think positively. But I also just want to get that first shot over with. It's always a nervous moment for me, and the sooner I hit the first shot the sooner I can breathe out and start relaxing a little bit.

I'm not at all sure, however, that it really works that way. The first hole is a pretty straightforward par-5, and I'm always relieved to escape with a bogey. Sevens and 8s are not uncommon. But once that first shot and first hole are done, I tend to settle into a bit of a groove. The front nine at White Lake is longer and harder than the back, but I very typically make the turn with a decent score. We re-group according to the standings after nine holes, and I'm usually in the second group with the leaders.

And that's where the trouble starts!

I can't tell you how many times I've completely folded on the back nine and kicked away a good chance to win. Pressure strikes again. To be fair, I'm not by any stretch the only one who has succumbed. The history of the White Lake Classic is littered with the soiled underpants of many an otherwise steely-eyed competitor. I've won my share of WLC titles, but most often because others choke worse than I do.

Over the years I've tried different strategies to alleviate the pressure I put on myself. The most common (and fun) is boastful trash talk. I love talking and making jokes about how I'm going to kick everyone's butts at White Lake. Somehow, I believe that raising the pressure on myself to absurd levels makes it all seem ridiculous. I brag about how I'm going to win every year – to the point where no one takes it seriously. If I win I can say, "See, I told you so!" with a smile. If I lose, I can laugh along with everybody else at what I blowhard I am. Win-win.

This also helps me keep my own expectations to myself. If I have high hopes in a given year, nobody but me knows that. So any added pressure from raised expectations comes only from within, not from without. Does that help? Probably not much. Because I can get just as tense facing an 18th tee shot needing a par to break 80 playing alone as lining up a two-foot tap-in to win the WLC in front of my buddies.

Bottom line is: I'm a wreck when the pressure's on. No matter where it comes from. And with the much-anticipated 26th Annual White Lake Classic rapidly approaching, I wanted to do whatever I could to get my mental game in order.

People often say that "golf is 90% mental." As a young man I questioned that assessment. *How can that be?* I thought. After all, we're not talking about chess, or a crossword puzzle, or algebra. Sure, there's a little math involved when you're figuring out yardages, or adding up your score, I suppose. But it's still about *hitting* the ball, a 100 percent *physical* act. Right? It just didn't add up in my puny, hormone-addled, adolescent brain.

But later in life, as I studied the game and learned from my own experience, I realized that it's true. On the PGA Tour, for instance, every golfer is capable of playing well enough to win on any given week. The *ability* to win is there. Yet some never do – while others win consistently. And while it's true that some golfers have more "tools" than others (such as Tiger Woods in his prime), it's their ability to play up to their potential on a consistent basis that separates the winners and also-rans on Tour. And *that* is primarily a mental challenge.

That 77 I shot – which could easily have been a 74 or 75 if I hadn't snapped out of the "zone" I was in – showed me what I was capable of achieving on a golf course, crappy swing and all. My "tools" were adequate to be a golfer who breaks 80 almost every time. But truth be told, that score was more frustrating than gratifying. Frustrating because the 75 was right there in my grasp, sure. But also because it made me wonder, "Why can't I do that every time I play? Why am I so … *mental*?"

An entire cottage industry has grown up around the mental – even spiritual – side of golf. Books about those topics line the shelves at the few remaining brick-and-mortar bookstores. A quick search online will unearth many dozens of titles. Not to mention that so many top professionals employ not just a swing coach but a "mental coach" or sports psychologist, as well.

"But Mike," you may be thinking, "I suck at golf. I can't break 100 to save my life. My drives go too short and my putts go too long and my friends laugh at my inability to get the ball out of a sand trap without kicking it. Are you saying it's all in my head?"

Not completely, my frustrated friend! Your mind will only let you hit a golf ball as well as your body knows how to hit it. If you haven't trained your body to swing in a fashion that allows your golf club to make solid contact with a golf ball, your brain is of no use to you once you step on to the first tee. In fact, in may well do you more harm than good. Why do you think so many casual golfers drink beer while they play!?

And who among us has not staggered off the 18th green and thought to himself: "I don't understand. I was hitting them *so well* on the driving range!"

That's the key. If you really were hitting them great on the range, that shows that your body already knows how to hit a good golf shot. The trick then becomes training your mind to stand aside and let it happen. As Romeo the caddy (Cheech Marin) said to Roy McAvoy (Kevin Costner) in *Tin Cup*, after he helped the squirrelly pro stop hitting shanks on the U.S. Open practice range: "Your brain was getting in the way!"

Keeping your brain out of the way is a struggle for pros and amateurs alike. And when you boil them down to their essence, that's what most of the books are about. Each just has its own way of approaching it.

As the White Lake Classic approached, I started thinking more and more about the mental game. One thing I tried to get my mind right was re-visit a book by Dr. Bob Rotella, a renowned psychologist who works with a lot of Tour pros. I had read *Golf is Not a Game of Perfect* a few years earlier, and it was eye-opening. It seemed to address all the mental issues I struggled with and offered some concrete ways of dealing with them.

A lot of it is simply about positive thinking. Little things like focusing on the positive *result* of a shot rather what might go wrong. When you're playing (as opposed to practicing), don't think about the mechanics of your swing, think about where you want the ball to go. If those things seem deceptively simple, they are. Easy to say, much harder to do. Rotella sums it up: "You cannot hit a golf ball consistently well if you think about the mechanics of your swing as you play."

It was revolutionary to me to compare a golf swing to a throwing motion. That is … back when I played softball, after I scooped up a ground ball I didn't think about what my elbow was doing or my shoulder rotation as I prepared to throw the ball to first base. I just focused on the target, the first baseman's mitt.

Ideally, that's where you want to get as a golfer – so that you don't think about your swing any more than you would about your throwing motion. Emphasis on "ideally." A golf swing is far more complex than a throw to first base – complicated by the fact that you have this long, funny-shaped stick between your hand(s) and the ball you're trying to propel.

Another important principle is that to play your best golf you have to play as if you don't care about the outcome. This frees you from over-thinking and helps you swing more freely. It's the state of mind I was in following my hospital stay – but it's a very difficult state to create. And it can be a very delicate balance to maintain a carefree attitude with focusing on what you're doing. That paradox is one of the things that makes golf so difficult.

Back in college, I played a lot of serious pool – a game that shares many similarities with golf when played at a high level. One of the books I read on the game – *Mastering Pool* by George Fels – contained an entire chapter on the mental challenge of pocket billiards. Fels observed that "so many top players were phenomenally good when phenomenally young." He theorized that this was because young guys tend to have less on their minds – they're less burdened by the responsibilities, pressures, and expectations that generally come with more candles on your cake. Thus they're better equipped to more readily slip into "The Zone" that athletes so often talk about, where everything just seems to click and performance is at its peak.

In golf, think of the "putt like a kid" concept we discussed in Chapter 2.

Another popular book on the mental game is *Zen Golf* by Dr. Joseph Parent, which applies principles of Buddhism to the challenges of golf, and came highly recommended by Rob. It's hard for me to get onboard with the Buddhist angle, but reading the book I realized the principles being taught are very similar to what Rotella preaches.

There are so many different approaches to achieving the ideal mental state for playing golf that author Josh Karp wrote a whole book about them: *Straight Down the Middle*. After traveling the world seeking out the widest variety of golf teachers, spiritualists, and mental coaches he could find to help sharpen his golfing acumen, he concludes in part: "Don't try too hard. Don't think too much. Enjoy the game. That's what it's there for. That's what I've learned."

In other words: Relax! Can that really be so hard?

At lunch one day, I told Coach Carl about my epic collapse at Stone Creek and talked about the mental game in general. I told him that I had relived those last two holes many times, and often concluded that I was more a victim of bad luck than bad shots. It was really just two bad shots, I explained: the bladed tee shot on 17 (into the sand trap) and the chunky 6-iron from the rough on 18. The tee shot on 18 (through the fairway into the rough) and the second approach shot (which hit the green and bounced over) were both very ... *understandable*.

But Coach wasn't buying it. Those two shots may have been "unfortunate," but they were also most definitely mental errors.

On the tee shot, I was overly cautious of the trouble on the right. Instead of visualizing a nice gentle fade down the middle of the fairway, I was thinking about *not* going into the rough and/or water on the right. And so I overcompensated by tugging it left. Sure, I hit it flush and it went far and straight – but too far and too straight. It would have been a great outcome on a lot of other holes, but not on this one.

On the recovery shot, it's easy to say, "It was just a bad lie." But I knew it was a bad lie, right? Yep. I even compensated for it by taking one less club than I felt I needed to get to the green. But the truth is I probably should not even have been thinking about getting to the green. All day long I had done a great job of "taking my medicine" when I found myself in a tough spot. Twice, in fact, I had saved par by punching back into the fairway, sticking my third shot close, and making the putt. But I lost sight of that strategy when the heat was on and tried to do too much with it.

The third shot, the one that bounced over the green, is the one where I really felt cheated. I hit it perfect. When it was in the air I thought it was going to end up near the hole. I was already thinking about saving my par. Instead it bounced through the green to the back fringe.

Just bad luck, right? Not so fast, said Coach Carl.

"Like you said, on the second shot you advanced the ball about 30 yards, and then knocked the 7-iron over the green. Probably because you were mad, you were pumped up. And of course a ball out of the rough is going to go farther [because it has less backspin], and you weren't thinking about that," he explained, effectively bursting my bubble of self-pity.

"Those are the timeouts you gotta take, and think to yourself, 'What am I trying to do here?' What's the condition, what's the situation? You have to be able to take those elements and analyze, quickly, what the end result might be. I got a flyer lie, it's downwind, or crosswind, or into the wind. If I do hit it short it's going to jump up because it's not going to have a lot of spin on it. As it was, you hit the green and it bounced over. Those are things you have to slow down and think about in situations like that."

So what your saying is … it *was* my fault? Dang!

And then there's the matter of the missed three-foot putt. Surely that was just bad luck, right? Well, maybe. But the truth is I could have taken a moment and asked for a ruling from my buddies. If I'd asked permission to move my ball to avoid the hole, they may have said "no" – and I might have missed the putt anyway. But at least it would have been "on the record" that I was putting over the Grand Canyon, which may have at least garnered a little more sympathy after I missed! Taking that extra moment to calm my nerves may have helped, too.

Instead, I'm doomed to play the "What If?" game for the rest of my life.

In my own experience, the most powerful tool for achieving relaxation on the golf course is *perspective* – as evidenced by my first 16 holes at Stone Creek that day. But there was one other time when I was able to put the game in its proper place and play the best golf of my life. And I have Jesus to thank for it.

It happened one summer in the late 1990s. After many years of wandering far away from God (I'll spare you my checkered and complicated religious past), and still conspicuously single, I started seeking higher meaning in my life. This led me back to church, to a "born-again" experience, and suddenly, unexpectedly, inner peace on the golf course.

The result was I started playing the consistently best golf of my life, breaking 80 about half the time. It wasn't because God had suddenly improved my swing or started supernaturally guiding my approaches to greens and my putts into holes. It was simply because I was more relaxed on the golf course than I had ever been. I realized that I had put far too much of my self worth into my golfing ability. Bad rounds or even bad shots had begun to feel like little personal tragedies. But "coming to Jesus" and the meaning it brought me put golf in a much better perspective.

I'll be the first to admit that this sudden surge didn't last forever. After that one glorious summer I settled back into a more "normal" mid/low-80s range of scoring. I'm not sure why the improvement didn't last longer. But I do know it wasn't a change in my swing that caused it, but rather a change of heart.

When Bubba Watson sank that one-foot putt – following his famous miracle hook from the trees – to win the Masters in 2012 (and become the first *true* lefty to win a major), he broke down and cried like a baby. Bubba is a *very* emotional guy, as we all learned that day. We also learned that he has amazing "tools" – he can do things with a golf ball, shaping his shots to curve left and right at will, that most others can only dream about doing. With his unconventional homemade swing, he also drives the ball farther than just about anybody else in the game.

So, why did it take Bubba so long to start winning? He was 33 years old when he won the Masters – and 31 before he won his first PGA Tour tournament in 2010. Before that, he labored on Tour for four years without a win, following three years on what is today called the Web.com Tour (golf's equivalent of the minor leagues).

Today Bubba is a two-time Masters champion and one of the biggest stars in the game. Not just because of his victories, but also because of his carefree personality and approach to life. His 2011 post-Masters media tour – including his now-famous appearance on David Letterman's show – endeared him to millions who had never heard of him. Along with Ben Crane, Hunter Mahan, and his good friend Rickie Fowler, he is a member of the notorious "Golf Boys," a popular boy band parody that produces silly videos (in which Bubba appears to be wearing nothing but an ill-fitting pair of overalls) and raises money for charity.

He is known for purchasing (and often driving) the original "General Lee" car from the old "The Dukes of Hazzard" TV show, and in 2013, a video about his new hovercraft golf cart went viral, adding to the legend of this fun-loving hillbilly from Baghdad, Florida who hits the golf ball a country mile.

But it wasn't always this way. There was a time, before he started winning, when Bubba was a completely different guy – at least on the golf course. He was known not for making videos and driving hovercrafts – and certainly not for winning – but rather for the temper tantrums he threw on the golf course. (Truth be told, he's still occasionally subject to this unfortunate tendency.)

It got so bad that his caddy – Ted Scott, a fellow Christian whom Watson hired in part to help keep him on the straight and narrow – pulled him aside and read him the riot act. If Bubba didn't get his act together and start behaving more like a gentleman on the golf course, he could find himself a new caddy.

He meant it, and Bubba knew it. The fact that his friend would be so blunt with him got the message across, and served as a wake-up call for Bubba.

It's no coincidence that Bubba started winning not long after. Following his win in the 2011 Zurich Classic, Todd Lewis of the Golf Channel asked him: "Your first 121 starts on the PGA Tour, no wins. Your last 19 starts, three victories. What has changed over the last few months?"

"Realizing that golf is nothing," Bubba replied. "It doesn't mean anything to me. I win today, tomorrow I'm hosting a Nationwide event, hoping to raise some money for some good charities in

Athens, Georgia. I'll be on a plane in just a second, and that's what it's all about. It's all about the stuff [away from] golf. It's all about raising the money for the kids, doing the junior tournaments that I do, that's what means more to me. And family means the most to me."

In the interviews I've seen, Bubba has never said outright that this transformation was what you might call "a God thing." And he's not one of those guys who first thanks God for a victory in the post-round interview. But Bubba is otherwise very outspoken about his Christian faith, regularly posting Bible verses and other words of spiritual encouragement on Twitter.

And when it comes to putting your golf game in the hands of a Higher Power, Bubba and I aren't the only ones who have found success. There are a lot of outspoken Christians on the PGA Tour, many of whom are not shy about thanking God first, foremost, and publicly after a victory. Admittedly, this rubs a lot of people the wrong way. "You can't tell me that God doesn't have better things to worry about than who wins a golf tournament!" is a common complaint.

But it's important to remember that these guys aren't claiming that God favored them over anybody else, or supernaturally guided their shots in any way. They are simply acknowledging the source of the inner peace that allows them to keep their wits and succeed on the golf course (a peace that's available to anybody, by the way, just for the asking!).

For most of us, golf is just a game. But a good portion of the joy of it comes from playing it well. So it can be very easy when a personal best score, or a free lunch, or even just bragging rights are on the line on the closing holes to forget about "perspective." Even more so when the goal is to win the coveted White Lake Classic trophy! Yet if I were going to be triumphant in my left-handed WLC debut, that's exactly what I would have to do: keep things in perspective.

Hmmm ... maybe it would be easier to just have a mild heart attack. Pass the cheese curds, please!

CHAPTER 10
The Final Approach

"Golf is deceptively simple and endlessly complicated; it
satisfies the soul and frustrates the intellect. It is at the same
time rewarding and maddening – and it is without a doubt
the greatest game mankind has ever invented."

–Arnold Palmer

For 23 years, Carl Unis was head professional at Brynwood Country
Club in Milwaukee. It was a great life, teaching Milwaukee's upper-
middle-class golfers how to improve their game while imparting
hard-earned wisdom gleaned from the fairways of life.

But things took a turn into the deep rough when his marriage
fell apart. A short time later, to make matters worse, he parted ways
with the club. He was 52 years old.

"Stuff happens," he told me plainly, and reluctantly. But he tried
hard not to let it faze him. He still had two boys to take care of.

"The problem was I didn't know where I was going with it," he
said. "It was day-to-day, you know? I tried to apply for other jobs,
but it was like ... you might call it a mid-life crisis situation. It's tough
to start fresh at that age."

On the plus side, time away from the daily grind left him with
some extra quality time to spend with C.J. and Alex. They went
fishing, hung out, and grew closer than ever.

Eventually, he got a call from Dennis Tiziani, a long-time
Wisconsin club pro best known today as the coach (and father-in-
law) of Wisconsin's favorite touring pro, Steve Stricker. Dennis asked
Carl if he'd be interested in taking over as executive director of the
Wisconsin Golf Foundation (WGF), which benefited all the allied

golf organizations in Wisconsin, such as the Wisconsin State Golf Association (WSGA), the Wisconsin PGA, the state junior golf association, and others.

Carl jumped at the new opportunity.

"As executive director I wore a lot of hats," he says. "Fundraiser, administrator, event organizer. I started the Junior PGA program we have now, but back then it was known as the Golf Foundation Junior Tour."

The Junior Tour was of special interest to Coach Carl, combining his love of the sport and his passion for coaching and mentoring young people. Over the years, a lot of highly successful golfers went through the program, including Mark Wilson, a five-time PGA Tour winner.

"A lot of good players that played that junior tour are now pros in the state or elsewhere."

He was also instrumental in starting the local chapter of the First Tee, a program run by the PGA of America that uses golf to instill "life-enhancing values" in young people. He secured a $5,000 grant from the USGA (United States Golf Association) and another $5,000 from local businessman Steve Marcus (of the Marcus Corporation).

Four years after he started, however, the foundation's board decided to "go in another direction," as boards so often say when personal politics are involved. It was another tough blow, as Carl had built the foundation from nearly nothing to a very solid organization.

"I left it in pretty good shape," he says. And Carl still takes satisfaction in knowing Wisconsin golf is in good hands.

"I would have liked to see it come to fruition a little bit more on my watch," he says. "Because that sort of thing, developing golf and golfers, has always been a passion of mine."

Once again, Coach Carl found himself without a definite career path to follow. It was a tough spot to be in, but again, he looked to his past to find the strength he'd need.

"I've always been a survivor," he says. "Never had a dad. Been working since I was 7 years old, selling peanuts at the Browns and Indians games down in Cleveland. Worked my way into the stadium selling programs, and selling ice cream after the games. And, you know, I've always been somewhat entrepreneurial. So I figured I'd just pick myself up by the bootstraps, and let's go from here! It's just another bump in the road. A couple bumps in the road. Well, we can survive that.

"My mom always told me if you have your health you have your wealth, and I didn't know what she meant by that. But I do now. So, fortunately enough, throughout my golf career I've been very, very healthy. I've had very few injuries. So I was able to pull myself up by the bootstraps and go."

He realized that the two things he loved most – playing and teaching – were still there for him. So he rededicated himself to playing and made his own opportunities to teach. The results have been pretty spectacular.

Previously, before he left Brynwood in 1990, Carl was the 1984 Wisconsin PGA Match Play Champion, as well as runner-up in the Stroke Play Championship in 1969 and '83. He also twice finished second in the Wisconsin State Open, in 1977 and '79. In 1979, he was named the Wisconsin Golf Professional of the Year.

On the national scene, he qualified for the National Club Professional Championship 18 times, earning medalist honors on four occasions.

As an administrator, he was president of the Wisconsin Section PGA from 1980-81. He also served on the board of the Greater Milwaukee Open from 1981-1994, and competed in the tournament 14 times.

In the senior ranks he really began to shine. He was the Wisconsin Senior PGA Champion and Senior PGA Player of the Year in 1990 and 1998, which qualified him to represent Wisconsin in the National Club Professional Senior Championship. From 1988-1990 he played eight events on the PGA Senior Tour (now the Champions Tour).

But it was as teacher where he made his biggest impact. Among his students that won statewide or national titles are senior player Gary Menzel, high schooler Tina Kocinski, and top amateur Mike McDonald.

Menzel won the Wisconsin State Golf Association (WSGA) Senior Amateur Championship seven times and the WPGA Senior Open four times, along with a bucketful of other titles. In 1999 he made it all the way to the finals of the USGA Senior Open. He was elected to the WSGA Hall of Fame in 2005. He credits Coach Carl for the bulk of his success.

"I've been very fortunate," he says. "I've won quite a few

tournaments. And it all goes back to what I learned from Carl, and all those lessons through the years. Carl's the guy.

"The other thing is, Carl has always been a friend. In thick and thin, he's there. He's always asking how things are going with the family and everything. And he's gone through some rough things in his life, too. Through it all, Carl has always been a good guy."

Another Coach Carl success story is Tina Kocinski (now Tina Stencovage), who won the Wisconsin State High School Girls Championship in 2001. Coach Carl worked with Tina from the time she was about 11 until she graduated high school and headed to Penn State University on a golf scholarship.

"Coach Carl was really inspiring and encouraging," she says. "He actually went out on the course and coached me, helped me find areas to improve my game. Not only on the driving range, but he'd always go the extra mile to help me out. If I needed some help before a tournament, or wasn't feeling confident, he would be there for me. So that was really nice.

"And I think it helped elevate my mental game, too," she says. "I had this little book, and every week or two he would write down something for me to work on or improve. It was always positive. That's one of the reasons I really like working with him, he always kept it positive. I can tell you I saw a lot of golf coaches over the years, other people's coaches could be so negative. I'm sure you know, the name of the game is confidence. So having someone that was able to bring forth positives was really great to have around."

Coach Carl is proud of all his students, of course, but he seems most proud of Mike McDonald, who he worked with since Mike was just 8 years old. Mike's dad started teaching Mike the game when he was just a toddler, but soon realized his son had a talent he wouldn't be able to fully develop on his own.

"My dad was at the Golf Dome and he started asking around about a coach," Mike says. "Carl came highly recommended by a number of people, so he gave him a call, and that's how it all started.

"He's been my first and only golf teacher I've ever known. I wouldn't have it any other way."

After finding a lot of success at the junior level, Mike led his high school team to the state tournament for the first time in its history. It was enough to draw the attention of Marquette University, which recruited Mike and offered him a scholarship after his sophomore year. College golf was a tougher transition than he expected, but Coach Carl was there to help guide him through it all.

"It's kind of funny to look at how a relationship progresses," he says. "Carl's and mine has gone so well that he's the only guy that I would ever go to to look at my swing. Because there's more in the relationship than just golf now."

It's a partnership that was instrumental in Mike winning the Wisconsin State Amateur Championship in 2011. After a strong 68 in the third round, Mike entered the final round just one shot out of the lead. It was new territory for him, but a phone message from the coach helped calm his nerves and get him in a winning mindset.

"Yeah, Carl called me, and he always would just tell me, just 'Stay within, Mikey.' He's ingrained that into me from the first time I played tournament golf. One shot, one hole at a time. You can't get ahead of yourself. Just stay in the moment.

"And that's exactly what I did out there. I stuck to my game plan, I stayed to that one shot, on every hole. I knew what I wanted to do, I knew what I needed to do, and it worked out, it happened."

He won the tournament by a stroke after a solid 72.

Even more important than landing on his feet professionally, I'm happy to report that Coach Carl has found the love of his life. After about five years of having no particular interest in romance, some friends introduced him to Carole Gray.

Carole's husband had died after 27 years of marriage. Like Carl, she wasn't really interested in meeting anyone new. It was too soon, she felt. But as it turned out, both she and Carl were born and raised in Cleveland, so they connected right away. A few days after their initial meeting, Carl called Carole on the phone.

"It was really funny," she says. "He said, 'This is Carl Unis, I don't know if you remember me or not, but I met you at the Range Line Inn the other night.' I said, 'Vaguely.' I was being silly! And he said, "Well, I was wondering if you'd like to go to a [Milwaukee] Bucks game.' I said, "Sure, I'd love to! When?' And he said, 'I'll pick you up in 20 minutes.' And that's how our life started!"

"She swept me off my feet!" Coach Carl told me on more than one occasion. "I can't say enough how instrumental she's been in my life. We have four children between us – C.J., Alex, Peter, and Betsy – along with eight grandchildren!

"We're a blended family and it's like we've been together all our lives. So life is good! Life is definitely good."

• • •

Life was good on that beautiful day in early October, too. Mee-Kwon Golf Course looked great. The leaves were just starting to turn and the sky was filled with sunshine. But I didn't notice those things. I was focused – probably too focused – on the task ahead of me. I really wanted to play well. And to impress Coach Carl, who was there to give me my first-ever "playing lesson."

Nerves were a factor on the first tee, I have no trouble admitting. My opening drive was not great, a pull to the left … I mean *right*! (It's weird how I still think of a pulled shot as going left.) Coach immediately offered up what he called a "lunch ball," a term I'd never heard before. Basically a first-tee mulligan. And since there's no driving range at Mee-Kwon for warming up, I always figure that's fair. So I took another with only slightly better results. Still to the right, but not as far.

Then Coach hit his opening drive – though I have no absolutely no recollection of that shot.

I'll confess right up front I paid very little attention to how Coach Carl was playing. As at Morningstar, I was too caught up in my own stuff. I do remember he was really consistent. And that I got the impression he didn't have his best game that day. But every now and then you could see flashes of the skills that helped him make that U.S. Open cut. He doesn't hit the ball very far anymore, but I could tell just by the sound, by the crispness of his shots, that he plays at a higher level than I ever have.

After I tracked down my ball in the first cut of rough, I was faced with about 150 yards to the green on the short par-4. I hit a 7-iron a little chunky, and left it short. I hit a good chip to about eight feet, but missed the putt and took a bogey 5. Not a bad way to start at all. I'd take an opening bogey any day.

Coach may have eagled the hole for all I know.

Things went downhill, literally and figuratively, on the number 2. From an elevated tee, the par-4 second hole doglegs to the right, with out-of-bounds on the left and trees to the right. I hit a driver high and to the left, but got a break when it stayed in play, short of the O.B. From the rough I hit a horrible second shot, and then a mediocre hybrid short and left of the green. A familiar spot! My chip was also mediocre, followed by a routine two-putt for double-bogey. But still not a disaster.

On the par-3 third I missed a five-footer for par after a good chip and settled for a bogey. On four, a tricky par-5, I left an 8-foot par putt short. I explained to Coach Carl that I've been kind of timid on putts, worrying about blasting it past. He said, "Well, do you know what the research says about the percentage of putts left short that go in?"

"Still zero?" I replied.

Point taken!

Another missed putt (a bad read this time) after another nice chip led to one more bogey on the fifth. And same again on the par-3 sixth: a bad tee shot, a nice recovery, a makeable par putt and another miss. I was avoiding disasters but wasting a lot of opportunities. I was shooting just what I deserved, getting away with some bad shots but missing makeable putts.

Same story on #7: three mediocre shots followed by a routine two-putt and a bogey. Through seven holes I had five bogeys and two double-bogeys. Not bad, really, but not good enough to break 90. It was frustrating not to have any pars yet.

Then things got very interesting on eight. Coach, of course, had been instructing me all along the way. Not in a big way, but little reminders here and there. On the eighth tee, he mentioned that he thought I was squeezing the club too tight at impact. I'm sure he was right; it's one of my consistent mistakes. Goes right along with my trying too hard, thinking too much about score, and putting too much pressure on myself. It adds tension – which I now know is the enemy when it comes to a nice, fluid golf swing.

Good advice, but of course I thought about it *too* much. While focusing on loosening my grip tension I forgot about nearly everything else. I pulled way up out of the swing and topped the ball badly. And that's probably putting it too kindly. It may in fact have been only the force of the wind I generated that knocked the ball off the tee. Whatever it was, the ball dribbled forward only about 10 feet. As bad a shot as I've ever hit.

"Hit another one," Coach said calmly.

So I did. This one was better, but again I pulled it badly; the ball settled near a pine tree to the right of the fairway. I was embarrassed by the first shot, frustrated by the second, and visibly agitated, I'm sure. Coach calmed me down and then told me to try again. He told me to focus on letting my arms "chase" the ball down the target line on my follow-through; that is, as opposed to trying to steer the ball. So that's what I did, and *Voila!* I hit the best drive of the day, by far. Flush down the middle, straight as an arrow, with plenty of distance.

As we made our way down the fairway, I asked Coach to explain the difference between those three swings.

"The first one you moved totally *up*," he said. "You were trying to use your body to create a lot of clubhead speed. [Probably to overcompensate for the light grip pressure, I thought.] So you changed, you went *up*, and you came right over the top of the ball.

"The second one, you just got too quick. It looked like you were up on your toes at impact, so you pulled with your hands over to the right. And on the last one, where you just *creamed* it, you just let the club do the work. You *swung* the club, you didn't try to *hit* the ball. You were more swing conscious than ball conscious."

So simple, right? If only! Why is it so hard to just get out of the way and let my body do what it already knows how to do?

Then I had to decide which ball to play. I had already picked up the first one, the terrible top, but I wanted to keep my score at least *somewhat* legitimate, so I picked up the perfect drive and went over to the second ball, which had just made its way under the branches of the pine tree. Ironically, if I were swinging right-handed, I would have been fine, but I couldn't really get at the ball left-handed. I thought about flipping a club over and punching it out righty, but decided to keep things "pure." So I backed into the tree the best I could, with razor-sharp pine needles tearing the flesh from my bones, and tried to whack it out.

I got it away from the tree, but not much further. The ball settled into the light rough to the right of the fairway, and from there I hit my best approach shot of the day: a flushed 7-iron that sent the ball on a laser line to the hole. Must have still had good thoughts in my head from the good drive that didn't count. The ball landed softly in the middle of the green, about 20 feet from the hole, and I two-putted from there for a bogey five – with a nice juicy asterisk because of the adventures on the tee. (If I had played the first drive, I would have been very fortunate to score a bogey!)

I closed out the front nine with a frustrating double-bogey on the par-4 ninth, including another makeable putt I left short of the hole on a perfect line. As we tallied up our scores at the turn, Coach and I found a discrepancy. I had put myself down for a double-bogey six on a hole where he wrote down a five. I couldn't say for sure he was right, so I decided to stick with the six, perhaps as further penance for going mulligan crazy on the eighth tee. The result was a semi-respectable 48. I would have to do something sorta special on the back nine to break 90.

The good news was, I like the back nine better. So I was reasonably optimistic that I could do well – even though I did not officially care about the score. Officially.

The back nine started out pretty routinely, with two-putt bogeys on 10 and 11, both par-4s. No terrible shots, no particularly good ones, either. On 12, a very short par-4 playing into the wind, I hit a solid drive to the left fairway, followed by a slightly fat wedge to the front of the green. Two putts later I was on the board with a par.

Thirteen, my "nemesis hole" at Mee-Kwon, is a par-4 that goes down into a valley and then back up to an elevated green. In the valley on the right, extending about halfway into the fairway, are several large bunkers. Up the hill, the left side of the green is guarded by another bunker. A tough hole. But it's also one that strikes me as unfair. That's because big hitters have no trouble blasting it over the fairway bunkers and back up the hill. Shorter hitters, regular people like me, have to deal with both the big sand traps and a tough, uphill shot to the green. But who am I to complain? Besides, that little chip on my shoulder probably gets into my head and makes it even harder for me to hit a good drive – because it's so much easier to picture a bad result than a good one.

In this case I got a little lucky. I hit my driver a little off the heel, but it faded just enough to avoid the traps and end up in the fairway, down at the bottom of the valley. I was looking at about 150 yards to go, straight up the hill. I decided to play it fairly conservative and hit a 6-iron. I wound up and hit it dead *flush*. I pulled it pretty far right, however, which kept me well clear of the greenside bunker, and also pretty far off the green. From there I hit a very nice sand wedge to about six feet, but couldn't sink the putt. Bogey 5, I'll take it on that hole for sure.

Hole 14 is the easiest hole on the course – or at least it should be: a short par-3, downhill to a nice, wide green. I pulled my 8-iron out of the bag, but switched to a 9 when the breeze, which was at our backs, picked up a little. Unfortunately, I bladed it and pushed it off to the right – I mean *left* – a little short of the green. Another nice chip, this time to about eight feet, and another missed putt for another bogey.

So far on the back, I was still avoiding big mistakes but also not taking advantage of opportunities. I was one shot ahead of bogey pace, but felt like I should be doing even better.

Fifteen is a double-dogleg (right then left) par-5, turning back up the hill. I hit my best drive of the day to the middle of the fairway! Too bad I was aiming right, which would have cut off some distance, but I was in no position to complain. I rushed my second, flaring it left and short with a 3-wood, then hit another pulled 6-iron to the right of the green, behind a big trap. A bladed sand wedge and two putts later I was in with another frustrating bogey.

Sixteen is another par-3, and I got lucky with a "good miss" with a 6-iron. My bladed shot faded ingloriously onto the front of the green, about 20 feet from the hole. I misread the first putt and missed by about five feet, but finally made a five-footer for another par.

Suddenly, I was two ahead of bogey pace, still with a chance for that 41 I was after.

Seventeen is that longish par-4 with a big sand trap guarding the right side of the fairway, tricky for me as a lefty. With the pressure mounting, I kept my cool and hit a nice driver that just skirted the left edge of the trap, rolling out into the middle of the fairway. A good hybrid left me just short of the green, in the rough by the trap guarding the left side. I hit down on the ball to make good contact and keep it low to run it up to the hole. I hit it just a bit thin, but it headed right for the hole. For a moment I thought it might go in – "Coach, look! Look, Coach, quick!!! – but it stopped just short. Tap-in par 4.

All I had to do now to break 90 was keep my head and make a bogey or par on the dogleg-left, uphill par-5 18th. I asked Coach if he thought I should hit a 3-wood or driver. He said to hit the big stick, since the wind was coming across from the left and into our faces a little bit. So I visualized hitting a nice little fade that would clear the trap, hang up in the breeze, and drop softly into the center of the fairway around the corner.

What I hit, however, was something entirely different. Almost the opposite, in fact. Instead of a high, soft fade, I hit a low, hard hook. It scooted down the side and settled in the rough maybe 150 yards out. Coach had me hit another, and I did the same thing again – though this time a little less severe. Not a great way to start the last, crucially important(!) hole.

Again, in the interest of integrity, I played the first drive, the worse one. When I got there I realized it wasn't really that horrible. It was in the rough, probably 180 or 190 or so yards from the green, up a fairly steep hill. I hit a fluffy hybrid that popped up and traveled maybe 120 yards. The good news was I was in the middle of the fairway, looking up the hill to a front pin placement.

I figured I had maybe 70 yards or so to the pin, so I pulled a sand wedge from my bag. But then I considered the hill and the wind and switched to a pitching wedge, figuring a low punch, a bit of a "bump and run," would be the shot to hit.

I struck it well, but too hard. It flew onto the green and kept going, just trickling off the back edge of what is probably the largest green on the course. Fortunately, I hit a nice chip and made a clutch five-footer to save my bogey.

Did I do it? Did I break 90? YES! The scorecard read 48-41 for a nice total of 89. The 41 was especially gratifying, with six bogeys and three pars. No double-bogeys! I considered a double-free round a nice accomplishment when I was at my peak as right-hander.

Yes, there was reason for celebration. But not too much. I had to keep in mind a few things. For one, Mee-Kwon is just a par 70, which makes breaking 90 a little easier. Also, it makes a *huge* difference to have your coach with you helping on every shot. (I once read a story about how Hall of Fame golfer Tommy Aaron won a big bet by teaming with an amateur. The condition of the wager was that Tommy's partner had to do what he said on every shot. He then went out and shot the best round he ever had, by a good margin.)

Plus, I did have that one mulligan.

But all in all it was very gratifying. I hit a lot of good shots, and confirmed that I had it within me to play some pretty good golf as a lefty. It was just going to take more practice to get more consistent.

On the other hand, thinking about that last hole, it was still a little frustrating that I so often would play a hole without feeling like I hit any good shots – and still come away with a bogey. That meant my short game was pretty solid, but it also meant my short game was covering up a lot of my deficiencies. That's not a bad thing, but hitting a heroic drive or sticking a long approach close to the pin is a lot more *fun* than getting up and down.

Afterward, I bought Coach a soda and we reviewed the round. I asked him what he thought I most need to work on. What he said next *shocked* me!

"Well, I saw a lot of, uh … anxiety," he began. (I wasn't actually shocked.) "You don't take time enough to set up and let yourself get in balance. If you don't get in balance right in the beginning, your hands are going to take over. When you're in balance, you can make your turn and feel your arms just *going* to the target. But when you're going to your toes, your hands take over."

Interesting. "Is that my most consistent problem," I asked, "getting my weight too far forward?"

"Yeah. On your forward swing. You tip to your toes. The biggest thing you should work on is keeping your chest away from the ball. That's the simplest way I can tell you to stay up: chest up. So that you can swing underneath yourself. Otherwise, you go down and you're pulling in. I hope that makes sense."

It did. But I asked him to elaborate on the anxiety part. What are the symptoms, how can he tell? Do I get a little hurried, a little quick?

"Yeah," he said. "The quick, jerky motions in getting set up."

"That's interesting," I said, "because in my mind I felt like I was taking my time. Which maybe says something about my internal clock?"

"Yeah. In your mind you were going slow, but physically it didn't seem that way. That's the only way I can describe it."

So I'm fast and jerky and instead of slow and smooth. I can work on that!

But Coach, isn't there anything *nice* you want to say about me?

"By and large I was very impressed, in this short period of time, with how you handled yourself out there," he said. "I mean, that one tee shot was the only one, the only scud that came into play today. But other than that, other than coming up a little bit, everything else was pretty good.

"I mean, you're breaking 90. I think that's outstanding."

Beaming with pride, I reminded him about the big weekend, the WLC tournament, coming up. I told him about how I always do well in the practice round, and always seem to fall apart in the tournament round. I asked him what I could do to *mentally* prepare myself for that.

"You gotta think that the tournament round is a practice round. It's about being able not to try so hard. One-and-two. One-and-two. Keep that rhythm in check Remember, the only person that makes it hard on you is you. If you're able to manage yourself and cope with your inner peace, if you allow the inner peace to happen, it will happen.

"It's like, I talked to my student that won the state amateur [Mike McDonald] before the final round. I told him that he had to have inner peace and let the golf course come to him, which he did. He started out bogey-bogey, but he got it together and won the tournament. To score you have to let the golf course come to you. You can't worry about scoring.

"You were thinking about scoring on 18 today. I mean, you weren't that bad off after the tee shot. And the second shot, you didn't catch it all. But all you had to do was get it on the green and possibly make your four. You're not going to hit every green. And I've learned that in the last few years, because I'm not as strong as I used to be, so I have to make up for it with my chipping and putting. When it's on I'm very good; when it's off I stink. But, you know, I'm still able to enjoy it. I'm still on this side of the grass. What am I going to do, go fight it now? Whatever happens, I'm going to go with it. Whatever takes place, I'm still going to enjoy it."

At first I thought he hadn't really answered my question, about how to prepare for White Lake. But the more I thought about it, the more I realized he had answered a *larger* one, about how to enjoy yourself on the golf course, no matter what. And that, as I already knew, is really the key to relaxing and playing well.

All things considered, it was one of the best days I've ever spent on a golf course. The next day at work, I sent this e-mail to Rob:

> I'm having a hard time at work today. Sitting in a couple of long boring meetings (right now!).
>
> Yesterday, in retrospect, was amazing. Not just playing well, but it was an amazingly beautiful day on a very beautiful golf course. The clubhouse is up on a hill overlooking the course -- "This is a country club view" was my comment to

THE WRONG SIDE OF THE BALL

Coach. We hung around a little bit afterward and talked about the round. I was just floating. Today, by contrast, I'm trapped in these stupid meetings talking about stuff I don't care about, thinking only about golf and my book (and a little about Jack's newfound love of swimming).

The thought that's in my head is, "I wonder if I could get a job at the golf course and supplement the meager pay by doing freelance work on the side?" (And writing best-selling books, of course.)

Even though it's a short week, it's going to be a long week. And I fear it's going to be even harder come next Monday.

"Next Monday" would be the Monday after White Lake. And I'd either be distracted by basking in the glow of a glorious victory ... or licking my wounds following a soul-crushing defeat.

But there I go, getting way too serious again! Somebody slap me.

CHAPTER 11
The Fifth Major

"If you watch a game, it's fun. If you play it, it's recreation.
If you work at it, it's golf."

—Bob Hope

"ROB TWARDOCK STEALS BAAA-ALLS!!"

The full-throated wail echoed through the still night air, resonating among the tall pines and majestic hardwoods that line the fairways of the venerable White Lake Golf Club. It was well after midnight – and even further past bedtime for the vast majority of those inhabiting the cottages dotting the shoreline and back roads surrounding Michigan's White Lake. Chances are, nobody but the raccoons and opossums and various other nocturnal species heard it. Yet as the final echo faded into the moonless night, six young men peered at each other through the near pitch-darkness, eyes wide open, mouths agape.

"Did he really just do that? Is he trying to get us all arrested?"

But Little Tommy ("L.T." for short – known today as Dr. Thomas Scaggs, an accomplished and respected emergency room physician and hospital administrator) was not happy. And who could blame him? He had been unceremoniously *ditched* by his six fellow "muckers." His offense? No one remembers. But his legacy endures. His frustrated accusatory outburst lives in White Lake Classic lore as one of the most memorable moments in nearly 30 years of the tournament we all consider the "Fifth Major."

It began as a free exchange of golf and accommodations for unskilled manual labor. In the spring of 1986, five years after our high school graduation, four of us (me, Rob, Mike, and Tom Lessaris) were invited by Rob's parents to spend nearly a week (a *week!*) at the family cottage, golf included. In return, we four young bucks would install the property's seasonal dock. In ice-cold pre-Memorial Day waters, it was a wholly unpleasant task. But still ... free golf! And lots of it.

Of course, there were more hours in the days (and nights) than it takes to put in a dock and play a few rounds of golf. And so it was that the remaining hours were filled with drinking beer, playing cards, eating, and (in the early years) "mucking" – known in more respectable circles as "sneaking onto the golf course very late at night and wading knee-deep into the mucky, muddy water hazards to surreptitiously swipe as many golf balls as possible."

Following that initial, ultra-exclusive event, our ranks began to swell – and the amount of work we were expected to perform diminished. The true reasons for this change are lost to the winds of history. But according to legend, it had something to do with shoddy construction, the frequent and unpredictable collapse of certain dock components, and possibly the occasional death and/or dismemberment of a beloved Twardock family member or guest. (Though that's never been proven in court.)

Within a few years, the field had reached full strength. Joining the original four (a.k.a. the "Founding Fathers") were Andy Stallman (of broken nose/cherry pie fame), Keith Staggs, and the aforementioned Tom Scaggs. And with the expanded field came a new handicap system. Rob and I were deemed to be the baseline "scratch" golfers, while others were assigned handicaps by the official "committee" (a.k.a. Rob, the tournament host), based very subjectively on past performance and some magical, mystical formula that existed only inside Rob's head. The only widely understood component of the formula was a strong bias against a defending champion. In 26 years of official competition, there had never been a repeat winner.

Back when all (or most) of us were still single, the Handicap Committee also chose an "honorary caddie" for that year's tournament, typically a young, blond, and buxom starlet. Once Rob himself tied the knot, the tradition mysteriously died away.

Since the inaugural event, various items and activities have been officially banned. According to most recollections, the smoking of cigars was the first to go. Unfortunately (for Rob), it didn't take Mike long to find a loophole. Just as quickly, the loophole was closed, and "pipes" were added to the list of contraband. Other banned items/activities include (but are not limited to):

- the melting of beer cans and bottles in campfires
- large black dogs that eat wicker furniture
- super-atomic wedgies
- mucking (though this pretty much died of natural causes as we aged)
- hitting old golf balls into the lake (related to item above)
- and, most recently, smoke bombs.

Due at least in part to the growing length of the "banned" list, the White Lake Classic has not always been held at White Lake. In fact, for a number of years the event became positively nomadic in nature, with tournaments held in Smith Mountain Lake, Virginia; Champaign, Illinois (multiple times); Door County, Wisconsin; Galena, Illinois; and even as far away as Portland, Oregon. The little cottage on White Lake, however, will always be the event's spiritual home, and remains (for all but the man who must bear the brunt of the hosting duties) the favorite locale by far.

Another sacred tradition in those early years was the post-tournament dinner at the nearby summer home of Rob's Uncle Wendel and Aunt Evelyn. I use the term "dinner" somewhat guardedly, because what began as a lavish, multi-course spread (featuring high-quality steak, premium beer, various tasty side dishes, and scrumptious desserts) gradually devolved into something closer to crackers and cheese washed down by store brand soda.

Perhaps I exaggerate a bit – or a lot. But that's the thing about White Lake lore. There's a lot of storytelling involved, and some events as we remember them may in fact bear little resemblance to actual, objective history.

But we cherished those gatherings, even as we joked about how the luxury level seemed to diminish. Truth is, Wendel and Evelyn were both getting on in years, and I'm sure it became more difficult for them as time passed to maintain the first-year standards. (Just as I'm sure our occasionally drunken antics had nothing to do with it!) That's also what made Uncle Wendel's participation in the tournament so special. For most of those early years, we assigned him a handicap and he took part as a regular competitor. Alas, we never got his handicap quite high enough to earn him a victory, but the year he won the "Andy Trophy" was special.

After Andy passed away at the young age of 29, his parents created a trophy in his honor. This fine traveling trophy, a fake brass cup on a fake wood base, is awarded annually to the maker of the weekend's most spectacular shot. The winner is named at the tournament's conclusion, after the competitors gather to nominate shots and vote.

Andy had always seemed to be a particular favorite of Uncle Wendel's, so when Wendel finally won, I can honestly say without hint of exaggeration or hyperbole that it was by far the proudest moment of Wendel's very long, eventful, and successful life. Thus is the power and prestige of the Andy Trophy.

And so there were two potential prizes at stake when I arrived at White Lake on Friday afternoon. On the heels of my 89 with Coach Carl, my hopes were reasonably high – though a final tune-up nine on Wednesday had gone a long way toward keeping those hopes in check. It was so bad I stopped keeping score after five holes – something I almost *never* do! Nonetheless, I was able to easily dismiss the bad round as "getting it out of my system."

Of more genuine concern was my back, which, after several weeks of feeling pretty good, seemed to be tightening up. Most likely it was due to the increased frequency of my play. But I figured as long as I did my due diligence regarding stretching, I should be okay.

By tradition, the golf begins on Friday with a practice/qualifying round. But the real drama began before we even arrived at the course, with the heated negotiation of terms for the competition to buy that night's dinner. After a lot of whining and bickering, we decided to keep the same teams from last year, but with a new, highly complex handicap system. Suffice it to say not everyone was happy with it. But off we went, nonetheless.

The first hole, a 529-yard straightaway par-5 with a creek about 80 yards short of the green, resulted in a fairly promising start: a popped-up drive, a couple of mediocre hybrids, a punched 8-iron, a chip, and two putts for double-bogey. Not great, but not bad considering the first-hole jitters.

The second hole was memorable for the irony of it. My second shot landed at the base of a tree near the green, on the "wrong side" for a left-handed to hit it easily. After sizing up the shot – and making a big show of pointing out the irony! – I flipped over my sand wedge, took a few short right-handed practice swings, and knocked the ball to the edge of the green. Two putts later I was in for bogey – and an "early favorite" to contend for the Andy Trophy.

A string of bogeys followed, with a pretty consistent pattern: Mediocre drive, mediocre approach (and a missed green), average chip, and two putts. Nothing great, nothing awful. Nothing new.

On number 6, a 330-yard par 4, I got my long-awaited first crack at revenge on the notorious "ball-eating tree" that guards the sharp dogleg left. All my life, such holes have vexed me. Any time a hole bends quickly left, my dependable fade/uncontrollable slice becomes a huge liability. And no hole has tormented me more than the dreaded sixth at White Lake.

In the early years, I simply tried to fly my drive straight over the ball-eating tree with a 3-wood. If I managed to hit precisely the right line, my ball would end up in a nice spot in the fairway, less than 100 yards from the green. But that almost never happened. In fact, I'm not sure it *ever* happened. The margin for error was extremely slim for a man of my slicey-ness. A little to the right and the ball would run through the fairway into the woods. A little to the left and the ball-eating tree (or one of its hungry neighbors) would gobble it up.

More often than not, however, the result was far uglier. It's a classic case of your body doing exactly what your mind envisions. Having never been able to develop a positive mental picture of what my ball was *supposed* to do, the negative images accumulated in my brain like stubborn scar tissue. And *no matter how hard I tried* to just flop the ball out to the right and safely into the fairway (even if that meant I was still a long way from the green), at the very last instant my brain would scream, "DON'T HIT IT INTO THE BALL-EATING TREE!" Uncontrollable spasms would seize my body, and my ball would fly straight into the tree. As usual.

Each year, the anxiety would build, and the effect would be multiplied – leading to one of the most infamous incidents in WLC history.

The exact year is lost to the ages, but what happened is burned in my brain. I remember trying especially hard to avoid the ball-eating tree, but as usual, I jerked it hard left, straight into its hungry branches. I reacted by expressing mild frustration in my usual, highly controlled fashion. Rob apparently thought I was trying to hit the ball *over* the tree, and expressed *his* frustration with *me* by saying something like, "Zim, why don't you just try hitting it out to the right?"

This was more than I could bear. So I tackled him. Right there on the 6th tee. It was not my best moment – and just one in a long list of embarrassing failures on the seemingly simple but nearly impossible hole number 6.

(Rob disputes some of the particulars of my recollection, but the essential facts are clear: I hit a horrible shot, Rob made an inappropriate comment, and I punished him for it.)

And so, ever since I began this left-handed quest, one of my foremost thoughts was that – assuming I didn't develop an uncontrollable left-handed *hook* – I would finally show that ball-eating tree who's boss. But on Friday, in attempt #1, I failed again. Perhaps in my eagerness to finally hit a perfect drive around the tree, I instead topped it badly, not advancing it far enough to even reach the corner. My recovery shot was good, however: a nice cut 3-iron around the bend to the middle of the fairway. A solid wedge followed, to about 10 feet, but I missed the putt for another routine bogey. As Charlie Brown might say: "RATS!"

On the next hole, the 155-yard 7th, I finally got my first par of the day. A solid 7-iron to the right edge of the green preceded two putts to bring me back to even bogey for the nine. My two best drives of the day followed on the par-4 8th and par-5 9th (with 3-wood and driver, respectively), but weak second shots took par out of play on both holes.

Still, when all was said and done I had seven bogeys, one double-bogey, and one par for a solid 45 on the front. I was thrilled! Of the five other competitors, only Rob had managed to beat me scratch, and only by one with a 44.

My goal for the weekend was not so much to win, but to "shoot a good score" – or break 90, if I had to put a number on it. And with the much shorter back nine lying ahead, I seemed to be in the perfect position to do that.

My confidence was soaring – most likely to my detriment.

In the team competition, last year's amazing comeback became this year's epic collapse. When the dust finally settled, and Serbo four-putted the 18th green (a large and difficult green, to be sure) the good guys, the defending champs, had lost by a single stroke. Of course, Scruffy and I were very eager to pin the loss on that final four-putt. But the truth is we had all thrown away many strokes on the back nine. I myself had ballooned to a disastrous 57, which included a stretch of triple-double-quad on numbers 12, 13, and 14.

I'll admit, I was pretty bummed to have blown my sub-90 round – and even more upset about having to spring for dinner! But by the time we sat down at our outside table, the fresh air, beautiful setting, and unmatched camaraderie had cleared my mind and soothed my soul. Before long, the beer, conversation, and post-round sh!t-giving were flowing freely. Looking back, the three hours that followed were the best of the weekend.

In the old days, we would have gone home, busted out the cards, and played poker until 2:00 or 3:00 a.m. But now, it was all we could do to keep our eyes open to watch the movie *Beerfest* – the viewing of which has become our newest tradition. And then we all went to bed to rest up for the big tournament.

Pretty sad.

Saturday morning dawned cool and beautiful, just as the morning before. But I barely tasted my stuffed hash browns at Gary's Restaurant as I worked hard at getting myself into a peaceful, Zen-like, pre-game mental state. After breakfast, we went straight to the golf course, where everyone else headed to the driving range. I stayed behind to chip, putt, stretch, and mentally prepare. It probably wouldn't have been a bad idea to go and hit at least a few balls, but I felt mental preparedness should take priority.

My back, unfortunately, was not in a good way, so I spent considerable time trying to work out the kinks. Maybe the back issues would help lower my expectations, I thought, which might in turn raise my level of play. But – doesn't just *thinking* such thoughts mean I'd already failed at tricking myself that way!?

Don't over-think it – but don't under-think it either! How do I find the right balance? If I over-think about under-thinking, doesn't that defeat the purpose of not over-thinking? It's so confusing!

So despite my best efforts to mellow into a nice, carefree zone, I instead was my usual antsy self. *Sigh.* What to do? I tried thinking about Jack, who always seems to play with such carefree joy. And I tried to remember all the things I'd been telling myself in preparation. That the project was *already* a success, no matter what happened. I tried hard (probably *too* hard) to convince myself that my results didn't matter, only the *process* did. But it was no use, really. I wanted to win! Well, that wasn't quite true. I would *love* to win, of course. But all I really wanted to do was play a round I could be proud of – that I could hang my hat on and say, "See! I *told you* I could do it!"

The ugly truth is, I wanted to *impress* people with my performance. Which is not the best mind-set with which to start a tournament.

When I heard the others return, I was sitting in the grass behind the first tee, stretching my back, furiously over-thinking everything with my head bowed slightly. "Are you *praying?*" L.T. called out when he saw me. I hesitated a moment and then replied, "Sorta!"

With my peaceful mood (such as it was) shattered by the return of my hooligan friends, it was soon time to tee it up.

After taking a few minutes for the traditional first-tee group photo, I teed it up between the white markers and prepared to knock one down the middle. Surprisingly, I felt pretty calm as I took my practice swings – and pretty smooth as I wound up and swung away with my driver. The results were not great, but a little better than the day before: My ball wound up on the right edge of the fairway. One for one in fairways hit!

As we walked off the tee, Little Tommy (who along with Keith would be my playing partner on the front) paid me a nice compliment. He said he was "amazed" at how well I seemed to be able to hit the ball left-handed. I don't think he meant that shot in particular, but I truly appreciated the sentiment. He was *impressed!*

In retrospect, I think that little stroke of my ego had a negative effect. (Tom, was it all part of your nefarious plot to undermine my performance?!) I don't think I went through my proper mental checklist before hitting my second shot, a solid hybrid pulled badly into the trees on the right.

After finding my ball in the right rough I made a pretty significant mental error. Knowing that the ideal layup spot is about 100 yards short of the green, I calculated that I needed 125 yards to get there. In reality, I realized later, I should have been thinking *175* yards, as I had mistaken the yellow 250-yard stakes for the 200s. After I pulled another shot, I was still left with about 175 yards to the green for my fourth shot. And I was still in the trees.

Thinking more about making good contact than getting all the way to the green, I hit another 6-iron and yanked it *hard* to the right. Fortunately, even though a pretty large branch came down, my ball somehow made it through the tree and just over the water, coming to rest about 60 yards short of the green. A solid punch pitching wedge put me on the back of the green in 5, from where I managed to make a stupid three-putt for eight.

Eight! A triple bogey on the very first hole! *Come on!*

Whoops. There I was, losing my cool already, just a little. I kept it inside, but … *Boy, that didn't take long!*

But it also didn't take long to calm myself back down. By the time we crossed the road to the second tee, I was doing better, and focused on the task at hand: the beautiful, 384-yard number 2 .

Like the day before, I pulled out my 3-wood and picked out a line heading up the right side of the fairway. But unlike yesterday, I opened the clubhead and popped the ball high into the trees overhanging the ladies' tees. *Crack! Snapple! Plop.* My ball came straight down near the red tee markers – and bad feelings returned. Another sliced/toed hybrid followed and I felt my self-control slipping away again as the ball settled at the left edge of the fairway, short of the 150-yard stakes.

"Nice shot!" Tom called out.

He meant it as a compliment, or at least as encouragement, but I didn't want to hear it. It felt like he was patronizing me. "Shut up and leave me alone!" I yelled back.

I meant to say it with an air of "banter," but it didn't really come out that way. I must have sounded pretty annoyed.

"Okay, fine," Tom replied … "*Hagan!*"

The words stung, because I knew I had deserved them. Mike Hagan, of course, was my high school golf team nemesis, about whose temper and overall irritability I'd always complained. To be compared to him based on my on-course behavior was an eye-opener. A few minutes later, after tapping in for another three-putt triple, I apologized to Keith and Tom and resolved to do better – in terms of both my behavior and my performance.

Lining up my 8-iron on the 129-yard par-3 third, I made a point – for really the first time since the opening tee shot – to focus on my pre-shot routine: check my balance, relax my arms, nice light grip, visualize the shot I want to hit, let my right shoulder be my motor, make a good full turn, etc. All the things I'd been forgetting to do thus far. It paid off with a nice solid strike to the center of the green, perhaps 25 feet short of the back pin.

As I pondered the resulting putt, Keith was having quite an adventure off in the trees to the left, and I let it distract me. Without giving it the proper amount of thought, my first putt stopped a good four feet short up the hill. I made a good stroke on the par attempt, but hit it a little firm and watched as it grazed the high side of the hole: my third three-putt in as many holes.

Well, a bogey is still an improvement! And I consoled myself by thinking, "If it weren't for the 3-putts …." But of course, thinking that way is like telling yourself that if it weren't for those half-dozen Krispy Kreme donuts you ate after lunch, you'd be doing pretty well on your diet today.

Just three holes in, I was seven over par (or four over bogey, my more-realistic measure), with three 3-putts – compared to zero for yesterday's front nine. I was four shots behind Friday's pace, and feeling like it was already over.

But as I was self-destructing, Tom and Keith were putting on quite a show. Both were playing in pain. Tom, of course, was still recovering from the ATV accident, and Keith – who apparently cares more about winning than he lets on – had an elbow problem. Though he rarely has time to play golf, he had been practicing pretty intensely in recent weeks and had a painful case of tendonitis to show for it.

He was playing it down, of course. He's the kind of guy who doesn't like to offer excuses, or admit weakness (or share his feelings), and he didn't want us to know how much pain he was in. But by the time we got to the second hole, there was no hiding it.

It was like playing with Steve Carell in the infamous chest-waxing scene from *The 40-Year-Old Virgin*, without the profanity (though just barely). Following his elaborate 73-second pre-shot routine, Keith would take a measured rip at the ball, then watch it fly off to the right. At the moment of contact, a primal scream would rise from deep within his bowels, squeeze past his larynx, and explode through his contorted lips before rattling (along with his ball) among the highest branches of the majestic White Lake trees. *YEEEEAARRRRRGGGGHHH!!!!*

If I hadn't felt so bad for him, it would have been pretty amusing. Okay, it *was* pretty amusing, despite my somewhat limited sympathy.

Somewhere around the sixth or seventh hole, however, Keith's fortunes seemed to change, just a little, when he took a small plastic bag out of his pocket, and washed down the contents with a few gulps of water. It seems he had been saving one dose of a leftover painkiller for just such a time.

"Keith, do you have a prescription for that?" I asked.

"Well," he said with a wry chuckle, "there *is* a prescription for it, it just doesn't happen to be in my name."

"That's fine with me," I answered, as I considered the implications. "But ... do you think you'll be able to pass the post-round urinalysis?"

Truth is, it wouldn't matter, even if there were such a thing. Keith clearly had no chance to win today. Besides, our other playing partner was a medical doctor. And I'm pretty sure I saw Tom unofficially "prescribe" the medication to him before he took it. It went something like, "Tom, is it okay if I take this pill?" Tom looked at it, shrugged, and said, "Sure." (The official examination must have come when I wasn't looking.)

By comparison, Tom's injuries were, though less recent, much more serious. His groans of pain were much more controlled – as were his shots, which were in fact downright remarkable under the circumstances. On the eighth hole, I hit what I thought was a good driver, right down the middle, on a similar line to Tom's shot moments earlier. Both balls were past the ridge, so we couldn't see where either ended up. As we walked up the fairway, we saw two balls right in the middle, one about 50 yards ahead of the other.

"Tom, what did you hit here?"

"A hybrid," he replied.

"Oh, then that must be mine, farther up, because I hit a driver."

"At least I hope that's mine," I added sheepishly.

Alas, it was not. My driver had gone about 200 yards; Tom had crushed his hybrid about 250. With a broken collarbone, no less. *Really!?* Great, just what I needed to inflame the tender remains of my shredded ego.

It was right about then that the sandbagging thoughts started to take shape. And after he hit another beautiful drive on the par-5 ninth, those thoughts spilled out into the open as I "interviewed" him on his play so far:

Me: "Tom just *crushed* another one-shouldered drive, probably 320 yards down the middle – reminiscent of when Tiger was pretending his knee hurt in the 2008 U.S. Open. So, Tom, why don't you tell the folks at home what you're pretending to feel?"

Tom [laughing, sort of]: "Well, it does hurt with every shot. [At this moment, Keith coughed loudly in the background, in a manner that sounded a little like a word containing the letters "b" and "s."] I think more of the pain is muscular than it is actually the clavicle [that's doctor talk for "collarbone"]. But I am trying to protect it with my follow-through."

(Translation: "I'm not swinging way too hard, like I usually do, so I'm actually making a *better* swing today.")

Me: "Well, whatever the reason, you're hitting the ball very well, despite your imaginary injury."

Maybe the sand-bagging innuendo got to him, because things got very interesting shortly thereafter. Number 9 is a tree-lined dog-leg right, and if you don't shape your drive or put it on exactly the right line, you can easily drive it through the fairway – which is exactly what had happened to Tom, as he found himself in the left rough under a large tree. Trying to keep the ball under the branches, he topped his second shot badly, advancing it perhaps 20 yards.

What followed was another Steve Carell chest-waxing scream – this time *including* the profanity. "At least I can hit it now!" he said almost as loudly when he saw the results. He was past the tree, and still had in mind to try to hit the green in regulation. His ball was about 255 yards out – it was easy to measure because the two-foot-high, yellow plastic 250-yard stake was just ahead, directly between him and the flagstick.

"With my luck, I'll probably hit that thing!" he said with a sarcastic laugh, trying desperately to show a little good humor.

As previously discussed, mental coaches will tell you that your body tends to do what your mind imagines. So, perhaps you can guess what happened next ...

After making incredibly solid contact with the narrow yellow stake, Tom's ball ricocheted sharply to the right, coming to rest at the base of a tree clear across the fairway.

I have to say that, given his hot-tempered history, Tom actually held things together pretty well. I reminded him that given his play thus far, he was probably leading the tournament by several strokes. And that if he could settle himself down and not compound his error, he could afford a double-bogey, which is probably what he was looking at.

Whether my advice helped him or not (now that I think of it, isn't giving and taking advice against the rules? He should probably be disqualified!), he punched out solidly from under the tree, hit his approach just over the small green, and got up and down cleanly for a double-bogey 7.

When Rob, Mike, and Serbo finished up a few minutes later, we compared scores and, sure enough, found Tom comfortably in the lead. Even with the double-bogey he had shot a 43. Nobody had bettered him – he was winning *gross*! And with his five front-nine handicap strokes he had a net 38. Such a low net score on the front was perhaps unprecedented.

As per tradition, we re-grouped after nine holes according to the net scores. The also-ran threesome teed off first, with Keith (who still had an outside shot with a 55/net 45), Scruffy (53/49), and yours truly in dead last with 55/50. Ten strokes worse than the practice round.

Oh, the humanity! I couldn't recall ever trailing the entire field at the turn before. Serbo slid into the second group with a 50/43, Rob was tied with a typically unexciting 43/43, with Tom and his suspect 43/38 leading the way.

He wasn't quite yet a lock, of course. A lot can happen on the back nine – and a lot often has. Perhaps the back nine's best defense is the false sense of security it can instill. The second nine is certainly very short, but it's also very tight, with lots of trouble, so the potential to blow up is high.

No question, there was still some golf left to play.

As for me, I was doing my best to forget about the title, forget about the front nine, and focus on shooting a good score on the back. If I could maybe shoot another 41 or so, I could at least tell myself that I had shot *two* good nines over the weekend, even if they weren't consecutive. I could console myself with a "what if?" 85 or

86 by combining those two scores. *Now that would still be pretty satisfying!* I told myself.

I also changed my strategy. My back wasn't getting any better – I was still pretty stiff and sore and struggling to make good swings with a good, full turn. But I realized I could probably do pretty well just by *punching* my way around. During my brief career as a lefty, I'd often noticed that my most reliable shot seemed to be my recovery shots. That is, half to three-quarter swings when all I was trying to do was make good contact and move the ball forward. The back nine demanded more control anyway, so why not take it a step further? I figured that if I could just keep the ball in play, avoid the big mistakes, and get at least close to most greens in regulation, I'd be in business.

Number 10 is a perfect example of what the back nine is all about: barely 300 yards, a dogleg left, and tight, with not a lot of room for error. I hit a weak hybrid, not far at all, but right in the middle of the fairway. I had about 140 yards left to a front pin, perfect for a punch 7-iron. My plan was working perfectly! It hit it just a little fat, but right at the pin, maybe 10 yards short. As I sized-up the chip, I tried hard to imagine that I was on the practice green – it was exactly the sort of shot I always think is fun to practice, but difficult to pull off when a real score is on the line. I opened up my sand wedge and plunked a nice little shot just onto the green about four feet from the pin. I missed the putt (crap!!) but was still "on plan" with a bogey.

On 11, the short par-3, I repeated yesterday's mistake, flaring an 8-iron short and left of the greenside bunker. This time, however, I recovered beautifully. The ball hopped cleanly off my sand wedge and onto the green, rolling right at the pin. It settled about a foot-and-a-half away for a tap-in par. I was on my way!

The next hole, the 12th, was another one that has gotten under my skin over the years. It's one of the shortest par 4 holes you'll ever see, officially measuring just 263 yards from the white tees. It's nearly impossible to drive the green, however, as it's so well guarded – particularly late in the year when the reeds in the pond in front of the green get really high. The green is very small, kidney-shaped, sloped steeply from back to front, with two distinct lobes above a small pot bunker. Its shallow depth and angle mean distance control and accuracy are both at a premium – much like the 12th at Augusta.

Strategically speaking, it's really quite devious. Yet I've never been able to make myself embrace the hole. As a right-hander, my fade/slice always worked against me, with trees and out-of-bounds on the left, and more trees on the right that block approach shots, even from the right side of the fairway. Making it worse, the fairway lies in the lowest, wettest part of the property, which gives the turf a distinctly "spongy" quality.

In fact, historical documents archived on the club's website show that the 12th fairway lies in a part of the property that used to be labeled "swamp."

With the deep divots I traditionally take, I've long had trouble making clean contact on the 12th fairway: I either take a massive divot and chunk the shot into (or even short of) the water, or blade it over the green or into the reeds.

The good news is, my lefty fade is much more conducive to finding the center or left of the fairway. And just like on Friday, I hit a nice easy hybrid to a good spot about 110 yards from the green. As I assessed my approach, I realized that the tree guarding the right corner of the green, on the near side of the water, was still a factor to consider – and that Mike was making a mess of things in the right rough.

Keith on the other hand, hit a beautiful approach. After punching out of the trees, his next shot plopped gently onto the green. With the pin back left, however, he still had plenty of work to do from the green's frontal lobe.

Maybe his shot put a good, positive image into my own frontal lobe. After settling on a wedge over a 9-iron, I pulled my punch shot just a little, and watched as it headed toward the very top reaches of the green-guarding tree. After clipping a few leaves, the ball dropped onto the green, five or ten feet inside Keith's ball on a similar line to the hole. *Yes!*

Following a lot of discussion of how much our putts would break – with memories of yesterday's runaway putts still fresh – Keith hit a beauty. At first I thought he had hit it too high, and too slow. But the ball kept breaking and breaking, and rolling and rolling, before finally settling about two feet short of the hole. He still had a tricky sidehill putt remaining, but from 35 or 40 feet out, it was a great effort.

Even with a great read from Keith, I *still* didn't hit mine high or hard enough. I left the putt about three-and-a-half feet short, again on a similar line. Terrified of rolling my par putt way past, I aimed at what felt like a 45-degree angle above the hole, tapped it up the hill, and breathed a sigh of relief – with a little baby Tiger fist-pump – as it trickled into the hole on the high side. *Another par!*

Keith was not so fortunate, missing his bogey putt on the low side. Mike ... I have no idea.

Even though I had no illusions about winning the tournament at that point, the adrenaline was kicking in again (uh oh!), and I started fantasizing about parring in for a 1-over 36. *That would be awesome!* Surely, at minimum, a sub-40 nine-hole score was in the works! Right?

Will I never learn?

Resisting the temptation to rip a driver or 3-wood on the fairly wide-open 13th hole, I stuck to the plan and hit a hybrid – weak and down the left side, flirting with the O.B. Fortunately, it stayed in-bounds, though not out of the trees. Trying to bend a 6-iron back out into the fairway and toward the green, I chunked the shot badly, leaving the ball in the trees on the left. Again, what I *should* have done is taken my medicine and chipped out safely. From there I had a little better luck with a 7-iron, but pushed the ball into the left greenside bunker. A nice sand wedge explosion shot later, I was looking at a four-footer to save bogey.

Slightly sidehill, a tiny bit left-to-right – hit it firm and don't give away the hole, I thought. I lined up and stroked it solidly toward the right-center of the cup. "Nice putt!" Scruffy proclaimed ... just before the ball caught the left lip and rolled a foot-and-a-half past. Maybe less.

"Scruffy! What the ...?!" He had committed a cardinal sin: He praised my putt before the ball actually dropped – a classic *jinx*. It's nonsense, of course, but I was mad that I had missed and stupidly took it out on him. With my blood beginning to boil, I needed a scapegoat. Then I made the *real* mistake. Rather than take a deep breath and regroup, I mindlessly stepped up and stabbed at the comebacker – and missed that one, too.

Suddenly, what had been a solid chance to save a bogey after a couple of bad shots became an inexcusable triple. Immediately I started counting strokes in my head. I was still at level bogey for the back side, four over through four, so all hope was not yet lost. I could not say the same about my composure.

It was a crucial point in the round. If I could calm myself down, there was no reason I couldn't still shoot a decent back-nine score. But I was also at risk of spiraling into despair. My last hope for finishing the round – finishing my whole *year!* – on a high note was slipping away. As usual, with the pressure on in crunch time, I failed the test.

Harkening back to the "plan" I had visualized in the days before the tournament, #14, a very short but very unorthodox par-5, called for a 3-wood tee shot. Under today's new plan, a hybrid would have been plenty. Call it throwing caution to the wind, or call it recklessly abandoning my revised strategy, I pulled out a 3-wood – and promptly hit a worm-burner about 75 yards into the right rough. A few deep, deliberate breaths later, I was calm enough to walk to my ball, where I found it sitting up nicely in some fluffy grass. Realizing I was still within a solid shot's reach of the second-shot landing area, I made what felt like a good swing with my 3-hybrid ... *right underneath the ball.* My TopFlite Gamer V2 went nearly straight up, coming to rest right on line perhaps 50 yards ahead.

And then I nearly lost it for real.

The dam was about to burst. The rage and disappointment rose up inside me, and I just barely managed to keep it from exploding out. I came *very* close to flinging my club high into a tree, tightening my grip on it at the last instant as I swung it furiously over my head. Curse words (I almost *never* swear!) very nearly escaped my tightly gritted teeth. My face, I'm quite sure, turned a deep and probably frightening shade of red. (In fact, L.T. would later say I "looked like a lobster.") Then I just squatted in the grass with my head down for a long time, breathing heavily, trying to calm down, thinking about how gloriously I was failing in my quest to master left-handed golf.

Was I praying? I'm not sure, I don't really remember. I hope I was, but I can't say. What I do remember is trying not to cry.

How had it come to this? Isn't this reaction exactly what I was trying to prevent with all the reading up on the mental game? The pep talks from Rob and Coach Carl? What happened to giving it all to *God?*

After what felt like a very long time, I gathered myself and walked to the ball. There was nothing left to do now but just try not to care. *A shot at a time, okay!?* I realized I had been getting way out of myself again – or way too *into* myself, thinking too hard about results rather than just letting things *come to me*, as Coach Carl likes to say. Gradually, the tension subsided as I reminded myself of all the things I'd told myself before the round. *The project is already a success, no matter what happens. Visualize good results, remember your pre-shot routine, and take it a shot at a time. Above all, relax and enjoy yourself!*

All that had gone out the window when the shots began to hit the fan.

But with all hope lost I finally began to relax a little. After the fluffy pop-up I hit a *good* hybrid into the middle of the fairway, leaving 120 yards or so to the green. It was then that I remembered again I was not alone, as I heard a few choice four-letter words leave Keith's mouth somewhere behind me. It was clearly time to rejoin the festivities.

Scruffy, meanwhile, was chopping wood in the left rough, working on his second or third provisional as he hacked his way through the trees and toward the hole. Wouldn't you know it, he found his original second shot just short of the water. In an effort to make sure he cleared the trap guarding the front of the green, he blasted it over the green, and over the trap *behind* the green. From there he blasted over the green *again*, then chipped on and two-putted for a double-bogey 7. Keith ended up with an 8. I punched a 9-iron to about 30 feet, then two-putted for a 6. After all that, a *bogey*. I was ashamed of my previous fury.

On the 15th tee I faced a 118-yard blind shot (thanks to more tall reeds in the water hazard) to the green. With the wind slightly at our backs, I pulled out a 9-iron – and promptly shanked it about 50 yards to the left, the ball coming to rest under two pine trees behind the 14th green. All I could do was laugh and shake my head. I could see from the tee that I would have no shot, so I declared the ball unplayable and re-teed. Hitting three, I struck what may have been my best shot of the weekend – certainly my best iron. The ball soared high and straight toward the right side of the green, falling from view on a line just right of the pin.

After retrieving my first shot I walked up to the green – where my ball was nowhere to be seen! *What the …!?* Glancing around I saw Scruffy preparing to hit his chip shot from just off the green, where I thought my ball should be. *Scruffy! Wait …! What are you doing!? Are you hitting my ball!?* "NO! I marked yours," he said, a little irritated by my tone.

Oh. Sorry about that, Scruffy. I was still a little tense, I guess.

When my turn to putt finally arrived I made the putt for the most unusual bogey I've ever scored.

I say "finally" because some additional theatrics preceded my holing out. Keith had hit his tee shot near the water on the right, in front of the 11th tee. So he had to wait – and wait, and wait, and wait – as we watched a player on 11 hit four or five shots off the tee, apparently unaware of, or indifferent to, Keith's presence. When he finally got to play, Keith hit a very nice approach (his third shot, following a drop) from awkward spot, that ultimately settled a few feet off the green – from where he chipped in nicely for bogey. (Remember that phrase: "chip-in for bogey.")

With the holes and the pressure winding down, it was time again to sit back and watch Scruffy try to drive the green on the 320-yard dogleg right 16th hole. Ever since that big tree came down in a wind storm a few years back, it's been very possible. The year before, Mike finally pulled it off, crushing a high, fading drive that rolled onto the front left of the green. He missed the eagle putt, but later claimed the Andy Trophy for his monumental effort.

With a repeat performance in mind, Mike reared back and crushed one of the longest, prettiest-looking drives I've ever seen. Unfortunately, it was also one of the *straightest* long drives I've ever witnessed. The ball didn't move an inch to the left or right as it cleared the far end of the fairway, seemingly still on the rise, before striking a tree and bouncing sharply to the right, toward the green. Keith and I were just about rolling on the ground in astonishment. Holy *crap*, what a shot!

Suffice it to say our own efforts were not nearly so impressive. Trying to play it really safe, I badly pulled a 7-iron into the right rough. From there I hacked my way up through the trees before blading a sand wedge onto the back of the green and two-putting for a 6.

The last two holes were relatively uneventful: on 17, a long three-putt double-bogey for me, a nice birdie for Mike, and a funny little dance of agony over a missed short putt for Keith. On 18 I had a bad drive into the right trees, a good punch recovery to about 135 yards in the fairway, and a slightly pulled 8-iron onto the upslope in the deep and grassy "Valley of Death" to the right of the green. A decent sand wedge followed, right on line but about 10 feet past.

THE WRONG SIDE OF THE BALL

Two putts meant another double.

Add it all up and I shot a 47, or three over bogey on the par 35 back nine. Which, after all that, is … not horrible. So all that was left was to wait for the championship flight to see who would take home the trophy for the 2011 White Lake Classic.

Unsurprisingly, it was Little Tommy, by a pretty comfortable margin. The sandbagging talk began again almost immediately. It felt as if we had given him too many handicap strokes to account for his injury. In fact, someone (could have been me) came up with a term that I think is going to stick: "Scagg-bagging." So yeah, it looks like L.T., who still bristles whenever we talk about the hypothetical asterisk we say belongs on the trophy the first year he won (in light of a very generous ruling in the face a mysteriously lost ball), may now have to endure the ignominy of being the inspiration for a new derogatory term.

That's okay. I'm sure he can handle it.

By the time we all piled back into my minivan to head back to the cottage, I was pretty much over it. At least, I was starting to put it all into perspective. It helped that we had important business to conduct back at the cottage: the drinking of ceremonial beer and awarding of the Andy Trophy.

They say that English is a living language, and this is certainly true regarding the WLC definition of "spectacular." On at least two occasions, no one felt strongly enough about any of the potential winners to bother with voting, and the trophy went un-awarded. More often than not, a spectacularly *bad* shot claims the prize – which is perhaps why Keith is by far the most frequent winner. One year, during a rainy long weekend in Virginia, we awarded the trophy to Serbo for throwing a triple bulls-eye during a round of darts.

After a very entertaining debate – which lasted a good hour – Keith's "Chip In for Bogey" won a narrow victory over Mike's "Almost Ace," which he had hit during the practice round. Mike's shot was clearly more impressive, but in the end the committee decided it would be more entertaining to add to Keith's legacy: He now has won the Andy Trophy for "Chip In for Birdie," "Chip In for Par," and "Chip In for Bogey." Keith wasn't thrilled, but the rest of us laughed long and hard at the thought of it. We also agreed that somewhere (perhaps in Japan, where we often theorize Andy went to sabotage the Japanese auto industry after faking his death) Andy was also laughing with complete approval of our selection.

That night we played bocce ball, grilled steaks, dealt some poker (I won 20 bucks!), and had a grand old time. In the morning we went out for breakfast, cleaned up the cottage, and headed home before noon. My one-year commitment to playing left-handed golf was officially complete. It had been an amazing adventure, but I knew I wasn't quite yet done.

After all, I had a promise to keep.

CHAPTER 12
Snips and Snails and Anthills

"Don't hurry, don't worry."
–Walter Hagen

Brookfield Hills would not fit everyone's definition of a "real" golf course. At just 4,430 yards from the white tees, with a par of 62, a "championship" course it is not. "Executive" is a better descriptor. But it has plenty of water, genuine rough, nicely groomed fairways and greens, and an abundance of mature trees. None of that mattered to Jack, though. It has the all-important *sand traps*. So it was more than real enough for him.

Back in the spring, when Jack won the four free passes to Morningstar Golf Club, I had promised him a "real" round of golf in addition to the Wii "Sports Resort" game I gave him in exchange for them. And while the Wii game had been a big hit, we hadn't made it to the golf course together ("real" or otherwise) nearly as much as I'd imagined.

Part of the blame for that goes to my back issues, but some of it lies with Jack himself. Many times, he had declined my offers to go play nine holes at one of the local par-3 courses, either because he was busy doing other things or, more often, because he'd ask if we could just go to the driving range instead. Or to the practice area at Brown Deer. Turns out, Jack (at least at this stage) approaches the game exactly *opposite* of the way his old man did. He'd rather *practice* than *play*.

So when the Sunday after White Lake turned partly sunny and somewhat warm (high about 60), I knew it might be our last chance to play the promised round before the snow began to fly. Not surprisingly, I had to twist his arm, just a little, to convince him to join me. (I also had to agree to take him out to sell some Cub Scouts popcorn before we went!) Fortunately, it was a big sports day in Milwaukee (Packers at noon; a Brewers playoff game at 7:00), so when we got to the course about 3:30 it was all but deserted. Perfect for a 9-hole father-son outing.

I had it in mind to make this a special occasion, so we rented a cart – just like my dad and I used to. And, in a fit of spontaneous generosity, I even bought him a new driver. How could I resist? I'd been looking for one for him (his current set included only a 3-wood), and they had some on the rack, just his size, for $15. Such a bargain!

In the blink of an eye, however, my true frugal nature returned in all its glory.

"Ooh, Dad – can I have a Nutter Butter?!"

"No."

Out on the practice green I realized right away that this would be a more relaxed round than I'd been playing lately. I couldn't help but smile watching Jack hop, skip, jump, and almost dance his way between chips and putts. He positively exuded the pure and simple joy of a child.

Why is it so hard for *me* feel so carefree on the golf course?

It would be something of an understatement to say I'd been taking the whole left-handed project a little too seriously. Well, that's not quite true. Taking the *project* seriously is okay, but I had been putting far too much stock in my on-course *results*. I needed constant reminding that success did not hinge on the scores I shot. Right? Truth is, my ego never let me stop thinking about my scores for too long. And all too often I found myself back in a place I was years ago: Getting way too stressed out playing golf.

It had been a week since the WLC and I was already feeling a sense of relief. For most of the past year, I had been spending as many lunch hours as possible practicing – either in the "Lefty Dome" at work, on the range, or at the practice area at Brown Deer. Sometimes I used that time to make phone calls or do research. Before the book, I went home most days to eat lunch and relax. Resuming that practice proved a surprisingly welcome relief.

And because my back was still an issue (it had been pretty stiff and sore since the second round in Michigan), I wasn't even really looking forward to *playing* the round with Jack. I wanted to be there, absolutely – but I wasn't relishing the idea of swinging a club. To get in the proper frame of mind before we went, I had to resign myself to stiff swings and poor performance. Even so, hidden away in a dark corner of my brain, I eagerly nurtured a notion about how my "not caring" might propel me to shoot an exceptional score. I know … I'm a sick, sick man.

Again, thank goodness for Jack, who almost immediately disabused me of any notions of doing anything other than enjoying myself. As we prepared to tee off after our warm-up session on the putting green (where, truth be told, Jack could happily have spent another hour), I said something like, "It's just too bad it's so windy, huh?"

Jack just shrugged. "I don't see much of a downer about wind."

Well said, Son! After all, wind is really only a big factor when you let it get to you. It's not a downer at all when your head is where it should be. I decided to file Jack's insightful words away with other famous bits of wind-swept wisdom, such as Gary Player's admonition: "When it's breezy, hit it easy."

Playing the back nine, we started on the 10th hole, a 360/335-yard (white/red tees) par-4 dogleg left around a large pond. Jack was mildly intimidated that he couldn't even quite see the green. "Don't worry," I reassured him. "This is the longest hole on the back nine, so they'll only get shorter from here. Just aim for that white stake out there in the middle of the fairway."

His ball – propelled by his new driver – found the fairway. Mine – propelled by the toe of my hybrid – found the pond … where Jack was thrilled to find a large snail shell. Jack carded a 9 (including four putts). I carded a … let's just call it an "X." And with that out of the way, I abandoned any idea of keeping score for either of us.

As the round progressed, Jack's natural creativity came to the fore. Somewhere around the 11th or 12th hole he "invented" a new putting grip, with his hands a good foot or so apart on the grip. He told me it was modeled after the long putters he sometimes sees the pros use on TV. With his first attempt he got good results, so it immediately became his new standard. "It works best on short putts," he explained later, drawing on his extensive experience and scientific study of the new technique. "But sometimes on long ones it helps with distance, too."

I just smiled – and resisted the (very strong) urge to correct him.

There'll be plenty of time for that next year, I reasoned. This round was about having fun.

Of course, it wasn't long before he was driving the cart. I know, I know … but this particular cart seemed to have a top speed only slightly above that of the dearly departed snail. And Jack is a naturally cautious kid, so I wasn't worried about him getting carried away or reckless. Except for the time we almost rammed that post because I had parked the cart with the wheels pointed sharply to the left, he did just fine.

One nice thing was how impressed Jack seemed with even moderately competent shots on my part. I wasn't swinging very well, but every now and then I hit one that at least *looked* pretty good in the air. "Nice shot, Dad!" he would say. Rather than explain, as is my wont, how that shot really wasn't all that good, it didn't go as far as it should have, etc., etc. … I just smiled and said, "Thanks, Bud!"

It made me realize (and regret) that he hadn't seen me hit a left-handed shot on a golf course in several months! But this led him to appreciate a fresh upside to the situation. I think it was on the 14th green, while we were letting a single player in a cart play through, that he explained that the good thing about me playing left-handed is that "we can play more even!" Again, I resisted the temptation to say, "Well, you know, I'm really a lot better than this, even left-handed, it's just that my back, you know, isn't quite right, and …."

Instead, I said, "You're right Jack! That *is* pretty great." And I absolutely meant it.

It was wonderful to play at such a leisurely pace, and let Jack hit do-overs and practice shots whenever they seemed warranted. Of course, that meant tossing a ball into a sand trap now and then so he could practice his favorite shot of all. Because what's the point of playing on a "real" golf course if you're not going to get to hit a few sand shots? Once, he spent several minutes raking afterward, taking great care to make sure the rake lines were all nicely concentric within the small, nearly round bunker.

The only downside to this approach was that by the 17th hole we were starting to race the darkness. The sun had fallen behind the trees, putting us completely in shadow. The wind had not let up, and without the sun's warming glow it was starting to feel pretty frigid. I asked Jack if he wanted to put his jacket on. After a moment's hesitation, he decided that might be a good idea, even though … "I wasn't cold at all," he said matter-of-factly, "until *you* started talking about it all the time."

As we approached the 18th tee I finally felt compelled to coax him along a little bit. It wasn't just the encroaching darkness; I could see there were only a couple of cars left in the parking lot, and I didn't like the idea of someone in the clubhouse having to wait for us to return the cart before they could go home. After all, the Brewers game would be starting soon!

"Come on, Jack," I implored gently. "We really have to try to hurry it up a little."

But that's the thing about Jack – he won't be rushed. I often tell people that I don't think he understands the *concept* of "hurry up." He does things on his own schedule – which is to say, he doesn't have one. His internal clock continuously flashes "12:00." And while this trait is occasionally endearing, it more often than not edges toward downright maddening. And so I was fighting a familiar feeling of growing impatience as I watched him take a number of leisurely practice swings … and then *stop*. "Dad …"

Jack, come on! I thought. *We need to keep moving!* I sighed, trying hard to stay patient. "What is it, Jack?"

"Don't you think," he said, casually and deliberately, "it's interesting how so many ants seem to build their anthills in divots?"

What? Oh, for crying out loud …

All I could do was laugh – and congratulate him on his very insightful observation. "Yes, Jack, that *is* very interesting! I wonder why that is?"

It was a classic "Jack moment," as his mom and I have come to call such things. Walter Hagen, one of my all-time favorite golfers and one of the game's most colorful characters, was known for saying, "Don't hurry, don't worry. And be sure to smell the flowers along the way." Some people smell flowers; Jack ponders anthills. Somehow, I think "The Haig" would be okay with that approach, too.

I was so moved, I resolved on the spot to buy him that Nutter Butter when we returned to the clubhouse.

I see so much of myself in my son, in both good ways and bad. But here's one area where we could hardly be more different: Where I tend to live and die on the golf course according to what the scorecard says, Jack couldn't care less. I've never *once* seen him get upset or frustrated playing golf. He not only doesn't care what he shoots for a round of golf, he doesn't care what he shoots for one *hole*! The closest he ever comes is when he makes up his own par for a hole based on how he feels he should perform. As often as not, his made-up par will have "and-a-half" tacked on. Otherwise, he plays completely "in the moment," thinking only of the shot at hand. When he hits it well, he rejoices. When he hits it badly, he puts it behind him immediately and moves on to the next shot.

Think maybe there's a lesson in there somewhere?

Putt like a kid? At the very least. How about *play* like a kid? Or *live* like a kid. Even Jesus said we should have *faith* like a kid. Why not take it to the golf course? Enjoy the game for its own sake, not for what you achieve in it. Enjoy life in the moment. Never hurry, never worry. Don't worry about tomorrow; tomorrow will worry about itself.

Easy to say, of course, but harder to do. And soon I would have a decision to make.

I spent a year learning to play golf left-handed. "Why?" That's what almost everybody asked – in various ways, spoken and unspoken – when I told them what I was doing. The answer is: lots of reasons. Because I wanted to learn something new. Because I was curious; I wanted to investigate a phenomenon that has long intrigued me. Because I wanted a challenge – one I could write a book about. And have an excuse to take golf lessons! Because I believe it's what God was coaxing me to do. All these reasons … and more.

I didn't know how it would turn out. Sure, I dreamed of becoming a scratch left-handed golfer and playing left-handed on the Champions Tour one day. Now I know that's not going to happen – at least not the Champions Tour part. I didn't get as far as I'd hoped, largely due to the injuries and personal obstacles I had to deal with. On the other hand, viewed more positively, when I consider how many physical problems I had, I'm very pleased to have performed as well as I did.

In the end, I hit enough good shots and played well enough at times to know that it's "in there." My *sinister* swing is more fundamentally sound than my *dexterous* version ever was, and I'm very confident the potential still exists to become a fine left-hander.

But my lefty game was still very erratic. My ability to score well on a given day seemed to depend on two things: 1) not making big mistakes, and 2) the strength of my short game. Even when I shot the 41, it wasn't so much because I was hitting a lot of good shots, but because I wasn't hitting a lot of really *bad* ones. And I was getting up and down consistently when I was close to the green. Point 2 can be viewed as a positive by itself, as much of the touch I developed over the years as a right-hander did indeed seem to carry over to the other side.

A lot of people asked me, "What happens at the end of the year?" I always told them, "I don't know." The plan was to do it for a year, take stock, say a few prayers, and then decide what to do next.

Now that I had done that, I decided to keep going. Actually, Rob pointed out that I'd already made that decision, whether I realized it or not, when I bought the new driver and fairway woods. "I guess this means you're going to stay lefty for a while," he said.

He was right! Even though I'd been thinking it for quite some time, the latest club purchases essentially sealed the deal. These clubs are the nicest ones I've ever had, and to switch back now would mean a fairly significant equipment downgrade. And there's *no way* I could justify buying a nice new set of right-handed clubs on the heels of the golf expenses I incurred during that year (not a fortune, but enough to affect our household budget).

There's also the lingering (nagging?) thought that I hadn't yet discovered my true lefty potential. That *if I just kept working at it*, I could still get really good. Maybe. But the reality is that going forward, without the ready-made excuse of doing it "for the book," it would be much harder to justify committing time and money to practice and play – let alone keep taking lessons. But you know … there's no reason to dismantle the Lefty Dome. And it would be nice to check in with Coach Carl on occasion to make sure I was still on track, even if regular lessons won't be a part of the program. One way or another, I hope that relationship continues.

However, now that I've had some time to think about it, the best reason to keep going as a lefty was simply the ongoing challenge of learning something new. Playing left-handed gave me a fresh perspective on the game (even as I admittedly continue to fight a few old demons). I love the challenge – and, truth be told, I love the novelty of it, too. I'm not typically one who likes to draw attention to himself, but I like the idea of doing something different just for the sake of doing it.

It would be interesting to see if I stayed motivated to practice. It was entirely possible that in a year I'd be utterly frustrated by my lack of progress and just plain sick and tired of playing bad golf.

And here's something else I hadn't considered: Rob expressed to me that he has missed our (mostly) friendly rivalry. "It would be interesting to see how you progress with your lefty game," he e-mailed, "but it would also be nice to have the old Zim back every once in a while to go toe to toe."

Well, you're right about that, Rob. One of the many fine things about our golfing friendship is that we've historically been very close in ability, so we're able to wage epic battles playing straight-up (the only way that really matters). Over the years, many a chocolate milkshake has changed hands following our occasional matches. And no milkshake tastes so sweet as one paid for by your just-vanquished best friend.

Trouble is, I had hit exactly *one* right-handed shot in the past year (not counting the flipped-club chip shot at White Lake), and at that moment the very thought of it felt quite foreign. So I imagined it would take a while just to return to "old Zim" form if I went back. Plus, what Rob didn't know is how close I really was to being able to start once again *kicking his pathetic little Waverly Avenue butt all the way back to Carrie Busey Elementary School* – from the left side *or* the right! *Take your pick, Glacier Boy!*

Ahem. Not that I care about winning or anything. I mean, you know … not *anymore*, since Jack has reminded me what's really important. But I digress …

How about I plan to give left-handed golf one more year and then re-evaluate? Besides, with the official "one-year commitment" period over with, there's no reason I couldn't play right-handed now and then if I felt like it, just for old times' sake. I'd take it a day at a time and let the *game* come to *me*.

And then there's the issue of my back. I learned during the year how important fitness is to golf, especially as you approach eligibility for the senior circuit. Before I started swinging the club again, from either side, I decided to let my back rest for a while, lose some weight, and work on getting in better golfing shape. Or better shape in general. I don't want to be "all used up" by the time Jack starts to really enjoy the game, as I think often about how awesome it's going to be 10, 20, or even 30 years from now when golf becomes "our thing" that we do whenever we get together. But I don't think he's going to want to play with me if I turn into a raving lunatic whenever I hit a bad shot!

So I also decided to work hard to remember what I love most about golf. To do my best to keep falling in love with the game anew. To relish the opportunities to spend quality time with Jack playing a silly game with sticks, chasing a little white ball across God's green earth under the clear blue sky. And continue to learn from him how not to take the game too seriously. (Maybe we can even convince his mom to come out and join us now and then.)

Most of all, I hereby resolve, on my honor, to always do my best to do my duty (as the Cub Scouts say), on and off the course, to never hurry, never worry … and always remember to take the time to smell the flowers, gather the snail shells, and ponder the anthills I pass along the way.

THE END

MIKE ZIMMERMAN

EPILOGUE
Oh, My Aching Back

"It is what it is."

—Tiger Woods

By the time we got the results of the MRI, the diagnosis was not much of a surprise: "You have a large herniation of the L5/S1 disc." Though it was that one word, "large," that caught my attention.

After that final round with Jack, I decided to put the clubs away and just *rest* my back for awhile. I stopped golfing, stopped exercising, stopped stretching … just *stopped*. Which probably wasn't quite the right approach. A few weeks later, I started feeling a little pain in my right butt cheek and upper thigh, so I went back to my regular doctor for some advice. He ordered an X-ray – which didn't show anything except some overall deterioration of my discs, not too abnormal for a guy approaching 50 – and some physical therapy. Okilee dokilee. I was happy to comply.

More than once my therapist asked me if the pain in my leg extended below the knee. And the answer was always "no." So a couple weeks later, when I started to feel some tingling and numbness in my right foot – like it was falling asleep, but while I *walking around* – I thought, "Hmmmm." And I made a mental note of it.

By that evening it had gotten worse, and with the tingling started to come a little pain. It was bad enough the next morning that I decided not to go to church. But I was loathe to pay the co-pay for a walk-in clinic or emergency room ($100 and $250) for something that could wait until Monday.

By Sunday evening I was uncomfortable enough to worry about

sleeping. And since I'm allergic to ibuprofen, I called the insurance company's "nurse hotline" to ask about an alternative. But I never quite got the answer I was seeking.

In the course of discussing what was happening, the nurse strongly suggested I be examined as soon as possible. Apparently, when you have pain and numbness in your leg you need to make sure your spinal cord is not being compromised. I didn't yet have the tell-tale warning sign (loss of control of certain bodily functions), but she thought it would be best not to wait until morning.

We identified a walk-in clinic that was open Sunday evenings, but it was clear on the other side of town. By then my leg was painful enough that I had fished out my old crutches from the rafters in the garage to help me get around. And as I awkwardly folded myself into the passenger seat of our minivan, the pain suddenly went from "very uncomfortable" to "excruciating."

I really can't describe how much it hurt. The only thing I could compare it to was the time I broke my leg when I was 14. No matter how I shifted in the seat, the pain would not subside.

"We're going straight to the Emergency Room," said my poor wife. And though I hated the thought of shelling out 250 bucks (it was guilt as much as cheapness), I was in no position to object.

At the ER, all they really did was examine me to make sure my spinal cord was not affected, and give me some *really* good drugs to dull the pain. Then they sent me home with an order to see my doctor the next day and schedule an MRI. A few days later, I got the "large herniation" diagnosis.

Fortunately, the painkillers they gave me worked well, so I wasn't in too much pain while we decided what to do about it. Ultimately, after a couple of unsuccessful cortisone injections, I decided to undergo a "microdiscectomy," the same procedure Tiger Woods had in March 2014. I had mine in March 2012, two years before it was cool.

The surgery, an outpatient procedure where they go in through a small incision to cut away the part of the disc that was bulging, went well. I was soon off the pain meds and thinking about golfing again. The only problem was that I seemed to have suffered some nerve damage in my right leg and foot. Some of the numbness never went away, and probably never will. It's annoying, but it's not debilitating.

The other thing is, though the surgery fixed my bulging disc and took away the leg pain, those were really just symptoms. I still have a "bad back" – and probably always will.

By mid-summer I was ready to start golfing again, still committed to the left-handed approach. I was eager to pick up where I had left off. For the most part, I was pleased with how easily it all came back to me. But with the official one year of left-handed golf experiment over, it became harder to justify spending as much time and money on golf as I'd like. And I realized that without more consistent play, it would be hard to maintain any sort of consistent form, let alone keep improving.

For a while, golf became pretty frustrating. *I've abandoned my right-handed game and now I can't play lefty either! I've ruined everything!* I didn't always think that way, but often enough. Still, I kept at it as best I could.

In May 2013, during a golf outing to raise money for Fort Wilderness, I hit what may have been the best drive I've ever hit – left- or right-handed. It was long, high, straight, and right on the line I was aiming. I finished with perfect balance in a beautiful position, with my belt buckle facing the target line, my left heel off the ground, and my left knee kissing my right. I "posed" in that position as I watched the ball sail off into the wild blue yonder. Yes, it was a short downhill par-4, with a good tailwind behind us, but in the end it traveled well over 300 yards – almost to the green. It was the best drive in our scramble group and led to an easy birdie.

Maybe I should have dropped the mic, declared the experiment a success, and quit playing lefty right then and there.

That fall, I even threatened to contend in the White Lake Classic. That is, after playing some practice rounds at a resort course in northern Michigan, I shot a very solid 44 on the front nine, beating everybody else but one – scratch. But again I collapsed on the shorter, much tighter back nine, where the trees, water hazards, and O.B. stakes always seem to take their toll. I finished with a 95. Still, with my 15 handicap strokes (yes, they talked me into taking a few more), I shot a respectable net 80 to finish third.

Again, I hit enough good shots to know that the potential was still there, and enough bad ones to keep me from shooting any kind of satisfying 18-hole score. I could break bogey for nine holes now and then, but never really came close to stringing two good nines together.

After an essentially golf-free 2014 – ongoing back issues and time commitments somehow managed to crowd out every playing opportunity – I seriously considered returning to right-handed golf for 2015 and beyond. I even asked for, and received, a nice new right-handed driver for Christmas. But abandoning my hard-fought lefty progress proved not so easy. For one thing, I was afraid that I would have to re-learn to play as a righty. And I worried that if I even tried I might screw up my lefty game and suck from *both* sides of the ball. Also, I still really like the set of lefty clubs I'd put together.

In addition, it seemed my body was now "tuned" for a left-handed swing. That is, whenever I tried to hit a drive right-handed, it felt like my muscles were all stretching and moving in the wrong direction. It felt forced and uncomfortable, almost painful. And occasionally my weakened right leg would cramp up on the follow-through. It apparently didn't like pushing off anymore. It was like my body was rejecting my right-handed swing. The muscle memory transplant seems complete.

As I (finally) write this it's the summer of 2015 and I've managed to get out and play a few times. I'm struggling to remember all the things Coach Carl taught me, but at the same time, I'm surprised how much of it is still in there, how natural the lefty swing has become.

I still hit enough good shots that I know the potential is there to get good. It's just going to be a matter of time and commitment – two things I'm unfortunately a little light on these days. I'm shooting in the 90s generally, but closer to 100 than 90. When I get in a groove I can shoot pars and bogeys, but there are still too many blow-up holes to keep me from breaking 90. And I still tend to fall apart once I realize I've got a good round going. I'm resigned to the fact that when it comes to the mental game, I'm more Bubba Watson (notoriously fragile) than Tom Watson (rock solid).

But I'm *enjoying* it more again. I take more satisfaction in the experience, and the good shots, and the good holes, and worry less about what the final score will be. So I guess maybe I *have* learned something from Jack – Zimmerman, that is; that now-13-year-old bundle of joy and hope and optimism. I could learn a lot from him, actually. And I still have snail shell we found. Unfortunately, it's been harder to get him out on the course, as his interests lately (namely cars) have taken him in other directions.

I also still have that right-handed driver. Perhaps with practice I can turn it into an asset. As a lefty, I still fade the ball pretty regularly. So sharp left-to-right doglegs can still give me fits. So maybe, just maybe, I can become an ambidextrous *driver* of the ball, to fade a righty drive around those troublesome bends. Phil Mickelson once carried two drivers in his bag at the Masters. Why can't I do it at Mee-Kwon?

Yeah, that's the ticket. I could become the first switch-hitting golfer to ever win the White Lake Classic! That would be something, at least.

Stay tuned, America.

ABOUT THE AUTHOR

Mike Zimmerman is a lifelong golfer who generally shoots in the mid- to low-80s, and occasionally breaks into the 70s – before he switched to left-handed, that is! He lives in Glendale, Wisconsin, with his wife, Elizabeth, and their 13-year-old son, Jack. In addition to golf, he enjoys photography, playing guitar (and ukulele) in church, and spending time with his family.

ABOUT THE COACH

Carl Unis, a life member of the PGA of America, was head professional at Brynwood Country Club in Milwaukee for 23 years. He is a former touring professional with a stellar reputation and nearly 50 years of teaching experience. He currently lives in Fort Worth, Texas, with his wife, Carole.

Made in the USA
Monee, IL
21 May 2021

68157625R00125